P9-AOV-606

Helping Out

Children's Labor in Ethnic Businesses

Helping Out

Children's Labor in Ethnic Businesses

Miri Song

Temple University Press
Philadelphia

Temple University Press, Philadelphia 19122
Copyright © 1999 by Temple University
Published 1999
Printed in the United States of America

Library of Congress Cataloging-in-Publication Data

Song, Miri, 1964–
    Helping out : children's labor in ethnic businesses / Miri Song.
        p.   cm.
    Includes bibliographical references and index.
    ISBN 1-56639-708-1 (cloth : alk. paper). — ISBN 1-56639-709-X
    (pbk. : alk. paper)
    1. Children of minorities—Employment—Great Britain.   2. Ethnic
restaurants—Great Britain—Employees.   3. Fast food restaurants—Great
Britain—Employees.   4. Chinese—Employment—Great Britain.   I. Title.
    HD6247.H82G77   1999
    331.3'1'08900941—dc21   98-51927
                                                                        CIP

For my parents

Contents

Preface

CHILDREN AND young people have been the subject of a burgeoning literature on the "new second generation" and immigrant adaptation but their productive roles in immigrant families, as both workers and social mediators, have received very little attention thus far. This book is about the central role that children play in Chinese families running take-away businesses in Britain and in ethnic businesses more generally. When I first arrived in Britain and started frequenting Chinese take-away businesses I was struck by the number of Chinese young people working in them. However, the vast literature on ethnic businesses and immigrant adaptation has not investigated the work roles of children in small, family-run businesses. What kinds of labor do children contribute to family-based ethnic businesses and how should we conceptualize this labor? Furthermore, how do children experience and make sense of their labor participation in immigrant families? I argue that in addition to concerns about economic rationality, an examination of the *intersection* of family relationships and obligations, the survival pressures faced by immigrant families, and issues of cultural identity is necessary for a full understanding of the nature and terms of children's work in ethnic businesses. By prioritizing the need to capture young peoples' views and experiences of their work and family lives, this study is necessarily limited in terms of exploring the myriad of issues that arise in relation to this topic. For instance, I focus much more centrally upon family dynamics and relationships than upon the business aspects of these enterprises. Nor do I focus upon community and wider kin ties in the formation of the Chinese catering sector in Britain—although these issues are discussed as background to the study. Throughout the book, I rely heavily upon excerpts from in-depth interviews. I have preserved the colloquial speech and slang (including awkward usage and mistakes in grammar) of the Chinese respondents because issues of language and cultural identity are important themes in the study. Although this book focuses upon the experiences of Chinese young people (predominantly in their twenties), I use the term "children" to refer to a family relationship, vis-à-vis parents, rather than to individuals of a particular age. Because this is a British study, a number of terms are explained throughout the text for North American readers. One important clarification concerns the use of ethnic categories: "Asian" in the British context refers to people of Indian, Pakistani, or Bangladeshi heritage, and does not usually include the Chinese (as opposed to "Asian American," a term that typically refers to people of Japanese, Chinese, and Korean, heritage).

Many people made this book possible, but I am especially grateful to all the individuals who participated in this study. Not only did they provide scarce time and energy, but they also shared insights and stories I will never forget. I especially thank Wong, who provided invaluable information and inspiration. In the earliest stages of this research, when I was trying to get my bearings, I knocked on a number of peoples' doors: James Curran, Jane Wheelock, and Floya Anthias all shared their ideas and expertise with me. This research, which began life as a Ph.D. dissertation, was conducted while I was at the London School of Economics. I owe a great deal to Jane Lewis, who went beyond the call of duty as a supervisor. Over the years, a number of people provided comments and encouragement in various ways, including Martin Bulmer, Ito Peng, Andre Sorensen, Monika Zulauf, Mark Liddiard, Soraya Cortes, Penny Vera-Sanso, and Mark Kleinman, all of whom provided good cheer and advice. Peter Loizos and Janet Finch lent valuable criticism and insight as examiners of the thesis. Both at the beginning and end of this research, Jan Pahl offered a keen eye and enthusiasm for this project. David Parker, whom I met when I felt very alone in my interest in the Chinese, generously shared his ideas and experiences with me. In the last few years, I derived much support and wisdom from the members of the Women's Workshop on Qualitative Family/Household Research; in particular, I would like to thank Ros Edwards, who offered great comments and company along the way. Since my move to the University of Kent, I would like to thank my colleagues in the Department of Sociology (and the Department of Anthropology) for allowing me the time to write this book. On the other side of the Atlantic, I have received valuable comments and assistance from Pyong Gap Min, Mehdi Bozorgmehr, Lane Kenworthy, Vilna Bashi, and James Watson. Michael Ames has been the model of efficiency as my editor at Temple University Press, and Bernadine Dawes and David Lee Prout provided real expertise in the production and copyediting of the manuscript. I would also like to thank the anonymous readers of this manuscript for their helpful suggestions. My parents, Moon-Won Song and Yung-Hee Park, and my siblings Viv, Paul, and Joe, have provided support and encouragement for far too long, so I hope they will finally read this. A big thank you also to Sung Hee Suh, and to Jan and Herbie for always being there. Last, but not least, I am indebted to Murray Smith for his encouragement, comments, and editorial labors over the years.

Helping Out

Children's Labor in Ethnic Businesses

1

The Role of Family Ties in Ethnic Businesses

CHINESE TAKE-AWAY food businesses (called take-out restaurants in the United States) have long been a common sight throughout Britain's streets and, indeed, in many other countries. It is not uncommon to see children and other family members taking orders or packaging food in such businesses. They are, to the public eye, visible as workers in these enterprises. However, very little is known about how children in immigrant families may contribute to the running of ethnic businesses. This book examines the various work roles that children play, how they negotiate their family labor, and the implications of children growing up, in Chinese families running take-away businesses in Britain.

The Chinese in Britain provide an interesting case study of children's labor in ethnic businesses because, perhaps more than any other ethnic group, the overseas Chinese have been depicted as paragons of hard work and collective family cooperation in the literature on ethnic businesses and immigrant adaptation. Furthermore, Chinese take-away businesses are small labor-intensive enterprises conducive to the participation of children, especially since these families' home and work lives are largely intertwined.

As an important means of immigrant adaptation, ethnic businesses include many kinds of enterprises, such as Indian newsagents, Pakistani market traders, and Korean greengrocers. Despite numerous and passing references to the importance of family labor as a key resource in many ethnic businesses, family labor and families' relations of production have rarely been examined or elaborated upon. In particular, children's labor in ethnic businesses has tended to be "invisible" in such research. The availability of family labor has tended to be treated as an unquestioned given.

For many immigrant families in North America or Western Europe, it is becoming clear that children may play key roles in the successful social and economic adaptation of their families. For instance, children in these families may not only provide labor in ethnic businesses, but they may also act as language mediators on behalf of their parents, as was recently reported in *The New York Times* (Alvarez, 1995; see also Park, 1997:83).

"Productive" roles played by children tend to contravene Western laws concerning child labor, as well as dominant norms about the experience of childhood.[1] In recent years, there has been growing interest in the rights of children and young people in Western societies such as Britain and the United States (James and Prout, 1990; Pond and Searle, 1991 Roche, 1996; Jenks, 1996)—as evidenced by the International Year of the Child in 1979 and the passage of the 1989 Children Act in Britain. Children's labor performed within a family business has traditionally been regarded as more benign than industrial employment (Maclennan et al.,1985).[2]

However, most depictions of family-run ethnic businesses in Britain have been largely disapproving. One reason why children's work in ethnic businesses may be negatively singled out in Britain, as in other Western societies, is that children's work in Chinese take-aways is performed in a racialized work niche. The work performed in these businesses is associated with derogatory images and stereotypes about "foreign" immigrant livelihoods and being Chinese. Work in a take-away business, as colorfully depicted in Timothy Mo's novel, *Sour Sweet,* does not evoke the wholesome images of children on an early morning paper route or helping out on the family farm. It is undeniable that working in a Chinese take-away business is anything but glamorous, given the very long and arduous hours required by such enterprises.

As Morrow (1992:150) has pointed out, however, "there is a danger of taking for granted the stereotypical (and racist) image we have of 'child labor' being an entirely immigrant form of work." In one of the earlier studies of Chinese children from the 1970s, Jackson and Garvey (1974) argued that the educational needs of Chinese children were not being met in the British school system, due to their English language difficulties, and that their school performance was affected by their work in their parents' take-away businesses. The authors also reported that Chinese children were often not registered in schools: "If there are any questions, there is always the switch routine. Children are moved onto another area and another business, until the inquiries peter out"(p. 12). More recently, in *Children of the Dragon,* Simpson (1987) argued that Chinese children led "two or three different lives," a "schizoid existence"—a product of having to work in their families' take-away businesses.

The most common way in which Chinese families and children have been depicted in Britain, by social workers and other practitioners, has been in terms of family pathologies brought about by the social isolation and alienation stemming from the long work hours and confinement associated with running take-away businesses (see Fewster, 1990; Pistrang, 1990).[3] The overall image conveyed of Chinese families, and presumably of other immigrant families engaged in ethnic businesses, has been that Chinese parents are rather ruthless and hard-hearted in their manipulation of children's labor. Chinese children's lives are filled with dirty work and misery—end of story.

Even in studies that refute such stereotypes of the Chinese, it is often assumed that children's work in family-run ethnic businesses can only have negative effects upon entire families. For instance, in her overview of the Chinese catering industry in Britain, Susan Baxter (1988:122) has categorically stated that, "The ethnic take-away family business is merely another locus for the continued oppression and exploitation of the Chinese and for Chinese women and

children in particular, generating on the whole, low levels of profit."
According to Baxter, running a take-away business can only be regarded in terms of the economic and social marginalization of the
Chinese, given Britain's imperialist history in the Far East, including
its colonization of Hong Kong.

Unfortunately, such dire assessments of Chinese families running take-aways in Britain discount the potentially complex and
contradictory experiences of Chinese children working in their
family take-aways. Without disputing the claim that Chinese peoples' concentration in the catering trade reflects, to a certain extent, their economic and social marginalization in Britain, I would
argue that such wholly negative depictions of these families' lives
are too simplistic, particularly with respect to the experiences of
children in these families (see also Pang, 1993). Although this
book cannot address the policy implications of children's labor
participation per se, these depictions of Chinese children and families provide a useful backdrop for an exploration of these children's work roles, and their importance for families running ethnic businesses.

Immigrant Adaptation and Ethnic Businesses

Over the last three decades, the influx of nonwhite immigrants to
North America and European countries has led to an increase in the
self-employment rate in these countries. This has generated a re-
vival of research on immigrant adaptation and ethnic businesses.
Although Europe provided the largest source of migrants to Britain
from 1945 to 1954, most contemporary immigration to Britain is
from India, Pakistan, the West Indies, and other new Commonwealth countries in addition to immigrants from old Commonwealth countries such as Canada, Australia, and New Zealand
(Solomos, 1989).[4] Since the 1965 Immigration Act, the vast majority of immigrants to the United States have originated from Asia
and Latin America (Rumbaut, 1994; Portes and Schauffler, 1996).

Ethnic businesses have received considerable attention because
they have been viewed by many analysts as an important form of

economic and social adaptation and mobility for various immigrant groups. The recent sociological literature on ethnic businesses has stressed their competitiveness in comparison with the small business sector as a whole (Watson, 1977a; Ward and Jenkins, 1984; Waldinger et al., 1990).[5]

Although some analyses of the "native" small business sector apply to ethnic businesses as well, the centrality of migration and of disadvantages associated with immigrant status have led analysts to treat ethnic businesses as a different kind of social phenomenon. Because many immigrant groups are relatively disadvantaged in the labor market, due to both limited human capital and the various forms of racism and discrimination they encounter, small business ownership has traditionally been a means of achieving economic and social mobility (Gans, 1962; Van den Berghe, 1970).[6] Immigrant groups have traditionally been attracted to businesses characterized by low barriers to entry. Low capital investment and low technical barriers apply to areas such as shopkeeping, clothing manufacturing, restaurants, and taxis.[7] In Britain, ethnic businesses tend to occupy rather different sectors of the economy in comparison with forms of white self-employment. While about half of white self-employment is located in construction, agriculture, and manufacturing, half of ethnic minority self-employment is located in the retail sector or catering—though a third of all self-employed Caribbeans are in construction (Modood et al., 1997:124).

Historically, early immigrant groups often started businesses in areas that did not compete with white "native" businesses, so that they could minimize racist hostility from the "native" population. Newly arrived immigrants also established businesses selling predominantly to other ethnic minorities in underserved markets, where there was said to be a gap between ruling and subordinate groups (Rinder, 1959; Blalock, 1967; Loewen, 1971). As "middleman minorities," these ethnic business owners were said to fill economic niches shunned by white people (Bonacich, 1973; Lyman, 1974; Watson, 1975). A similar phenomenon has occurred in the form of immigrant groups replacing white businesses in "changing neighborhoods" (Aldrich and Reiss, 1976; Aldrich, 1980). For instance, in the United States Korean shopkeepers play a contemporary middleman role in minority neighborhoods: Korean greengrocers, fish stores, and liquor stores have moved into predominantly poor African American and Latino neighborhoods in Los Angeles, New York, Chicago, and Atlanta (Light and Bonacich, 1988; Min, 1996b). In Britain, Asian (mainly Indian) shopkeepers have dominated some inner urban areas of London not served by large grocery chains (Ward, 1985).

Operating ethnic businesses was understood to be a form of economic adaptation that suited immigrants who would eventually return to their "homelands" (Siu, 1952). As a key proponent of this view, Bonacich (1973) argued that middleman minorities usually traded with the indigenous community but otherwise had very little interaction with them. Most commonly, the first waves of ethnic business ownership involved male migrants who were separated from their families and relatives, to whom they sent remittances. Since middleman minorities remained oriented toward their countries of birth, their concentration in small businesses was regarded as a temporary arrangement, and they attempted to save as much as possible so that they could eventually return home.

However, the emphasis upon temporary migrants' marginalized economic, social, and political positions is now less easily applied to societies such as Britain, where the children and grandchildren of various immigrant groups have been born and raised in Britain. The settlement of migrants was founded upon the arrival of family members, including wives and children from abroad, and the gradual growth of various ethnic communities (Castles et al., 1984). Furthermore, the establishment of thriving ethnic business communities is now generally regarded as a key indicator of the success of particular immigrant groups.

"Ethnic enclaves," which are usually inner-city minority communities, such as the Cuban enclave in Miami or Chinatown in New York City, are based upon industries characterized by vertical integration and co-ethnic cooperation. Such enclaves have been said to provide newly arrived immigrants with more promising job opportunities than those in the wider labor market. Immigrants' contacts with ethnic business communities have been said to be invaluable in terms of their social, as well as economic, adaptation to their new environments. Countering depictions of vulnerable immigrants confined to dead-end jobs, some analysts have argued that waged work in ethnic enclaves can provide a means of working toward self-employment (Wilson and Portes, 1980; Portes and Bach, 1985; Portes and Manning, 1986; Zhou, 1992). This is achieved in enclaves by established business owners employing relatively recent co-ethnic immigrants. As co-ethnics, various forms of networks and assistance can benefit both employees and employers. Although some analysts such as Sanders and Nee (1987) have challenged the view that ethnic businesses are indeed as successful as many researchers have suggested, trust, familiarity with in-group norms, and ethnic solidarity have been said to be crucial elements in the operation and cohesion of these enclaves (Portes, 1987; Waldinger, et al., 1990).

Immigrant Groups' Ethnic Resources

A recent national survey of ethnic minorities in Britain revealed that rates of self-employment were relatively high (Modood et al., 1997:122): "A result is that about a third of Pakistani, Indian, African Asian and Chinese men who were in paid work were self-employed. For whites and Bangladeshis it was about a fifth, and for Caribbeans it was nearer one in eight." Of all groups, the Chinese in Britain have the highest rate of self-employment (most of it in catering)—30 percent of Chinese men and 26 percent of Chinese women in paid employment.

Why have some groups developed high levels of ethnic business activity while others have not? There has been growing interest in examining the role of ethnic enterprise as a means of adaptation by various immigrant groups (Rumbaut and Portes, 1990). Explanations for the differential "success" of groups in ethnic enterprise have been hotly debated (see Glazer and Moynihan,

1963; Sowell, 1981), especially in the United States, where "model minority" Asians, such as the Chinese and Koreans, have been compared with the black and Hispanic populations (with the exception of most Cubans).[8]

Both structural (e.g., stressing institutionalized forms of racism) and culturally based explanations have been important in analyzing various groups' differential status attainment. There is certainly no question that some groups have had better access to certain resources, such as information networks or informal access to capital and cheap labor, than others. For instance, levels of African Caribbean self-employment in Britain are considerably lower than those of other ethnic minority groups (Jones, 1993; Modood et al., 1997). In the United States, given the historical legacy of slavery, as well as unabating forms of racial discrimination, black people have always faced many barriers in the establishment of small businesses (Feagin and Imani, 1994). Nor are most black business communities large enough or sufficiently integrated for black people to obtain gainful employment within them in significant numbers (Wilson and Martin, 1982). Therefore, structurally based arguments (e.g., Steinberg, 1981; Omi and Winant, 1986) have emphasized the centrality of each group's class resources, demographic characteristics, and the historical context of settlement (including the group's experience of racism).

However, analysts such as Sowell (1981) have argued that racial disadvantage, per se, is not an adequate explanation for disparities in groups' success. By pointing to the experiences of some racialized groups such as the Koreans, West Indians, and Japanese, he has argued that race is not an insurmountable barrier to mobility, despite its historical importance (see also Nelson and Tienda, 1988).[9] In fact, culturally based explanations have tended to emphasize the importance of ethnicity and a group's ethnic resources as social capital (Light, 1972; Sowell, 1981). For instance, Jewish immigrants to the United States, many of whom arrived as refugees from Russia, South Africa, Israel, and other countries (Gold, 1992), have been seen by many analysts as possessing predispositions that stress hard work, frugality, and a future orientation (see Sowell, 1981). Such qualities have been likened to those characterizing the Protestant work ethic (Sombart, 1967; Hsu, 1971).

Culturally derived ethnic resources and strategies, which are not available to or adopted by the "native" small business sector, have been key to the business success of certain immigrant groups (Light, 1972; 1980; Bonacich and Modell, 1980). According to Light and Bonacich (1988), ethnic resources are sociocultural features of a group that ethnic business owners may utilize to their benefit. In a classic study, Ivan Light (1972) argued that, in comparison with African Americans, who were characterized as individualistic in their business pursuits, culturally based forms of economic organization by the Chinese and Japanese in America facilitated their success in ethnic enterprise. Light pointed to the importance of business partnerships and rotating credit associations, which enabled members to obtain the start-up capital to open businesses.[10]

Thus ethnic businesses are said to use similar strategies and resources in the ways they resolve various business problems, such as access to capital, information, and cheap and reliable labor—often that of family members. Perhaps more than any other factor, culturally based difference in family structure and norms have been regarded as a key explanatory variable for the differential success of groups in ethnic businesses. In fact, a number of studies, including Waldinger et al. (1990) and Sanders and Nee (1996), suggest that an important determinant of immigrant self-employment is the family.

Comparative studies of ethnic enterprise, such as Boyd's (1990), have contrasted black family structures with those of other groups, most typically groups including those from East Asia and the Indian subcontinent.[11] In general, black family structures have been said to be more "diffuse" than those of other ethnic groups; as such, black families reportedly have more difficulty in recruiting family labor for their businesses. For instance, in a comparison of Chinese, Indian, and Creole businesses in the Seychelles Islands, Benedict (1979) argued that Chinese and Indian businesses were more successful than Creole businesses due to cultural factors. Unlike the Indian and Chinese businesses, which were characterized by strong family structures, frugality, and long-term planning, Creole businesses were characterized in terms of leisure, consumption, and limited family involvement—a finding echoed in a study of Surinamese entrepreneurs in Amsterdam (Boissevain and Grotenbreg, 1987).

The Family as an Ethnic Resource

Many ethnic businesses are family businesses, and there are numerous types of businesses in which family cooperation is central. Gypsy fortune-telling, for instance, is a family-based operation, often involving three generations of family members (Sway, 1988). Garment manufacturing operations by the Chinese in New York City, as well as by Asians and Cypriots in Britain, are also often kin-based, as are a multitude of ethnic restaurants and cafés.

The competitive edge provided by family labor is stressed in the literature on small businesses more generally. Families are said to engage in "self-exploitation" as a strategy to stay competitive (Bechofer and Elliott, 1981; Rainbird, 1991). Staying in business requires the use of every cost-saving method available. Relying on family can reduce labor costs in two ways. Family and friends often work for less than market wages, and they are particularly reliable employees, with less labor turn-over (Waldinger, 1986; Wilson and Stanworth, 1986; Boissevain and Grotenbreg, 1987). Thus, the family is said to embody a form of social capital in immigrant self-employment (Sanders and Nee, 1996).[12]

The centrality of the labor of wives has been noted in a number of different types of businesses, such as bakeries, family farms (Bertaux and Bertaux-Wiame, 1981; Delphy and Leonard, 1992), and small mom-and-pop stores (Bechofer et al., 1974b; Scase and Goffee, 1980a). There is now growing recognition of the key work roles provided by wives in various kinds of ethnic businesses. For instance, the wives of Korean immigrants to the United States often play a crucial role in the running of businesses, such as greengroceries and dry cleaners (Kim and Hurh, 1988; Min, 1988; Min, 1998; Park, 1997). In Britain, Chinese women have been central to their families' catering businesses (Baxter and Raw, 1988; Song, 1995), while Cypriot women work alongside their husbands in their cafes and corner stores (Josephides, 1988).[13] Family labor can also refer to the labor of other kin, such as siblings, aunts and uncles, and grandparents. For instance, Lovell-Troy (1980) documented the ways in which Greek brothers established pizza businesses together in the northeastern United States.

However, in comparison with other forms of family labor, *children's* labor has been overlooked in studies of ethnic businesses (see Light, 1972; Glenn, 1983; Sanders and Nee, 1996). What is often implied, but rarely stated, is that children may be central to the viability of such businesses. For instance, Waldinger, Aldrich and Ward (1990:144) note that ethnic businesses constitute "a family mode of production": "The ethnic enterprise is thus a *family mode of production* for three reasons: First, it contains an in-built dynamism keyed to the development cycle of the domestic group. Second, it is a unit of production ideally poised to exploit open resources in an expanding market. Third, because it can call on loyalty and sacrifice through lower incomes and longer working hours, it can also cope successfully with periodic market recessions" (my emphasis).

These analysts argue that the maturation of "the domestic group" (meaning children) provides a built-in expansionary potential for small ethnic businesses to grow and diversify. In one of the few explicit acknowledgments of children's contributions to ethnic businesses, Pnina Werbner (1987:224) notes their importance to Pakistani market traders in Manchester: "As families mature, the labour both of wives and of teenage sons and daughters becomes available. A market trader may then open a wholesale or manufacturing concern, depending also on his information network, supply contacts, expertise, and the demographic composition of his familial workforce."

The dearth of research on children's labor in ethnic businesses may be due to the assumption that they rarely participate in most contemporary forms of immigrant ethnic businesses. However, another possibility is that various forms of children's labor (particularly performed in the family context) are simply overlooked. As discussed before, sensitivity surrounding the issue of children and work in Western societies may also make investigation of this topic difficult.

The question of how and why groups engaged in ethnic businesses may or may not rely upon various forms of children's labor has received little attention. A few studies have suggested why children may *not* figure centrally in immigrant groups running various types of enterprises. In the case of Soviet Jews in the United States, Gold (1992:184) found several cases of parents who limited their children's connections with their stores, with the hopes that their children would enter into higher education instead. In the case of Korean business owners in the United States there is no clear documentation of or consensus about the degree to which business owners rely upon their children's labor. For instance, Min (1996b) suggests that Korean business owners are more likely to rely upon co-ethnic or Latino employees than their children, presumably, for similar reasons as the Soviet Jews. However, Park (1997:83) argues, "They also see other Korean immigrants use their children's labor as a simple and cost-free way to save wage expenses in businesses. A few immigrants adopt an orphan or other peoples' children for the specific purposes of using their labor in small business."

Children's labor participation could be especially important in small family-run labor-intensive ethnic businesses, such as Chinese take-away food businesses in Britain. Chinese immigrants' marginalized occupational status means that they start with little capital, and many cannot afford to hire employees. In such a situation, children, particularly as they grow older, can provide key forms of labor in a family-run business.

Conceptualizing Children's Labor in Ethnic Businesses

How should we understand and conceptualize the labor of children in families running ethnic businesses? While ethnic businesses are not a new phenomenon, they represent an example of a family/work configuration not easily theorized within rubrics of contemporary Western families or labor markets. Parents running ethnic businesses do not engage in waged work, which is the norm, and children in such families may be invaluable in providing various forms of labor and assistance. This too is atypical by dominant Western norms.

By contrast, children in most studies of Western family economies (with parents in waged labor) are usually seen as dependents who require economic resources, rather than as active producers for the family economy.[14] Despite some degree of reciprocity, most research on parent-child exchanges and forms of support over the life course have tended to emphasize a net transfer from parents to children (see Cheal, 1983; Rossi and Rossi, 1990). The most commonly recognized form of children assisting their parents is when children, as *adults,* help their parents when parents reach old age.

Another reason why children's work in ethnic businesses may be under-researched is that children's productivity in Western societies is usually assumed to be a thing of the past, and that family modes of production (outside of agriculture) are virtually unheard of in most Western societies today. To generalize, children were often key workers in Western family economies before the predominance of waged labor accompanying industrialization. An important aspect of children's labor in the past was its diversity—not only did they engage in waged work, but they also engaged in artisanal work for the family, and older children often provided child care. Before the growth of waged work, which was gradual and did not entirely displace family-based livelihoods, children's labor in Western societies was more often justified in terms of family needs (Elder, 1974; Davin, 1982).

In Britain, this gradual change in children's work roles was also motivated by the introduction of protective legislation aimed at limiting children's labor and mandatory schooling (Anderson, 1980; Lewis, 1986). Although the changes in society's view of children had their inception centuries before industrialization, there was a gradual transformation in the way that children and child-hood were socially defined, so that childhood was recognized as a different social stage from that of adulthood (Ariès, 1972; Allan, 1985; James and Prout, 1990).[15] The Western idealization of child-hood, as a stage that should be relatively carefree and concerned with social and creative development, is now a normative expec-tation, if not an unwritten "right", of children in contemporary Western societies (Ariès, 1972).

There have tended to be contrasting characterizations of chil-dren's work in so-called first- and third-world societies, with dif-ferent economic and social implications of this work for families. Children's labor in Western societies has been considered primar-ily in terms of their contributions to household tasks (see Pleck, 1977; White and Brinkerhoff, 1981; Brannen, 1995). In contrast with contemporary Western norms regarding children and work, there is usually ready acknowledgment of children's 'productive' labor in many developing countries, in terms of industrialized waged work, agricultural family economies, and informal forms of work.[16] Studies of child labor in developing nations have pointed to the importance of children's labor for family survival strategies. For instance, Judith Ennew's (1982) study of Jamaican children's work demonstrated that the vast majority of children in poor families, many of which were headed by single mothers, were often responsible for their subsistence needs when they were quite young. Poor Jamaican children, who left school in their early adolescence, typically entered into informal earning activities like hawking and street-peddling.

Poverty has been key in explaining the economic importance of children's labor for family survival in many developing societies (Cain, 1977; Lai, 1982). For instance, in Hong Kong it was not un-common (at least in the 1970s) for working class families to have three or more persons contributing to the total household in-come. Children in these families, and in particular elder daugh-ters, often left school early and pursued full-time employment in the garment or electronics industries (Easey, 1979; Salaff, 1981).

However, the case of children working in ethnic businesses in

Western societies, such as Britain, cannot solely be explained in terms of poverty, for these families possess some capital. The issue of children working in ethnic businesses, such as Chinese take-away businesses in Britain, raises questions about the interpretation and assessment of children's labor in a context in which parents' waged work and children's dependency is the norm. Ethnic businesses not only provide a livelihood, but they actually constitute an entire way of life for families who have to adjust to a new life in the aftermath of immigration.

Children's Understandings and Experiences of Their Labor

Although little is known about the ways in which children may contribute various forms of labor in ethnic businesses, even less is known about how they experience their labor participation. Many studies of migration and immigrant families have tended to emphasize the collective needs and cooperation of families. Themes concerning collective family behavior have been stressed in relation to Turkish adolescents in Germany, who must subordinate their individual life plans to the family strategy (Auernheimer, 1990). Also Pakistanis in Britain, Werbner (1987:160) has noted, "conceive of their immediate family, usually members of a single household, as constituting a joint enterprise having corporate aims and strategies. Each member of the household or joint family is expected to make a contribution, in accordance with his ability, to what are perceived to be shared objectives."

Glenn (1983:40–41) has also stressed collective family needs in describing the Chinese "small-producer family," which was characteristic of the Chinese in the United States between 1920 and 1960, as one of various family strategies adopted by them: "Finally, there was an emphasis on the collectivity over the individual. With so many individuals working in close quarters for extended periods of time, a high premium was placed on cooperation." These depictions of immigrant families point to both material and normative pressures for family members to work collectively. Therefore, a common assumption underlying explanations of "successful" ethnic businesses is that family members' obligations to work in these businesses is unwavering. This is because, as Boissevain and Grotenbreg (1987) have noted, there is an undeniable normative dimension in operating a family business. Meanings and ideologies of "the family" are intimately linked with the relations of production and reproduction in small family businesses more broadly. According to Rapp et al. (1979:177): "It is through their commitment to the concept of the family that people are recruited into the material relations of households. Because people accept the meaningfulness of the family, they enter into relations of production, reproduction, and consumption with one another—they marry, get children, work to support dependents, transmit and inherit cultural and material resources."

More than any other ethnic group, the Chinese have been mythologized as paragons of a strong family orientation, which is said to be conducive to the success of ethnic businesses. A prominent theme found in studies of Chinese families is that of familism (*chia*)—the ideological and social importance of family kinship as an organizing principle (Wong, 1985; Niehoff, 1987; Gates, 1987; Oxfeld, 1993).[17] Similar arguments valorizing the benefits of Confucian ideologies for immigrant entrepreneurship have been made in the case of Korean immigrants to the United States who have established small businesses (see Kim, 1981, and for an opposing view, see Min, 1996a).

However, in a recent article about Chinese family firms in Taiwan, Greenhalgh (1994) has rightly argued against relying upon tired, stereotypical understandings of "traditional Confucian culture" that stress familism, collectivism, and mutual benefit (see also Glenn, 1983; Li, 1988; Baxter, 1988). While traditional cultural norms and practices provide part of the explanation for successful family-based businesses, such enduring depictions of the Chinese family bring us no closer to understanding the *specificities* of how Chinese families who run take-aways in Britain elicit and maintain their family members' labor participation over time.

We cannot simply assume that family members are unproblematically committed to working in ethnic businesses, based upon enduring and "natural" norms of family obligations and feelings of affection (Song, 1997a). Although researchers on ethnic businesses have pointed to the positive contributions of unpaid family labor for the success of these businesses, feminist research has challenged the putatively benign characterization of family labor, in particular of women working unpaid for their families (see Hartmann, 1981; Finch, 1983; Phizacklea, 1988; Delphy and Leonard, 1992). In fact, Greenhalgh (1994) has argued that Chinese family firms rely upon the exploitative use of family labor by the family/firm head and that they operate on the basis of sharp inequalities by gender and generation.

A number of questions arise in reference to children's labor in ethnic businesses. First, in what ways do children contribute their labor in ethnic businesses, and how should this labor be conceptualized? Second, how do children experience and make sense of their labor? Third, how is children's labor elicited and maintained for the viability of these businesses? The fact that children are subject to their parents' authority does not preclude the possibility that they may want to provide their labor. It is also certainly possible that children may experience a number of tensions in relation to their labor participation.

What is lacking in many studies of immigrant adaptation and ethnic businesses is not only a focus upon the roles of children but also a rigorous understanding of the processes and means by which such an emphasis upon family needs and cooperation is actually achieved (see Moen and Wethington, 1992; Tilly and Scott, 1978; Hareven, 1982, for historical work on family strategies). Much more needs to be known about the *negotiation* of family labor and about how tensions between children and their families are worked out.[18]

Children in families running ethnic businesses need to be accorded agency, and not simply seen as constituent parts of families (Segalen, 1987). Rather than depicting children in ethnic businesses either as passive dependents, in relation to their parents, or as unproblematically and unquestioningly willing to work on the basis of "natural" family obligations, we need to examine how children understand and make sense of their labor participation (Qvortrup, 1985; Leonard, 1990).

Although the moral and material pressures for family members to provide their labor apply more generally to all small family enterprises, the intertwining of normative and material expectations in immigrant family businesses may be even more intense (Benedict, 1968; Kibria, 1994). In addition to disadvantages related to language difficulties for some groups, such as the Chinese in Britain, their status and experiences as immigrants and ethnic minorities in Britain are fundamental for the formation of family values and cultures. Key aspects of their experience, inevitably, include forms of social marginalization and racial stereotyping. As such, ethnic minority individuals have to rely upon their families for emotional as well as material support, given their experiences of racial marginalization and discrimination (Stack, 1974; Carby, 1982; Brah, 1992).

In light of such racial marginalization, there has been growing interest in documenting the lives and identities of young Chinese people, particularly in the context of their association with the Chinese catering industry (see Chung, 1990; Parker, 1995). The fact that many first generation Chinese families from Hong Kong's New Territories have relied so heavily upon take-away businesses, as well as the fact that Chinese people are often popularly linked with the "Chinese" food they sell to the wider British public, have meant that the take-away has been, and continues to be, an absolutely central part of many Chinese peoples' cultural identities and experiences in Britain. A number of American studies have also pointed to the link between a group's ethnic entrepreneurship and a strong sense of ethnic solidarity. Bonacich and Modell's (1980) classic study of three generations of Japanese in the United States argued for the economic basis of Japanese ethnic solidarity. That is, economic ties and obligations among the Japanese business community strengthened their ethnic ties (see also Patterson, 1975). Min (1991) also found that Korean immigrants' economic segregation in a limited range of small businesses, as well as their conflicts with non-Koreans (1996b), enhanced their sense of ethnic attachment. As Yancey et al. (1976) have argued, rather than relying upon a primordial understanding of ethnicity and ethnic group solidarity, it is only *after* immigration that a common sense of ethnicity emerges.

In the case of Chinese families running take-aways in Britain, their concentration in such a specific economic niche is bound to shape Chinese young peoples' sense of cultural identity. In addition to survival pressures and the pull of family obligations, the formation of their cultural identities is likely to be related to the ways in which Chinese young people understand and experience their labor in families running take-away businesses in Britain. What is needed is an exploration of how survival pressures, family obligations, and issues of cultural identity combine in shaping the nature, terms, and dynamics of children's labor participation in these families.

This book provides an in-depth study of children's labor participation in which we privilege children's own understandings and experiences of their work and family lives (James and Prout, 1996). I rely centrally upon the views and experiences of Chinese young people. Although I use the terms "young people" and "children" interchangeably throughout the book, I use "children" to refer to a family relationship vis-à-vis parents rather than to individuals of a particular age.

This research is based upon a small sample of forty-two young people in twenty-five Chinese families running take-away businesses in the southeast of England. The mean number of children in these families was three: Eight families in the sample had three children; eleven families had four children; five families had two children; one family had seven children. The number of children in these families per se was potentially significant because not only could larger numbers of children enhance the autonomy of these businesses but these families could also rely upon their children's labor over the long term.

A small scale in-depth study is imperative for examining the complex web of views, meanings, and experiences that may be associated with working in a family-run ethnic business. Ethnographic detail is crucial in making sense of and in avoiding an artificial compartmentalization of Chinese families' home and work lives. Details about a typical work day, for instance, or the interactions between family members and their customers, are crucial in understanding the roles that Chinese young people play in their family livelihoods, as well as how they understand and experience their work and family lives (Hammersley and Atkinson, 1983).

The fact that I am a Korean American who interviewed Chinese people in Britain created both opportunities and constraints in the research relationship. In recent years, there has certainly been growing sensitivity to how Western researchers may study and depict the Other (Said, 1978; Bhabha, 1994). In particular, there has been a heightened emphasis upon how racial and ethnic *difference* may shape both the relationships between the researcher and researched and the research findings (see Hammersley and Atkinson, 1983; Clifford and Marcus, 1986; Phoenix, 1988; Edwards, 1990; Reissman, 1991). However, this literature, with its emphasis on the researcher as white and the researched as black, did not easily apply to my own situation, as a Korean-American interviewing Chinese people in Britain (Song and Parker, 1995). In relation to the Chinese interviewees, I found myself neither a total insider nor a complete outsider. Although not being Chinese meant a lack of social contacts and my inability to speak a Chinese dialect (such as Cantonese or Hakka), I believe that my being Korean and my Asian appearance helped me to gain the trust of many of the respondents. A number of young people told me that I looked Chinese, and that my surname, Song, was Chinese.

Reactions to my proposed research, however, were not always favorable. In fact, some Chinese community workers and social service workers discouraged me by telling me that Chinese families were extremely private and would never speak to a stranger and that, even if I did get parents to speak with me, they would never discuss their family relationships or businesses. I discovered early on in my fieldwork that running take-away businesses was, in most respects, an intensely private affair. There was a great deal of sensitivity surrounding my probing about Chinese children's labor participation in families running take-away businesses. Many Chinese parents I contacted expressed worry and mistrust when told about my research. Given their sense of vulnerability, and the intense competition among Chinese take-aways for trade, I had to convince a number of families that I was not linked with any government agency or insurance company. One woman asked sarcastically if I wanted to start up my own shop and learn peoples' trade secrets. In addition to access difficulties, I also realized that it would be very difficult to conduct interviews with parents who were not reasonably fluent in English—since I did not speak a Chinese dialect. Therefore, I decided that any parent interviews I obtained would be a useful supplement to interviews with the young people who constituted my primary respondents.

The forty-two young people in this study, comprised of twenty-seven female and fifteen male respondents, were at least 17 years old. I focused upon this age group because I wanted to interview "children" who had finished school (in Britain, most children complete their secondary school education at age sixteen).[19] Most of these respondents were in their early to mid-twenties. I was able to interview two siblings in seventeen of the twenty-five families for a total of forty-two participants. This was because in addition to examining children's work roles, I wanted to explore the sibling dimension of working with and for one's family. I also interviewed the mothers in five of the families as well as some other Chinese people who were associated with the catering sector, such as an accountant specializing in take-away businesses, and a few members of a younger generation of take-away owners in Britain. Some names and details about families were changed in order to protect the privacy of the participants.

I made initial contact with families through Chinese community workers, who then called families that might be interested in participating in my research. Given my difficulties in gaining access to families, word-of-mouth snowballing was absolutely crucial to this study. Typically, young people who agreed to participate in the study contacted friends whose families also owned take-away businesses. When a young person agreed to be interviewed, I sent a short letter explaining my research, and then followed up with a phone call to arrange a meeting. I conducted two sets of interviews with almost all of the young people in this study (only one interview with mothers), with most interviews lasting between one-and-a-half and two-and-a-half hours. Two interviews were necessary, given the semi-structured nature of the interviews, as well as the extensive amount of data that was required. Interviews were usually conducted in my home or respondents' homes or businesses, or, in a few cases, cafés and restaurants.

Throughout this study, I rely upon case studies of particular families (see Mitchell, 1983). I chose to highlight families that provided particularly rich stories about their family relationships and business experiences, as well as families that provided a range of different experiences among Chinese families in Britain. Therefore, my discussion of children's work roles in these chapters is fleshed out by reference to specific family histories and dynamics over time.

Given my focus on families in the southeast of England, as well as the difficulty I had in recruiting families for this study, the families in this sample are not statistically representative of all Chinese families running take-aways in Britain (see Appendices). It is possible that this study underrepresents the experiences of Chinese young people who had very negative experiences of working with and for their families; such children may have felt unable to discuss their experiences with a researcher, particularly one who had not shared such experiences herself. Nevertheless, these families were typical in that they shared similar circumstances of migration and a heavy reliance upon family labor in their take-away businesses. In fact, I would argue that despite regional differences, the lifestyles and pressures entailed in Chinese take-aways, as well as the issues arising for Chinese young people, were likely to be very similar for such families throughout the country.

2

Chinese Migration and the Establishment of Take-aways in Britain

THIS CHAPTER elaborates upon how the majority of Chinese families who migrated to Britain, especially in the 1960s and 1970s, came to rely upon the take-away trade as their main form of livelihood.[1] The bulk of Chinese overseas migration in the last 150 years has been from the provinces of Kwangtung and Fukien in south China. Most of these migrants were peasants, artisans, and small merchant traders, although there has also been the migration of Chinese students and professionals to various Western nations (Ng, 1968). Many early studies of the overseas Chinese noted the relatively nonassimilated nature of Chinese communities abroad (see Crissman, 1967; Loewen, 1971; Bonacich, 1973). The arrival of cheap Chinese labor in Western societies engendered fears of the so-called "yellow peril" in the latter part of the nineteenth century, especially in North America, Australia, and New Zealand (Ng, 1968; Li, 1988). Thus it was in very hostile circumstances that overseas Chinatowns emerged, with the first generation Chinese, in particular, confined to such enclave communities.

According to the 1991 Census, which asked people to specify their ethnic origins for the first time, there were estimated to be about 156,900 Chinese in Britain, with 77,700 males and 79,200 females (Owen, 1993).[2] The Chinese constitute the third largest ethnic minority group in Britain, after people of Asian (Indian, Pakistani, Bangladeshi) and African-Caribbean origin. According to Owen (1992), the Chinese population is comparatively young, with approximately 7.1 percent under 5 years old, 34.2 percent between 5 and 24 years old, 41.2 percent between 25 and 44 years old, and with only 17.7 percent over 45 years of age.

The majority of Chinese immigrants in Britain are British subjects who were born in the (former) Commonwealth of Hong Kong (Watson, 1977a:183).[3] However, the Chinese in Britain actually constitute a much more diverse group of people than the term suggests; not only are there regional differences (and corresponding dialect differences, such as Cantonese, Hakka, and Hokkien speakers) among the Chinese from Hong Kong, but there are also Chinese people from Singapore, Malaysia, and more recently, Vietnam (Bozorgmehr and der-Martirosian, 1994). Nevertheless, approximately 75 to 80 percent of the present Chinese population originates from the rural New Territories of Hong Kong, and they are primarily Cantonese and Hakka speakers with relatively little formal education (G. B. Parliament, 1985b:5). It is this group of Chinese that constitutes the focus of this study.

Chinese men first came to Britain in the early part of the eighteenth century to serve as seamen on British merchant ships (G. B. Parliament, 1985b). Jobs as seamen provided the basis for the establishment of Chinese communities in Britain, such as in the Limehouse area of London and in Liverpool, which has one of the oldest Chinese communities in Europe (Broady, 1955; Lin, 1989). Since World War II, however, strict trade union rules made it difficult for non-British seamen to be recruited (Ng, 1968:3). As a result, Chinese men settled in major port areas and started to provide laundry services. But with shipping hit hard by the Great Depression, and the advent of modern laundrettes, Chinese migrants' traditional opportunities for employment quickly dwindled (Jones, 1987).

Levels of immigration to Britain became much heavier during the late 1950s and 1960s. According to Jones (1987:245), "The Communist take-over in China indirectly provided the initiative for a fresh wave of immigration. The massive refugee influx into the New Territories after 1949 brought new agricultural skills and a competitive drive in vegetable farming which forced many traditional Hong Kong rice farmers to look elsewhere for a living."[4] The collapse of traditional rice-based agriculture in the New Territories of Hong Kong came about in the context of migration from villages, as a result of rapid urbanization, as well as villagers' inability to compete with the influx of high-quality rice from other regions, such as Thailand.

As a result, villagers who had few skills other than rice cultivation and little education tended to view emigration to Britain as a relatively good opportunity. The migration of the Chinese to Britain in the 1950s was almost wholly comprised of unmarried men, or men who had left families behind in their villages. Many of these villages grew to rely heavily upon the remittances sent back by these men (Watson, 1977a).

In addition to the changes in rural Hong Kong's economy and society, variations in immigration controls and the growth in demand for ethnic cuisine in Britain were key underlying factors that led to increased levels of immigration to Britain (Parker, 1995:63). The "pull" factors of the restaurant boom in Britain during the 1950s and 1960s were crucial for the formation of a more permanent Chinese community there. According to Jones (1987:245), the establishment and expansion of a Chinese catering industry was facilitated by the fact that it did not compete with any sector of the host community (except perhaps fish-and-chips shops) but rather, with other Asian (e.g., Indian and Pakistani) and Mediterranean groups (e.g., Italian and Greek people).

The settlement patterns of the Chinese in Britain have been integrally shaped by the need to find new markets for their restaurants and take-aways. Besides London, significant numbers of Chinese have settled in Manchester (now with the second largest

Chinese community), Liverpool, Birmingham, Glasgow, Edinburgh, and Cardiff.

Family-based take-away businesses tend to operate in a relatively individualistic manner. This is reflected by the fact that, in addition to their concentration in metropolitan areas, the Chinese are quite geographically dispersed: "The distinctive feature of Chinese immigration is its dispersion. While Indian and Pakistani newcomers head for centres of Punjabi or Gujurati culture in Leceister, London, Bradford, the Chinese have learned that their only niche is to be a service to each individual community. . . . When there are too many take-aways in one area the Chinese move on. Community friendships, even family contact, is sacrificed to the aim of making a living" (Garvey, 1993).

In fact, the Chinese population does not constitute more than .8 percent (eight in 1000) of the population in any region or metropolitan county (see table 2.1) (Parker, 1995:77). Some Chinese restaurateurs and their families have even left Britain in the last few decades to establish catering businesses in Continental countries, such as the Netherlands and Germany.

Table 2.1   Regional Distribution of the Chinese Population in Britain

Region	Number	Percent of Chinese Population
Greater London	56,800	36.1
South East	27,100	27.1
North West	16,400	10.4
Scotland	9,500	6.1
West Midlands	8,600	5.5
Yorks/Humberside	8,100	5.2
East Midlands	6,400	4.1
South West	6,100	3.9
North	5,200	3.3
Wales	4,700	3.0
East Anglia	4,000	2.5

Source: (Owen, 1993)

The location of the twenty-five take-away businesses in this study (see Appendices) reflects the heavy concentration of the Chinese in the Greater London and the southeast areas.

Chinese Family Migration to Britain

The concentration of many Chinese families in take-away businesses underscores the importance of the family basis of Chinese economic activity in Britain. A marked shift in the nature of Chinese migration, from individual male migration to permanent settlement and family-based migration, occurred especially during the 1960s and 1970s, with the peak of family migration between 1963 and 1973 (Shang, 1984). Accompanying this family migration was the growth of Chinese associations and societies catering to the social, educational, and welfare needs of Chinese communities throughout Britain.

The parents in the sample families tended to be representative of the vast majority of Chinese people who immigrated to Britain from the 1950s to the 1970s. Most parents (39 of 50) were in their forties and fifties; another ten parents were in their sixties, while, exceptionally, one was in her late thirties. Most (31 of 50) of the parents in these families were born in the New Territories of Hong Kong. Parents who were born in China (17 of 50) had typically immigrated for work in Hong Kong before their move to Britain. Two parents were born in Singapore. With the exception of two families in which the grandfathers of the children had gone to Britain to work on merchant ships, the parents constituted first-generation immigrants to Britain.

For many Chinese families, the timing of migration, as well as their concentration in catering, were crucially shaped by changing immigration laws over time. While the 1948 British Nationality Act had enabled all Hong Kong citizens, as well as subjects born in other colonies, to gain a British passport, the Immigration Acts of 1962 and 1971 withdrew these rights (see Solomos, 1989). The 1962 Act rescinded the automatic right of citizenship from Commonwealth countries and was aimed to restrict entry to skilled or qualified workers or those who had jobs arranged in Britain, for instance in the Chinese catering sector (Williams, 1989:164). As a result, there was an increased migration from Hong Kong in the early 1960s to "beat the ban," which made family reunions much more difficult after the passage of the 1962 Act (Baxter, 1988). Despite the fact that much of the migration from the New Territories in the 1960s and 1970s increasingly involved entire families, migration tended to be staggered, so that spouses or children often migrated to Britain at different times.

Staggered Migration

Staggered migration could entail a significant period of separation between spouses and between parents and children, particularly between fathers and their children. While six parents (all fathers) immigrated to Britain in the 1950s and ten parents in the 1970s (mostly mothers), the vast majority of parents (34 of 50) arrived in Britain in the 1960s. Most fathers in these families arrived in Britain before their wives (the case in 18 of 25 families). This widespread disparity in immigration between Chinese men and women occurred because, after initially immigrating to Britain, Chinese men often went back to Hong Kong to marry after some years in Britain.[5] In other cases, married men left behind wives and children in Hong Kong and sent for them later. This separation was usually due to the fact that these men had to arrange employment and accommodations before their wives could join them, especially in light of increasingly restrictive immigration policies.

Parents and children could be separated in the course of these families' settlement in Britain in various ways. The timing and place of children's births could result in parents (especially fathers) being separated from their children. In the case of fourteen families, all the children were born in Britain. In three families, all the children were born in Hong Kong before immigrating to Britain. However, in the case of eight families, some children were born in Hong Kong, while others were born in Britain. Furthermore, five of the children born in Britain were sent back to Hong Kong to be raised there, typically by grandparents, and rejoined their parents later. In the case of British-born children sent back to Hong Kong, their parents were very busy working long hours in Britain and did not have the time or energy for child care (Watson, 1977a). Another motivation for sending children to Hong Kong was that parents wanted their children to be socialized in Chinese traditions and wanted them to learn Chinese.

In one family, Kam (age 26), the eldest of three children, was born and raised in Hong Kong and came to Britain in 1983 when she was 17 years old. Kam barely knew her father when she arrived because he had been in Britain since 1961, working in catering. Kam's mother had stayed with Kam in Hong Kong until 1972, when she also left to join her husband in waged work. Kam remained with her grandmother in Hong Kong. Although her father returned every few years to visit, Kam had to re-establish a relationship with him when she finally moved to Britain. Clearly, staggered migration could have significant effects upon the social and educational adaptation of Chinese children in Britain (G. B. Parliament, 1985a) and the development of family relationships, as discussed more fully in chapter 5.

In some families, not only were parents and children separated, but siblings could also be separated from each other, as a result of differential points of immigration to Britain. For instance, Pue-man (age 19), who was the third of four children, all of whom were born in Britain, reported that her two older sisters were sent back to Hong Kong:

They [her two older sisters] went back to Hong Kong with my grandparents. My elder sister stayed [in Hong Kong] until she was 5, and the second, until she was 4. They lived with my grandparents. My mum was always moaning that she had to look after my sisters after they came back [to Britain], and they didn't mix with me. They played together. I was about 2. My mum told me I didn't get on with them. That's why I don't have much to say to my sisters now. They're closer to each other. The Chinese, they have a language they call Hakka. My sisters didn't speak Cantonese, and only spoke Hakka. When they

were brought back to England, my mum made them speak
Cantonese. I didn't understand what they were talking about.
We didn't communicate very well.

Therefore, family reunification in Britain was often protracted
and gradual. In addition to the difficulties arising from family members being separated from one another, spouses' and children's immigration to Britain could also be motivated by the start-up of a
take-away business, which relied upon family labor.

Chain Migration and Clan Ties

Especially in light of increasingly restrictive immigration laws, as-
piring migrants usually had to rely upon their clan "relatives." Influential Cantonese clans (based upon a common ancestral lineage) in the New Territories, such as the Tang, Hau, Pang, Liu,
and Man, were well-organized in ferrying over clan members to
Britain (Shang, 1984). Often, distant relatives from the same village in the New Territories relied upon kin in Britain as a means
of chain migration, in which prospective migrants learned of opportunities and were provided with transportation, accommodation, and employment arranged by previous migrants (see Watson, 1975, for a discussion of how this worked with the Man clan,
or Anwar, 1979, for Pakistani chain migration to Britain).

Families who had "pioneered" the move to Britain were often
subject to obligations to bring over other eager relatives. In addition to brothers, sisters, aunts, uncles, and cousins, village ties
made it very difficult for families to turn away clan relatives. Not
only would a failure to assist them have risked their reputations in
both their home villages and in Britain, but many of these families wanted to maintain ties with their villages because, for example, some planned to return and build new homes or buy burial
plots there. Regardless of whether or not Chinese families had
space to accommodate others in their living quarters, pioneering
families could be subject to a seemingly endless stream of relatives over the years. According to Pue-man, whose family lived in
council housing [state subsidized housing administered by local

councils roughly equivalent to a housing project in the U.S.] prior to shop ownership,

> Usually it was distant relatives. My mum and dad lived in one village, and in that village, they all kind of respect each other like brothers and sisters, and if anyone comes over, we have to look after them. So they all come to our house. So people were coming in, going out, it was like a hotel. . . . I enjoyed it. New faces, strangers coming to live with me. Like a little girl or boy I could play with, but my mum and dad. I remember them moaning, because my mum and dad was very poor, they couldn't afford anything. Still they had to cook dinner for them.

Often, the relatives who came to live and work with a family used the visit as an opportunity to learn the trade themselves, and sometimes these newcomers even bought their relatives' shops. According to Jacqui (age 22), "My parents' relatives and friends were coming from Hong Kong, and my parents were helping them out. For example, in the early years relatives or friends would come and stay, and my parents would show them what happens [in the shop]. And then the newcomers would decide to buy the shop that my parents had, and my parents would move elsewhere. The kitchen and front were set so that if friends or relatives came over, they could watch what was happening, how to do things."

Most families who were assisted by relatives did not actually pay them a "real" wage, for such arrangements were often seen in terms of mutual advantage, where the arrangement benefited both parties. Or in other instances, relatives who came to study in Britain helped out in the shop in return for room and board. It was fairly common for these young peoples' grandparents, aunts, uncles, and cousins from Hong Kong to come and live with them at various points in these families' histories.

From Restaurants to Chinese Fast Food Take-aways

The Chinese are much more concentrated in one niche—catering—than other ethnic groups in Britain, who are more economically diversified. Turkish and Greek Cypriot entrepreneurship has been heavily based on clothing manufacturing (Constantinides, 1977; Anthias, 1983; Ladbury, 1984; Josephides, 1988). Asians, such as Pakistanis, have also been heavily concentrated in clothing manufacturing (Anwar, 1979; Bhachu, 1985; Werbner, 1987). However, both Asians and Cypriots are also heavily represented in the catering trade, as well as other services such as hairdressing and travel agents, in the case of the Cypriots.

The demand for fast food grew within the context of major demographic and social changes: The move of the British population to suburbs and council estates, the increasing labor force participation of women, and the growing number of single households all facilitated the market for fast food (Parker, 1995:65). According to Jones (1987:245), fast food had been preceded by a restaurant boom that had "its roots in wartime London, where, despite rationing, fortunes could be made out of restaurants catering for the thousands of servicemen then on leave in the metropolis."

The explosion of Chinese family take-aways was an outcome of the growing dominance of large fast-food chains started in the late 1960s, which made the "chop-suey houses" of that time obsolete. Chinese restaurants were hurt by the introduction of the value-added tax (17.5 percent for many products and services) and the selective employment tax (now abolished), with the latter increasing the costs of employing a larger number of employees (Parker, 1995:70). Take-aways sold foods similar to that at the chop-suey houses but did not have the overheads of restaurants and could often rely solely upon family labor (until recently, take-aways did not have to pay VAT) (Baxter, 1988).

In this research, I concentrate exclusively upon family-run take-away businesses, as opposed to Chinese restaurants, because take-aways entail a different division of labor and a different kind of reliance upon family labor, unlike restaurants in which "outside" labor is usually required. In fact, in a study of Taiwanese family firms, Greenhalgh (1994) found an inverse relationship between business size and the use of family labor, with larger firms more able to afford outside labor than small firms. The Chinese take-aways in Britain constitute extremely small enterprises, in comparison with such family firms.

Labor-Intensive Family Businesses

The small scale of Chinese take-aways is an important factor in making these businesses viable for families. In larger ethnic businesses, family members may adopt increasingly managerial, as opposed to labor, roles (Ram and Holliday, 1993). There are a number of ways in which family labor, and in particular children's labor, is well suited for the needs of a take-away shop, compared with some other types of ethnic businesses. Chinese take-aways must cook and sell simultaneously, and they tend to need a larger labor force during shop hours than do small retail shop owners. For example, small newsagents in Britain, which tend to be dominated by Asians, may operate during opening hours with just one person; newsagents and other shopkeepers sell, but do not actually produce any commodities (which is not to say that shopkeeping is not arduous work). By comparison, family members in Chinese fast-food shops still act primarily as a pool of labor, who must work together intensively. As will be discussed in more detail in the next chapter, family members spend a lot of time together in these businesses; for instance, they can congregate in the shop for their evening meals. Depending upon the level of trade, most take-aways operate with a minimum of two people present in the shop during opening hours—at a minimum, one person at the counter, and another in the kitchen, with the counter person often having to do some packing and cooking, in addition to taking orders.

The labor-intensiveness and relatively low overheads of take-aways mean that they do not rely upon new, expensive technology, as do large-scale fast-food chains. Unlike the commercial fast-food sector, which relies heavily upon "scientific management" and expensive labor-saving technology, Chinese take-aways rely primarily upon the physical and mental labor of family members (Baxter, 1988). Of course, families running take-aways have had to invest in some new technology, but it is still very limited in most of these businesses—there may be a chip-cutter for potatoes and modern deep fat fryers. Most of the labor-intensiveness of take-aways is due to the work involved in food preparation, which is not mechanized, such as cutting up numerous vegetables and meats and the preparation of various sauces. A great deal of work needs to be done outside of shop hours, such as cleaning the shop, going to wholesale markets, and seeing solicitors and accountants.

Also, much less capital is required to open a take-away, compared with restaurants, so it is much easier for individual families to start a take-away business. Because of the typically heavy involvement of family members, take-aways are often stable in terms of labor continuity, in contrast to many restaurants, which have to manage high labor turnover and maintain a good chef. Therefore, Chinese family members, engaged in both production and consumption, have made the transition from restaurants to take-aways possible.

Chinese take-away businesses tend to vary somewhat in terms of the food that is served. While eighteen families ran "pure" Chinese take-aways (which served only Chinese food), three families ran fish-and-chips shops, and four families ran combination shops that served both Chinese food and some traditional English meals, such as fish and chips, roast chicken, and beef with vegetables. Families that ran pure or combination shops usually offered about one hundred different dishes on their menus. Many of the young people interviewed explained that fish-and-chips shops tended to be less profitable than either pure Chinese or combination shops, given that fish-and-chips were cheaper than most Chinese dishes. Despite of the fact that shops serving Chinese food were more labor-intensive than fish-and-chips shops, given the food preparation involved, there was no significant difference in the family labor involvement in these types of take-aways. Although the growth in the catering industry enabled families to enter self-employment, starting a take-away business was no easy task, but one that required much hard work and saving.

Waged Work, Partnerships, and Shop Ownership

Chinese families who started take-away businesses had not necessarily planned on opening a shop, but given the very limited job opportunities available to most parents, shop ownership seemed to be a logical goal to work toward. A key reason why the catering industry was such a viable niche for these Chinese families was that most parents were limited in their livelihood opportunities by relatively low levels of education and limited English language abilities. In this respect, while the New Territories Chinese who immigrated to Britain in the 1960s and 1970s may share some limitations with some contemporary immigrant groups to Western societies, they differ (in terms of their backgrounds, skills, and resources) from other contemporary groups immigrating from Asia.[6] For instance, many immigrants to Britain from India or from the Philippines arrive with a working knowledge of English, given these countries' experiences of British and American colonialism, respectively (Cariño, 1996). This has enabled these groups to enter various forms of waged labor in Britain (e.g., construction and nursing). Nevertheless, English language ability per se does not automatically open doors to good job opportunities in the wider labor market. Nor can immigrants easily apply human capital and educational qualifications that were earned overseas.

There tended to be a very common employment trajectory for these Chinese immigrants in Britain, beginning with waged work in Chinese restaurants and take-aways, to restaurant and take-away partnerships, then culminating in sole business ownership. As is shown in table 2.2, most parents' work experiences before immigration did not prepare them for work in the catering sector.

Given the three mothers who had been teachers and the two fathers who had been tailors in Hong Kong, table 2.2 suggests that the parents in this sample constituted a slightly more diverse class and educational background than the norm of relatively poor parents from farming families in the New Territories of Hong Kong. Once in Britain, however, it was common for parents to have had multiple jobs before shop ownership for the purposes of accruing capital or savings. The majority of parents in the sample had work experience in either restaurants or take-aways before opening their own shops—this experience was often crucial for they were literally learning the skills of the take-away trade.

Table 2.2 Employment of Parents before Immigration

	Father	Mother
1.	farmer	housewife
2.	not known*	kindergarten teacher
3.	radiographer	nurse
4.	tailor	teacher
5.	dim sum seller	farm worker and construction
6.	farmer	teacher
7.	no occupation (young)	no occupation
8.	tailor	textile factory worker
9.	farmer	house keeper
10.	textile and noodle maker	nurse
11.	not known*	nurse
12.	factory worker	factory worker
13.	sailor	farmer
14.	student	student
15.	farmer and builder	farmer
16.	not known*	textile factory worker
17.	fisherman	clothing factory worker
18.	factory worker	housewife
19.	grocery employee	grocery employee
20.	chef	factory worker
21.	(refused information)	(refused information)
22.	chef	machinist
23.	not known*	not known*
24.	not known*	not known*
25.	dock worker	not known*

*The respondent did not know this information.

However, men's and women's catering jobs within the Chinese ethnic economy tended to be gendered, with women usually working in lower status, more poorly paid jobs as kitchen assistants and with men working as chefs or as waiters. Therefore, in terms of waged work, most Chinese women in Chinatowns in both Britain and the United States did not reap the same benefits as Chinese men. For instance, Min Zhou's (1992) study of New

York City's Chinatown found that Chinese women were very confined to the garment industry, in an enclave characterized by rigid occupational sex segregation.

It was not uncommon for Chinese women to engage in forms of "homework," such as home sewing on a piece-work basis—an area of work Chinese women shared in common with Asian and Cypriot women in Britain (Hoel, 1982; Phizacklea, 1990). Sometimes this homework was performed in addition to work in a take-away or restaurant. This extra work was designed to amass savings for the family nest egg, which was crucial if the possibility of opening one's own take-away was to become a reality. In this respect, most of the Chinese families came to Britain with much less capital than, for instance, Korean immigrants to the United States, many of whom arrived with substantial savings for the purpose of starting businesses (Min, 1988; Min, 1998).

Because waged work in Chinese ethnic economies was often the only employment available to Chinese people who did not speak English, and because these newly arrived workers were often indebted to Chinese employers who had supported their immigration applications by offering work vouchers, these workers could be very vulnerable to exploitation in the Chinese ethnic economy (Baxter, 1988). According to the Chinese Information and Advice Center (1985:7): "Catering workers face low pay, job insecurity, tied accommodation which is often overcrowded, poor working conditions, long unsocial hours and employers' failure to pay National Insurance for their employees. These factors combine to afflict especially the older catering workers, when, for example, they are unfairly dismissed through ill health."

However, a few exceptions to the trajectory of waged work in catering to shop ownership occurred in the sample. For instance, Chris's (age 17) parents started a take-away business, although they both had jobs as a radiographer and a nurse. Their case was rather distinctive in the sample because both parents were not only fluent in English and well-educated, but they had held professional jobs. Chris explained that his parents had wanted to try self-employment because they had felt that their waged employment provided limited opportunities for upward mobility. As Chris explained, "My father wants to be the next Alan Sugar" [the British entrepreneur who launched Amstrad computers]. Another incentive for Chris's parents was that they wanted to send their children to fee-paying schools, which they could not afford with their salaries. In the case of two other families, the mothers had trained as nurses in Britain but gave up their nursing careers in order to open take-away businesses with their husbands, both of whom lacked qualifications for other work in Britain.

During the phase of waged work in the Chinese ethnic economy, many families endured some hardship as a result of long work hours and frugal consumption patterns. Many families lived in very crowded housing with other Chinese families in similar situations. Long, antisocial hours in waged work in the catering industry also meant that some families tended to spend very little quality time together. For instance, Sai (age 25) saw very little of her family when she was a young child: "I remember that during those years [before shop ownership] my father got a job, and my sister and my mum had a job, and my brother went to college for a few months, but his English wasn't up to it. And he went to work for my dad, for someone he [dad] worked for, so during those years, I didn't see much of my father. I didn't see much of my family either, because they were working. So I was on my own, in this house with other Chinese people; it was fine. . . . I just accepted it as our way of life."

As a precursor to individually owned take-away businesses, it was fairly common for Chinese families to go into partnerships in restaurants or take-aways with one or more families before going it alone (see Light, 1972). Eight of these twenty-five families had been in restaurant or take-away partnerships before sole business ownership (with the exception of one family who, at the time of interview, had a sleeping partner in the business—someone who provided money to buy the business, and who received a percentage of the profits). Partnerships were a way of breaking into the trade, once one or both parents had learned enough about the catering industry through waged work. Moreover, partnerships were attractive because two or more families could pool the capital required to open a business, which spread out the risk of business failure. Partnerships were formed with the aim of each family eventually owning their own shops, and they typically lasted only a few years; conflict and mistrust around financial issues could dissolve partnerships prematurely. Tensions arose particularly in situations where the profits could not adequately sustain more than one family comfortably. The transition from partnership to sole business ownership was also found in the case of Greek brothers who co-owned pizza businesses in the northeastern region of the United States. These Greek brothers were very clear about prioritizing the needs and interests of their own spouses and children and understood that their partnerships were temporary (Lovell-Troy, 1980).

As Baxter (1988:122) has argued, the transition from restaurants to take-aways resulted in the shifting of the class positions of Chinese families with take-aways, from waged workers to self-employed business owners. In addition to aspirations for a better standard of living, autonomy was clearly valued by most parents, and it was thought that shop ownership would enable them to achieve more control over their lives.

Autonomy and Control in Shop Ownership

At the time of interview, both parents in twenty-three of the twenty-five families worked full-time in their shops, without any other form of outside employment. Two families were exceptional in the sample, in that the fathers worked full-time in their take-aways, and the mothers worked only part-time (although they previously worked full-time). Furthermore, three of the twenty-five families had recently sold their shops at the time of interview (all within the past year and a half). I decided, however, to include them in the sample, given that the children in these families were keen to participate in the study.

Families running take-aways could exercise a degree of autonomy and control over their work and family lives, which was an important need, in particular for first generation immigrants who could easily feel marginalized and disenfranchised in a new society. According to Anna (age 24),

> And I do feel that my family has made a lot more of themselves than if they'd worked for somebody else. They have control over their lives. They work damn hard, and they're constrained by finances and economic survival, and because of that, they have to do certain things. But they don't answer to any white person in a job. You don't have to bow down to a white person who's shouting you orders, which my dad thinks is really demeaning. He'd never work for a white person. And that's been his sort of dignity all along. "Maybe I don't have as much money as you have, or as big a house, but I don't have to answer to any of you lot."

In addition to concerns about autonomy, Gold (1992:175–78) also found that Vietnamese and Soviet Jewish refugees in the United States started small businesses in order to limit contact with an unfamiliar culture, to provide employment for relatives, and to pass the business onto their children. However, upward mobility via migration and self-employment did not guarantee an overall sense of increased well-being, as Foner (1978:226–27) found with Jamaican immigrants in London:

> Among Jamaicans in London, as well as among migrants in other settings, the impact of occupational mobility may be influenced by changes in the symbolic meaning of being black or being a member of a minority ethnic group. Where migrants' racial or ethnic status declines when they move, upward occupational mobility may not be consistently associated with satisfaction in the new place of residence. . . . even those [Jamaicans] who were proud of their occupations, income, and life style advances were still bitter about their position as blacks in Britain.

Most young people reported that the formation of a family business was also an important means of obtaining and maintaining economic security. This emphasis upon security was interesting, given the high risks actually involved in starting small businesses (Curran and Burrows, 1987; Light and Bonacich, 1988). One aspect of economic security derived from a family business was that Chinese families did not have to rely upon others (at least beyond the initial reliance upon Chinese patrons and networks) to assure a secure means of making a living. As owners of a means of production, family labor and commitment were usually sufficient to guarantee at least a subsistence living. A number of young people remarked that one of the benefits of running a take-away was the abundance and availability of food—illustrating that the availability of good food was by no means taken for granted. According to Pue-man: "When my family was all together, we lived in a council house, and my grandma said, 'Why don't you get a shop? Look at the children, they haven't got a lot of sweets to eat'—what Chinese call children's food. When we were living in a council house we didn't have crisps, sweets, like other children have. . . . And my mum knew lots of friends and relatives who had shops, and their children had crisps, fried rice, chow mein foods. And we hadn't had those before." Although none of these families were actually going hungry before take-away ownership, the availability of good food in the take-away was something which Chinese young people referred to with appreciation.

Owning a take-away business was also a way of finding housing, as well as a way of both working and raising a family. As Susana, a mother of two children, explained, "We didn't have a plan to open a shop. Having a shop is a way of, for that period of time, I think is the best outcome, or best solution for making a living and looking after children. Having a shop provided a place to live too." Lily, a mother of four children, explained that shop ownership, although requiring very hard work and stress, was preferable to a combination of jobs, over which she had had very little control:

I didn't know sewing in Hong Kong. I had four children, and my husband not make much money. He was a cook. We need more money. One day, I stand outside a door, and see English people pushing large boxes, and I ask, 'What is it?' Homework: stuffing envelopes. So I get work. The pay is bad, but I do it at home because I can see the children. When the children go to school, I find a different job. I look for machining work. I ask the governor, and he says, what can you do? I say I will do anything. I like it. He says, 'OK, you can do overlocking.' In an English factory, no Chinese. Then I switch to pickle factory because it's near my house, and near children's school as well. I go early morning to pickle factory, and when I come home, I can do the airplane toy assembly or do sewing. On Friday and Saturday nights, when the children go to sleep, I go to another restaurant and help as well, do everything in restaurant. So, you see, the shop is better for me. I do myself.

It was evident from Lily's experience that her main concern was to see to her four children's needs while still playing the role of a key breadwinner.

Business Turnover and Incomes

Although few families have actually become wealthy from running take-aways, almost all the young people and parents reported that running a take-away business had enabled their families to have a much better standard of living and more economic security than they would have achieved through waged work. The ten families that owned the freeholds on their businesses, as opposed to the ten families who had leaseholds of variable lengths (interviewees in five families did not know), were able to exercise more long-term control over their businesses.

Obtaining information about the financial aspects of these families' businesses was difficult, for some interviewees who had been very open about discussing personal family matters were clearly nervous about broaching financial issues about the business. One issue that was reluctantly acknowledged was the potential for tax evasion. Some under-reporting of income was implied in interviews with young people.[7] While young people from thirteen families reported that they did not know about their business turnover (gross sales), one interviewee refused to discuss it outright: Given the intense privacy surrounding financial matters, it is possible, of course, that those reporting ignorance could have done so to avoid discussing this matter. As a result, I had to rely upon the information I obtained from young people in only eleven families.

Like most small businesses, Chinese take-aways were negatively affected by recession and increased competition over the years, and as a result, many shops were reportedly less busy than in the past. Many of these young people said that their parents spoke wistfully of "the early days" of their shops as the period when business was good. There was considerable variation in how well families fared financially, despite a general downward trend in business revenues.

According to Charles Ho, a Chinese accountant dealing primarily with Chinese business owners, £1,500 to £2,000 weekly gross, (in August 1992) was an estimated average for most shops in the Greater London area, whereas £1,000 was "barely breaking even" and over £3,000 was considered to be very good.[8] According to Mr. Ho, profits were usually higher in shops located in small towns, rather than in metropolitan areas such as the Greater London area, where there tended to be much more competition. Among the eleven families, £4,000 was the highest weekly amount, £600–700 the lowest, and the average amount reported was £2,100.

According to the respondents, ever-increasing competition from other fast-food shops near their take-aways, in addition to recession, was the main culprit for drops in revenue. As Chris observed, however, "The good thing about food is that people still have to eat." Given the explosive growth of various ethnic take-aways, pizza, and hamburger eateries, as well as supermarkets introducing ready-to-eat ethnic meals (including Tesco's, Sainsbury's, and Marks and Spencer's Chinese dinners!), Chinese take-aways' share of the market did not increase in the last half of the 1980s (Baxter, 1988:136). However, despite market saturation and ever-growing competition, Chinese take-aways are still quite numerous. For families running shops with decreasing revenue, young people reported that they relied more than ever upon their regular customers as a cushion from economic slumps.[9]

In spite of increased competition and decreasing turnover, a number of young people reported that their parents, particularly their fathers, were very reluctant to institute any changes in the way their businesses operated; parents apparently clung to an established routine. It was often the children who suggested initiatives, such as introducing new dishes, home delivery, shop refurbishment, and the undercutting of competitors. A number of interviewees reported that they had introduced half-portions for sale, in response to customer demand. As one interviewee explained, "It's better than getting no trade at all, if customers don't want to pay for a full portion." Of course, shrinking profits tended to put more pressure upon families not to hire any employees, and to rely solely upon family labor. With hard times, family members were under more pressure to contribute as much as they could to the business.

Families on the Move

If their businesses were not doing well, families could "sell up" and move, because their main resource was the family, rather than fixed capital. As discussed before, Chinese take-aways constituted relatively autonomous units of production; they were not heavily dependent upon a chain of other producers or upon specialized labor. A number of families at the time of interviews had run several businesses in the course of their family histories. While twelve families were running their first shop, nine families were running their second shop, three their third shop, and one their fourth shop.

One family's history in Britain represented one of the longest business histories in this study. Mr. X first came to Britain in 1955 and married his wife in Hong Kong in 1962. All four of their children were born, in relatively close succession, in Britain from 1963 to 1968. At the time of interview, this family was running their fourth shop; they had experienced a great deal of change in their lives, not the least because of the many times they had moved. In fact, one of their ventures had included a brief move to a small town in Belgium, which proved to be disastrous. They bought a shop based upon information from a Chinese contact, but after only a few months, they were homesick and realized that the shop would not survive. They returned to England, where they remained without a shop for a few years. These four businesses spanned a quarter of a century, but they were not all continuous ventures. At two different points in their history, this family experienced two periods of unemployment, when they were "between shops." Each new shop necessitated a source of capital, and they often had to rely upon Chinese networks for financing.

Families in the sample varied in terms of the number of years they had been running take-away businesses. For instance, one family had an exceptionally short history of shop ownership: Kam's family had been running their take-away for only five years at the time of interview. In contrast, seven of the twenty-five families had been running catering businesses for over a total of twenty years (with one family in their twenty-eighth year, and another in their thirty-third year, though in this latter family, there had been two short periods between shops).

The most common reason for moving shops was that business had not been good in a particular location. The fortunes of take-away businesses often changed as more Chinese take-aways and other fast-food businesses such as kebab and pizza businesses, opened nearby. However, some interviewees, such as Colin, whose family was now running their third shop, also reported that their families had moved because of racial harassment (an issue discussed in subsequent chapters): "Stoke-on-Trent [a town in the British Midlands] was very good business but very dangerous because we had the National Front on our backs all the time. The school I was going to was really racist. It was mostly 16-year-old thugs, and we didn't know how to handle the situation. We've put people in court, and it's vindictive. Our insurance company refused to insure us because our windows were smashed every so often." Therefore, families moved in search of a place where they could operate a thriving business and where they could comfortably settle and feel safe and accepted.

Given the tendency toward geographical dispersion, with some take-aways located in areas with few other Chinese families, and family histories characterized by moves and resettlement, family members had to rely upon each other for emotional support and ongoing adaptation to new surroundings. It is within this context—the intertwined work and family lives of these Chinese families running take-aways—that the importance of children's labor participation in their family economies is examined in the next chapter.

3

"The Shop Runs Our Lives"

THE NATURE and range of children's labor in Chinese take-away businesses is not easily discerned from the outside or from the shop counter. If one were to walk into a Chinese take-away, one might see a Chinese young person working at the counter and a glimpse of the kitchen. However, given the typical spatial demarcation between what young people called the front (the counter area and shop front) and the back (the kitchen and living areas), much of how family labor is organized is not ordinarily visible (Goffman, 1969). I gained a sense of the rhythms of family labor through my visits to some of these families' shops and homes.

All the young people interviewed in this study stressed that the shop ran their lives. This was because small labor-intensive ethnic businesses, such as Chinese take-aways, constituted a family mode of production. Production and consumption were organized around the household, and several family members had to participate in the work process to meet basic needs. As family businesses, most Chinese take-aways required a counter person working out front, as well as a few people working together in often crowded and small kitchens in back—cooking and packaging food. As a result, family members typically worked in very close physical proximity to each other, particularly when business was brisk. Most take-aways had four woks in a row in the kitchen, with each wok for particular kinds of cooking. According to Ming, "When it gets busy, you need a couple of people at the woks. One wok is primarily for deep frying, another one's primarily just fried rice, and there's two for other dishes, say chop suey, chow mein. Four in all."

Chinese take-away businesses involve extremely long and arduous work hours. While most families (16 of 25) opened for both lunch and evening hours, nine families opened only in the evenings. Although evening hours tended to vary slightly, most families opened at 5:00 or 5:30 p.m. until 11:00 or midnight (often with later hours on weekends). Many of the families with only evening hours had opened for lunch in the past, but it was commonly reported that there was no longer enough passing trade to make lunch hours worthwhile. Instead, rather than opening between 12:00 and 2:00 (the most typical lunch hours), these families preferred the greater freedom they gained during the day. The grinding routine of shop hours was especially felt by seventeen families, who were open seven days a week, while the other eight families closed either Sundays or Tuesdays. Some families never took time off for a holiday, closing for only a few days of the year. Rather than taking a family holiday, it was more common for individual parents or children to go away, separately, to Hong Kong, leaving other family members behind to run the shop.

Given the labor-intensive food preparation that had to be done before the shop opened and the clean-up that followed shop closing, work days could stretch twelve to fourteen hours. Families would often finish cleaning up between 1:00 and 2:00 a.m. on weekends, and not get to bed before 3:00 or 4:00 a.m. Often, family members ate a late meal and watched videos from Hong Kong to wind down after a long evening. Given that families' lives revolved around shop hours, these Chinese young people reported that they never seemed to have enough time. According to Annie, "We're busy, always rushing, we're used to rushing, even when we're at home [it's a fifteen minute walk to the shop]. My mum rushes all the time, because when there's a customer, she takes an order, and she has to cook very fast. Even with driving, she's always rushing. And it's not good for eating, having to catch times to eat, so you don't eat at a regular time, at all odd hours."

Most families also had a weekly routine of shop work that revolved around the preparation of food, with weekends as their busiest days. According to Jacqui:

It depends on the day. There's a kind of weekly routine. Almost all the days involve some different work and preparation. Tuesday and Sunday's lunch is not open, otherwise the shop is open for lunch and dinner, seven days a week.

Sundays

Usually a lie-in day [a relatively slow day] because Saturday nights are usually quite busy, with a massive cleaning job [in the kitchen]. In the morning my dad gets up before my mum, and cleans the outside fan shutter thing; he does this for half the morning. It's the fan that takes in all the grease, like a funnel. When mum gets up, she prepares food for the evening, or takes food out to defrost, and makes lunch for us. Once that's done, my parents spend the afternoon watching a Chinese video, until 5:00, when they have to open the shop. They'll make the rice beforehand, take all the food out. Depending upon how busy Sunday night is, if it's not busy, they peel prawns or slice meat. It's quite an easy day, Sunday. Before they close, dad prepares the meat for the spare-ribs, for Monday morning. They close at 11:30 and clean up.

Mondays

Dad gets up first. Preparing spare-ribs is a long process, so he starts Sunday night. He soaks them in a sauce, and cooks them before you actually fry them. Dad does that Monday mornings. Recently, since I've started college in London, mum usually comes down with me to London on Monday mornings because she wants to see a Chinese herbalist doctor. Throughout mum's working experience, she's had increasing problems with her hands, so she sees the doctor once a week, and I suppose it's an element of release for her as well, going into London. During the evening, dad might do the potatoes for chips. Mondays are usually a slow day.

Tuesdays
It's like Sunday in that the shop's closed for lunch, so it's a bit of a lie-in day. If Dad didn't do the chips on Monday evening, he'll do them on Tuesday morning, and they'll do a bit of food preparation. By the afternoon, both mum and dad will go into town. Tuesdays is the day off for most Chinese take-aways, so it's a good way for meeting up with everybody. Some families close for Tuesday evening as well, but we only close for Sunday and Tuesday lunch, no entire days off.

Fridays and Saturdays
These are the busiest days for custom, and lots of food preparation. Fridays are the days mum goes to market for all the fresh vegetables or fruit. A local market.

M.S.: So when your mum goes to market, she gets food for your family meals as well?

Jacqui: Yes, well, it's all together. The shop food and the family food is one; there's only one kitchen—in the shop.

As in Jacqui's family, the merging of family and work lives was intensified in the case of eight families who lived above their shops (however, one of these families owned a house that was rented out). For instance, domestic housework had to be done around the needs of the shop, except in the case of a few families, where the grandparents stayed home and were responsible for much of the cleaning and laundry. When asked how and when housework was done, young people who lived above their shops, such as Fai, seemed somewhat amused by this question: "Well, there is no housework as such; the shop *is* the house" (his emphasis). Seventeen of the twenty-five families owned and resided in their homes, which were often near their businesses. However, in one of these families, the parents lived above their shop with the youngest of their children, while the other two children lived in a house nearby. As Laura explained, "It's more convenient for my parents to stay in the shop; my father's always at the shop, so he'd rather live there. We spend most of our time in the shop; the house is just a place to sleep."

The Nature of Children's Work Roles

Given the centrality of work and the shop to many of these families' lives, it is not surprising that Chinese children came to contribute their labor as a part of family life (Pang, 1993). Business start-ups usually have a great need for family labor (Wong, 1988). Most families opening a business tend to have little capital left over to afford employees (Scase and Goffee, 1980b). Although some families had no choice but to rely upon waged employees, relatives (both blood and clan relatives) could be an especially important labor source for families at the start-up of their shops, since businesses are often established before children are old enough to work in them. In four families, young peoples' grandparents either lived with them at the time of interview or had lived with them in the past. These grandparents could provide child care, perform domestic housework, or work in the kitchens of these families' take-aways. However, in most families, reliance upon relatives' or employees' labor was not as widespread or as continuous as reliance upon children's labor.

The Incorporation of Children's Labor

Children in most of the sample families (20 of 25) were gradually "incorporated" (Finch, 1983) into their take-away businesses when they were relatively young (often by the age of 7 or 8), either at business start-up or in the early years of the shop. The young people in five of the families reported undergoing a marked transition from noninvolvement to working in their businesses. Typically, these latter young people had started helping out in their teenage years. For instance, Jack was the eldest of four children who had grown up without working in the shop. Jack's grandparents, who had lived with them, worked with Jack's parents. However, Jack's grandparents moved out to live with his uncle's family when he was 16 years old. His grandparents' departure precipitated his parents' insistence that all the children start working in the business. Working in the take-away business, therefore, involved a major transition for Jack and his siblings:

"None of us really like it because it's such a big change. We used to never do anything. We just took it for granted that our parents and grandparents did everything. I know it sounds a bit selfish, but we just didn't think of it at that time. We'd say, "No, we don't want to do this", because it was such a big change. . . . I think it's because we used to be so pampered by our parents."

Young people in three of these five families reported that their parents had not wanted or needed them to start working until they were in their teens. Furthermore, children in a few families did not begin working until they were in their teens because these families had started their businesses relatively late (in relation to the age of their children).

However, for children in twenty families, incorporation into the business evolved as an important part of family life:

M.S.: Can you tell me how you started working in the shop, how you got involved?

Foon: I don't know. They've never asked us. It's almost as though it's just expected. We just watched and learned when we were young. There was no training course or anything. . . . When we came back from school, we came back to the shop and hung around. That's where the TV was—at the counter, in the shop. We didn't have a TV upstairs [their living quarters].

What was stressed by these young people was that it all seemed "so natural"—in other words, working in the shop was second nature to their everyday lives. While they were aware that their experiences of childhood differed from the Western norm of childhood, most young people characterized their work roles as developing in the context of family needs and circumstances rather than a purposeful mode of socialization (James and Prout, 1996).

Such an understanding of children's labor participation thus departs from analyses that primarily emphasize patriarchal authority and power in explaining how women's and children's labor may be incorporated into various family livelihoods (Finch, 1983; Walby,

1990; Delphy and Leonard, 1992; Adkins, 1995). Despite the strength of patriarchal authority, which is legitimized by means of tradition and personal loyalty (Newby, 1977; Hood-Williams, 1990), such authority cannot, on its own, fully explain children's committed labor on behalf of their families. These children's experiences and understandings of working for their parents was much more complex than the notion of parental authority suggests, as illustrated below.

> *M.S.:* How did you start helping out in the shop? Did your parents ask you?
>
> *Shirley:* Well, we were just there. It wasn't even like "Come and help us." We were naturally there. We went there to eat.

When I asked young people if their parents had told them that they needed their help, they commonly responded in the following ways:

> *Sui:* No, they've never said, "We need you." You don't need to say it really.
>
> *Fai:* If you ask me, yes, they needed us, but they're not saying it in that way. It was understood.

In addition to the fact that their parents needed their help, and the fact that much of family life revolved around the shop, some young people reported that they had spent a lot of time in their take-aways because of their parents' protectiveness toward them. According to Wong, "At the time, I just thought that it was her [mother] forcing us to work in the shop and everything else, but it wasn't that. . . . But it was purely because she was such a protective person. My mother looks at the world from the worst possible angle, and she expects life to be full of badness. It was more the protective feeling because my parents are always saying, 'Yes, you have to remember that you are in someone else's country,' which I think is crap, basically."

Typically, children who started working at a young age started out doing "easy things" in the kitchen, such as washing dishes, peeling prawns and potatoes, and other tasks which were considered suitable for young children. While the performance of these "simple" labor intensive tasks was clearly productive for the family business, keeping children busy at such tasks was also a means of managing child care for parents who needed to work extremely long hours in their shops.

The availability and potential productivity of children's labor tended to increase as children grew older. Children's work responsibilities increased over time. This was usually signaled by their learning new skills in the kitchen, such as cutting vegetables and meat with knives, or using woks, which are quite heavy, and not easily handled by young children. As children grew older, they were able to move from the back to the front to work at the counter. Although parents with very limited English language proficiency could take orders at the counter (the dishes were numbered), children who were fluent in English were better able to deal with customers, as Wong explained: "The moment you have, 'Can I have the chicken chow mein, but I don't want some bean sprouts, and I want extra onions,' then you know, that's exactly the scenario. I just want to show you where it [his parents' communication with customers] breaks down. To say 'chicken chow mein,' that's fine, no problems, but as soon as you say more. . . . That's the sort of thing they'll [his parents] have problems with." Not only did the increased diversity and responsibility of children's work roles over time mean that children could relieve their parents of some work pressure, but their availability as mature workers meant that families were much less reliant upon paid employees and extended relatives.

Complementing Parents' Work Roles

Children's work roles complemented the parents' division of labor, which tended to be concentrated in cooking, various forms of kitchen work, and the management of the business. This was because while the children in a few families knew how to cook all the dishes, in most families, parents possessed the cooking expertise.

The most common division of labor between parents was in terms of a gendered kitchen hierarchy (Song, 1995): both parents' main roles were in the kitchen, with fathers as the chefs, and mothers working as kitchen assistants. In these families, fathers' and mothers' work roles in the kitchen were demarcated by the fact that fathers tended to do the "more skilled" work, such as marinating and spicing food, making the sauces, roasting meats, while mothers did work that was more labor-intensive and "unskilled." Before business ownership, the mothers in these families usually had experience in catering as kitchen assistants, while fathers had worked as chefs or as waiters. As a result, more fathers than mothers had professional cooking experience. This gendered hierarchy accords with Chinese women's subordinate status in the Chinese catering industry in New York City's Chinatown (Zhou, 1992). Although her study focused upon much larger Chinese firms in Taiwan, Greenhalgh (1994:754) also found that while 19 percent of male family members worked in managerial positions, nearly 85 percent of working female family members occupied nonmanagerial posts. This gendered hierarchy also reflects the traditionally subordinate status of women in Chinese families (Wolf, 1972; Salaff, 1981; Greenhalgh, 1994). According to Wong,

> There's a very kind of male chauvinist attitude from my father in that he gets to do all the, I was gonna say glamorous work, but you can't call it glamorous work in a take-away. But out of all the tasks that are there, all of the, you know, the better jobs you can do, like all the roasting, all of the preparation, making all the sauces, my father does that. But my mother, in certain respects, is just as good. Her frying is better than my father's, but she doesn't get to do that. So my mum gets to do things like peel the potatoes, chopping the potatoes, buying the groceries, the stuff that's a real pain in the ass, especially when it's cold and raining and everything. She has to do.

Mothers who worked as kitchen assistants tended to do more labor-intensive work than fathers. Not only did fathers tend to work as the chefs, but with the exception of a few parents, fathers also tended to do the business management. Perhaps not surprisingly, mothers (and daughters) performed the bulk of domestic housework, such as cleaning or doing the laundry (Song, 1995).

Gendered divisions of labor have also been found in other studies of immigrant families. For instance, Korean wives in the United States carry a double burden in that besides outside employment or work in their family businesses, they are responsible for the vast bulk of domestic housework (Kim and Hurh, 1988; Min, 1998). Men's refusal to perform "women's work" has also tended to be the norm in Cypriot and Asian families running businesses in Britain (see Westwood and Bhachu, 1988).

Despite the fact that many of these Chinese mothers were, on the whole, subordinate to their husbands, the mothers in a few families managed their shops and took the initiative in planning and strategizing around their livelihoods. Though not a typical case, Annie reported that her mother "[wore] the trousers in her family," and planned everything. According to Annie, "My father's not very responsible. He just turned up and did what he had to do. But my mother had to organize everything. She planned everything; she ran it [the business]. My father just worked there." In her study of Vietnamese refugees in the United States, Kibria (1994) has argued that in the context of migration, the economic power of Vietnamese men declines vis-à-vis women, so that their male authority could be weakened. In such households, wives' waged labor could be crucial in countering men's authority, especially if their husbands encounter any periods of unemployment.

In addition to gender roles, the differential way in which cooking and business skills were acquired by Chinese mothers and fathers was clearly important in shaping the parents' division of labor. Although many of these young people (both male and female) noted gendered practices and norms in relation to their parents' division of labor, they also stressed parent-child division of labor. Children in these families tended to note *both* their parents' limitations, particularly in relation to English language proficiency. Parents' division of labor and their limitations were key in shaping Chinese children's labor participation. Work not performed by the parents had to be performed by other sources of labor, such as employees or relatives, but more often the children. A crucial factor shaping the degree to which parents relied upon their children was English language competence.

Children and Caring Work

Chinese children's labor participation in their family take-aways was relatively widespread in these twenty-five families. Few children in the sample had any part-time jobs outside of their family businesses while they had been in school. Only one respondent (of forty-two), Lisa, had a Saturday job at Boots (a drugstore chain), "for the experience" in addition to working in her family's take-away. Most children who worked in their take-away businesses had little extra time for any other part-time jobs. At the time of interview, many of the young people in this study were contributing their labor in their family take-aways, although a number of them were pursuing higher education or waged employment. Of the 42 respondents, 13 were pursuing higher education (university and postgraduate degrees), 14 were in full-time outside employment, 6 worked full-time in their take-aways, 5 were looking for work, and 4 were in the sixth form (the last 2 years of secondary school devoted to studying for "A-levels"—examinations used for university entrance). (See the Appendices for details on higher education and outside employment).

Although the popular image of Chinese children in these families usually involved them working in their take-away businesses, either at the counter, or in the kitchen, these young people also performed important forms of caring work—such as assisting, accompanying, and translating for their parents. To date, little research on the Chinese in Britain (or on any other immigrant group in Western societies) has examined the key kinds of caring work that children often perform for their parents. This caring work transcended the boundaries and rhythms of the take-away for it was performed around the clock. Children not only did labor-intensive kitchen work or took orders at the counter; but they also acted as translators and intermediaries for parents who knew little or no English. As a result, some young people grew up with a great deal of responsibility and became privy to adult concerns from a young age.

A hallmark of such responsibility was a very pronounced sense of feeling needed by their parents. According to Anna, "You knew your parents depended upon you. Half the reason they were pleased to have kids was that they needed these kids to maintain the business and they were really stretched when they had to hire any staff, and their lives got easier as you grew older, and you took on more responsibility. And I just feel that my mum and dad could never have had a shop of their own and not had children."

Some of the work performed by Chinese children seems to suggest some parallels with the caring labor performed by adult children, usually daughters, for their elderly parents (see Finch and Groves, 1983; Ungerson, 1987; Lewis and Meredith, 1988). Described as a labor of love, looking after elderly parents is based upon intense feelings of obligation and guilt, as well as love and concern. Such caring work for elderly parents is said to be difficult, in part, because it seems to reverse the traditional parent-child relationship—rather than parents caring for their children, adult children, in turn, look after their parents in infirmity and illness. While this kind of work seems almost universal for adult daughters, the performance of caring work by children or adolescents, rather than adults, is relatively unusual in most contemporary Western societies.

Chinese young people who had to act as mediators and translators for their parents could contribute to key decisions made in their families and their take-away businesses—a finding that accords with those of Sung (1987) and Wong (1988) in their studies of Chinese immigrants in New York City. In fact, children's roles as interpreters was highlighted in an article in the *New York Times* (Alvarez, October 1, 1995): "With immigration now at a postwar high in the United States, there are literally millions of children who, like Seong, are thrust into awkward positions of power within their families. Serving as their parents' English interpreters, they also serve as their cultural interpreters, translating unfamiliar customs as pint-sized liaisons between the old world and new." Nevertheless, I found some variation in the degree to which children performed caring work for their parents. For many children, their daily lives were fundamentally structured by their parents' reliance upon them for mediation and various forms of labor, while for a minority of children, their parents' reliance upon them was minimal. The performance of caring work was strongly linked with other forms of children's labor participation in the take-away. Therefore, I categorized children's labor participation in terms of the variable degree of caring and shop work these children performed for their parents.

Children in most of the sample families (eighteen of twenty-five) had *integral* work roles in relation to their parents and their family businesses. These children tended to have a great deal of responsibility in the running of their families' take-away businesses. Children in these families tended to work fairly regularly in their shops, for instance, in the evenings, after school, or during weekends. Children who had to be at their shops when they opened (usually 5:00 or 5:30 p.m.) had lives that were very structured by shop hours. According to Sai, "I was there every night. I had to be there at 5:00, when it opened. I had to be there, even if I wasn't doing anything. Certain things, like making chips, that was my job. So I did that after school, and got it sorted out before 5:00."

In another family, Wong and his brother Foon, as the two eldest children, grew up helping out in the shop almost every evening. Their parents had no formal education, spoke no English, and did not drive. Not only did Wong and his brother accompany their parents to most appointments and places, but Foon was responsible for the bookkeeping and business management of the shop by the time he was 15 years old. Furthermore, the two brothers knew how to cook most of the dishes and worked at the counter. In this respect, they were much more flexible workers than their parents, who were largely confined to the back of the shop. In addition to the fact that many of these children contributed their labor regularly in their take-aways, integral children reported a strong sense of being needed by their parents, which stemmed primarily from the caring work they performed. As Wong put it, "We are our parents' guide dogs to the world. It's providing a lifeline to the outside world. Because you've got to understand. Sorry, that's not [*pause*] you've got to remember that my parents, o.k., they live in such an isolated world, that it's really difficult to comprehend, without speaking English. They can't write it, I mean, they can't even write their own language. They don't have the freedom to go about helping themselves. How are they gonna cope with old age, and we hear stories all the time, that even to be English and to be old is such a nightmarish proposition, that in my parents' situation, it's at a level much more lower, and it's terrifying, and that's why the guilt gets even more, because you know that the severity of their difficulties is going to increase, as well."[1]

Typically, neither parent in families in which children were integral spoke, read, or wrote more than very limited English. Many of these parents, in fact, had little or no formal education in Hong Kong. In one family, Richard, age 24, worked full-time in the shop for his parents. Richard worked at the counter and managed all the accounts. He did the bookkeeping, the quarterly value-added tax payments, and had meetings with the accountant and the bank manager. In another family, Mary, age 26, started managing her family's shop when she turned 16 and was described by her sister as "basically my parents' secretary." Not only did she manage the financial aspects of the shop, but she also assisted them, for example, with doctors' appointments or returning purchases in stores.

Older children, particularly daughters, often took on semiparenting roles with younger siblings. For instance, Ming, age 19, had a younger sister who was 11 years old. Because her parents spoke very little English and had very little knowledge of the British school system, Ming attended meetings with her younger sister's teachers to arrange for the transition from primary to secondary school. While sons and daughters did not systematically perform separate tasks in the take-away, caring work was more clearly gendered, especially in relation to meetings with doctors and teachers. This kind of work seemed to be regarded as appropriate for daughters, particularly by parents, but also by some sons, who reported that they would be highly embarrassed to translate medical, and particularly gynecological matters for their mothers.

Given the substantial amount of responsibilities that integral young people had, many of them reported common themes around a loss of childhood. They had grown up as "little adults," given the responsibilities that caring work and working in the shop had entailed. As Anna put it, "A lot of that feels like a loss of childhood, almost. I don't feel in a sense, we were ever really young, because we were working so young."

Themes about children being little adults have also been described in a very different context. Ennew (1982:552) described poor Jamaican children as "proto-adults," who were key contributors to their families' survival strategies: "As children learn the skills of the casual sector [the informal economy], they grow into proto-adults for whom physical, intellectual and emotional immaturity do not preclude either social and economic independence or the assumption of a high degree of responsibility for self, and frequently also for others."

One daughter, Sue, recalled the difficulty of having to divine adult information and knowledge in her efforts to mediate for her parents, especially in business meetings, which required very detailed translations: "It was a lot of work, especially, at a young age, when you don't know that much about the outside world, mortgages, etc. You just don't know the background to all that. And all of a sudden you're flung to the deep end. Your parents often show a letter in the middle of a transaction, or from a source, and your Chinese isn't at the level where you can explain exactly what's going on." Therefore, the performance of caring work for parents was significant in terms of children's intense sense of responsibility for their parents. It was not just working in the take-away business but also feeling relied upon in particular ways, that compounded children's sense of their importance to their family livelihoods.

In addition to the eighteen families in which children were integral workers, there were four families in which children played a *supplementary* role in their family livelihoods. On the whole, supplementary children were in families where they performed less caring work than integral children. In these families, there was one parent with some (albeit limited) English language skills; as such, these children did not always need to translate or to accompany their parents for all errands and/or appointments.

Young peoples' evaluation of their parents' English language skills was subjective and not assessed in a systematic way. Even if parents of supplementary children did not *objectively* speak more English than the parents of integral children, the former may have felt more able or willing to try communicating in English. Some parents were reportedly unabashed about trying out their limited English with customers, grocers, and sales clerks, but others were very self-conscious and intimidated by such encounters. Therefore, supplementary children sometimes had to provide caring work in certain situations that were simply beyond their parents (or for the parent who did not speak English). For instance, some of these children reported that their mothers were effectively "helpless," because they spoke little or no English. These mothers did not feel confident about going out on their own or using public transport without accompaniment, so they could be extremely isolated in their homes and had to rely upon their children or spouses to accompany them to various places. According to Richard, one key reason why his mother seemed so helpless was not only her lack of proficiency in English but also her lack of education more generally: "My mum's very quiet; she argues very little unless she's very very upset. She can't be bothered to argue. It's the way she's been brought up and the very little education she got. She's helpless. If she had more education, she would put up more of a fight."

Children who were supplementary also tended to work regularly in their shops and could be involved in some of the business management. Nevertheless, their overall work responsibilities were more limited than those of integral children. Because these children's caring responsibilities were more limited, their sense of their parents' reliance upon them was diminished compared with integral children.

In contrast with both integral and supplementary children, children in three of the twenty-five families had *minor* work roles: Minor children did not perform any caring work, and unlike the integral and supplementary children, they did not grow up working regularly in their shops. Furthermore, the children in these families had relatively little knowledge of how their shops ran. None of the children in these families knew how to cook the dishes on the menus and tended to be limited to occasional counter work or forms of food preparation when they did work in their shops. Perhaps the most striking difference between integral or supplementary children and minor children was that minor children did not feel that their parents really needed them; these children reported that their parents could manage without their help.

In fact, these children were quite marginal to the operation of their shops. Young people in these families usually worked only occasionally in their shops, for instance, as back-up labor if the shop became very busy, or perhaps during school holidays. As a result, these children did not experience the time constraints, in relation to school work or social lives, or the family and work pressures that most integral and supplementary children reported.

For instance, in one family, Theresa and her two younger brothers performed minor work roles. Most significantly, they did not have to translate on behalf of their parents, who both spoke English. Theresa's mother had been raised in Singapore (where English is widely spoken) and worked as a nurse in Britain before shop ownership, and her father had worked at various odd jobs in Britain for many years and had gradually learned English. Moreover, Theresa's labor participation was only occasional, and when she did work, she was mostly confined to counter work; she didn't know how to cook most of the dishes. According to Theresa, "I quite like it [working in the shop]. A lot of customers say, 'I remember you when you were this high.' You see, I'm not stuck down here [at the counter] every night. If I was to work every night, I'd be like, 'oh go away.' My friends hate it. They're so rude to customers. They're bored." This family's business reportedly did well, and this enabled Theresa's family to hire employees, thus freeing up their children for school work and leisure time.

Furthermore, the parents of minor children had different educational and occupational backgrounds from the parents of integral and supplementary children. In two of these three families, both parents were reasonably fluent in English; in the other family, the mother was fluent in English, and her husband was taking English lessons at the time of interview. In one family, both parents had worked in an hospital, as a nurse and a radiographer, before opening up a take-away. In the other two families, both mothers had also worked as nurses in Britain before shop ownership.

In addition to the fact that the children in these families did *not* feel needed by their parents, their parents did not necessarily expect them to work in the shop (an issue elaborated upon in chapter 5). The young people in these three families noted that their parents, and their families more generally, were atypical of most Chinese families running take-aways in Britain. They reported that their parents were less traditional than most Chinese parents in Britain. For instance, Colin said of his parents, "My parents are very liberal for Chinese parents. They're different, they're pretty easygoing." Although Colin reported that his parents would be pleased if he wanted to work more in the take-away, they had not pressured him to do so. Moreover, the parents in two of these three liberal families were in their early forties, and were younger than most of the parents in this sample. In addition to educational and background differences, there may also have been some attitudinal and lifestyle differences between the older parents and these younger parents, which shaped the differential reliance upon their children's labor.

However, the three families in which children had minor work roles were somewhat exceptional in this sample. As discussed before, most of the families in this study tended to be headed by parents with little or no formal education and limited English language skills. Although I can only speculate on this point, based upon my conversations with these young people and with Chinese social workers and community workers, children with integral and supplementary work roles seemed to be more wide-spread than those with minor work roles among Chinese families running take-aways in Britain.

To summarize, the nature and degree of Chinese children's labor participation seems to have been integrally shaped by their parents' *need* for their labor and English language skills. While in practice, the performance of caring work, domestic housework, and shop work were often combined, and part and parcel of children's lives, the regular performance of caring work in a variety of social situations made children's work roles qualitatively different from work that did not involve caring for their parents. This was because, for integral children, looking after their parents usually entailed a great deal of responsibility and a strong awareness of their parents' reliance upon them.

Birth Order and Gender

Thus far, we have discussed variation in the degree to which parents relied upon their children across different families. However, there were also some patterned differences in the labor participation of children within families, particularly by birth order and gender. Overall, birth order was recognized as an important factor in organizing divisions of labor between siblings within families (see Brannen 1995 for a discussion of children's housework). This was found to be the case in Glenn's historical study of Chinese family strategies in the United States: "Third was the division of labor by age and gender, with gradations of responsibility according to capacity and experience. Elder siblings were responsible for disciplining and taking care of young siblings, who in turn were expected to defer to their older brothers and sisters."

In general, older children performed more caring, shop, and domestic work than their younger siblings, and this seemed to be a widely held practice among these Chinese families (however, exceptions are discussed in chapter 6). The emphasis upon older children doing more work was intensified in cases where there was a significant age difference between older and younger siblings.

Often, differences in work roles by birth order combined with disparities by gender. Twenty-one of twenty-five families had children of both sexes. Both daughters and sons in most families reported that daughters were expected to perform more caring work and domestic housework than their brothers. For instance, Sui, age 33, reported that she had felt like a "little mummy" to her younger siblings:

M.S.: You're nine years older than the others, right? Do you think that that meant more work responsibility for you when you were growing up?

Sui: Oh yes, I think so. My parents relied upon me not only to work in the shop, but to take everybody to the doctors, be the communicator. And also, as a babysitter. My parents don't speak any English. My dad speaks broken English. I had to read all the correspondence for my parents. Any queries. Also traveling.

M.S.: That must have been such a great responsibility.

Sui: Well [laughs], I grew up with it, so I didn't know otherwise.

M.S.: Did your brothers and sister, when they got older, also help out?

Sui: Yes. My sister worked the next hardest because she was the next oldest, and she was more willing than my brother. My brother tended to be let off more because he was naughty. He didn't do things properly. The little one [another brother] got off completely.

M.S.: How did you feel about that?

Sui: I think I treated my brothers and sister as somebody who is really young. I was quite paternalistic with them. But my sister did resent my brother because he was only one year younger, and he got let off from all these things. My brothers not helping with things was a big mistake. They don't know how to look after the family. They never learned how to do it.

My mother always kept it away from them. She thought it was a privilege for them, but it's really [*pause*] they [brothers] don't understand things as quickly as we do.

As an integral and oldest child, and as a daughter, Sui had a significantly greater set of work responsibilities, compared with her siblings, particularly her brothers.

In contrast with the experiences of eldest children, the youngest children in families tended to grow up doing less work than their siblings for they were often protected by parents and older siblings from shop work in particular. Most respondents who were older children accepted, to a certain extent, that they would be more relied upon, given the widespread norm that older children do more than younger children. For instance, Kam, age 26, had a younger sister, age 21, and a younger brother, age 12, and had a much greater work role in the shop than her younger siblings:

M.S.: When you say your brother helps occasionally, how often is that?

Kam: It depends. Not regular [*laughs*]. Maybe once a month. When I am busy. He is 12, but he is not serving the people. He is doing other things. I am serving the people and do everything because I am the biggest.

M.S.: Do you feel that you have certain responsibilities that they do not have?

Kam: I did more because I am the elder one, I have to. This is my job, my duty to do it, so I just do it. I don't mind it.

Unlike Kam, however, some of the daughters who reported doing more work than their brothers resented this disparity. For instance, Tina, age 19, and Kelly, age 18, were two sisters who worked a great deal in their parents' take-away business. They had two older brothers, age 22 and 21. Tina reported that she and her sister grew up doing much more work and that they had been more "responsible" than their brothers had been: "My parents might say [to her brothers], 'Why don't you just go home if you're not gonna help out?' It gets me so uptight when I hear that. I'd rather he had to just sit there, doing nothing, than going home. Cause he's the older, and he should show me the way through, really. He's older, and he should show me how to. He's not incapable of doing it; he just doesn't want to do it." Not only did Tina feel that her older brothers received preferential treatment on the basis of their sex, but what compounded her dismay was the fact that her two *older* brothers were not behaving like older brothers—the norm of birth order was contravened. Interestingly, daughters who reported that their brothers were privileged in terms of their work responsibilities were generally more accepting and resigned about this if their brothers were younger than they were (as in the case of Sui, above).

Like Parker (1994), who reported that Chinese daughters tended to perform more labor than sons in the take-away, some daughters in these families performed more work than sons, but this disparity was clearest in terms of daughters' performance of caring work and domestic housework. In fact, I found no clear-cut and systematic disparity in the labor contributions or work roles of daughters and sons in the take-away.[2]

Given the small sample, it is difficult to generalize about the combined effects of birth order and gender, or to be able to disentangle the effects of the two. However, being female, and the eldest, often meant that such children carried an especially heavy work role in relation to their siblings. The opposite example of this was the experience of the youngest son, who by virtue of both his birth order and sex, often did less work in comparison with his older siblings. We will return to the issue of differences in siblings' labor participation in chapter 6, when we discuss differences between siblings in more individualistic terms.

Children's Labor Participation in Broader Context

One important reason why children's labor was so central to these family economies was that it tended to be very reliable and continuous over time, particularly in comparison with other sources of labor, such as employees and relatives (Sanders and Nee, 1996). Nine families never had paid employees (nonrelatives) in the history of their shops, while the remaining sixteen families had employees off and on over the years. Only two of these sixteen families had employees almost continuously.

I would argue that reliance upon children's labor cannot be understood solely or even predominantly in terms of financial considerations (although this surely played a part).[3] Children's roles as translators and mediators could not easily be replaced by employees, because some parents had to rely upon their children for English language assistance and guidance in almost every facet of their lives. Hiring employees was often a very fraught matter, and children were especially valued as workers because of the various difficulties associated with relying upon employees.

While employees did lighten the workload, they still needed to be supervised by a family member. Most families who had employees relied upon them as low-level kitchen assistants; typically, families aimed to employ a relatively inexperienced, and therefore inexpensive, employee who would work *under* the direction of the chef. Employee turnover was high because many employees were paid low wages as inexperienced staff. Furthermore, relying upon employees for counter work was considered risky because, according to respondents, family members, rather than employees, needed to do the public relations aspect of the job—this included chatting with regulars and in some cases listening to their personal problems. Showing a family face to the shop was seen as imperative in establishing and solidifying a regular customer base. Employees simply could not be trusted, or expected, to put effort into the work involved in customer relations. In addition, a number of young people reported that they had had trouble with dishonest counter workers who stole money, or who gave away free food to their friends. Gold (1992:187) also found that ethnic business owners' reliance upon co-ethnic labor could be problematic: "In contrast to their positive characterizations of Latino labor, Soviet Jewish and Vietnamese employers described co-ethnic workers as disrespectful, overly ambitious, unwilling to do hard physical labor, potentially criminal, and generally more difficult to manage and fire."

Only one of the families in this study employed a white British man to do home deliveries. Based upon my observations, a few take-aways (other than those in this study) did employ white British people, either for counter work or for home delivery, but this still seemed far less common than hiring Chinese employees. One reason why some families may hire white workers at the counter is that they hope to avoid, or at least minimize, racial harassment from their predominantly white customers.

A key difficulty with relying upon co-ethnic employees was that most Chinese employees expected (as in the wider Chinese ethnic economy) to receive housing and food, in addition to a wage. For families who lived above their shops, this also meant living with employees. Sharing living quarters with employees was problematic from several points of view. For one, crowding in living quarters was a serious problem for a number of the families who lived above their shops:

M.S.: When did your employee from the early days leave?

Yee-ling: She left about two years after we came [Yee-ling and her siblings had joined their parents in Britain when Yee-ling was in her teens]. After that, no more outside labor. Actually we cannot afford outside labor. Not so much in terms of money, but in terms of reliability. It's not easy to employ somebody. You have to provide accommodation as well as wages. We all lived upstairs [above the shop], and there's only three bedrooms and a bathroom. My mum and dad had a room, my grandma, my two sisters and me and my brother, the five of us in one room. Can you imagine? While the employee was with us, my brother was in the room with us because the employee had her own room. Not having a wardrobe, all the beds. It was very messy.

Another difficulty was that neither family members nor employees enjoyed much privacy, not only in their home lives, but also in terms of the work environment. In addition to concerns about trusting employees, working with employees introduced new forms of stress:

M.S.: About outside labor, was affordability the main issue?

Anna: Distrust. You can't trust people with money because a lot of it's counter stuff and it's like you had to know the people you were hiring, otherwise you'd have to have all the modern technology like the till-toll. . . . The part-timers we had for a short while when my brothers weren't there didn't work anyway. I think it affected the way the family worked. I think with the family, there doesn't have to be this politeness around; it's just like do it, and peoples' tempers get frayed, and it's OK to get frayed because people know where you're coming from because you've lived there. But there's a stress when there's someone there. You have to keep a united front as a family, you have to pretend you were happy, you didn't want people to look down on you and say, hey, look, they fight all the time. So it's constantly a front. If there's someone else there, you have to play the role of the dutiful daughter, the caring parent.

Therefore, parents' reliance upon their children as workers was motivated by a range of difficulties that hiring employees entailed for families, such as affordability, trust and privacy. Outside employees, both Chinese or British, "spoiled" the family basis of these enterprises.[4]

The centrality of children's labor in Chinese take-aways stems from a combination of factors, including parents' limited English abilities and educational backgrounds, the labor intensiveness of take-aways, and the unusually intense intertwining of family and work lives. In fact, these Chinese take-away businesses constitute a family mode of production. I found that the dominant Western paradigms of dependent children and breadwinner parents and of clear divisions of work and family (or home) were not applicable to these Chinese families. Chinese parents were not the sole economic providers or decision-makers in most of these families because they relied heavily upon their children in various ways. This is not to deny these parents' authority and power as parents; however, integral children in particular were acutely aware of their parents' dependence *upon them,* and knew that they were crucial to both their parents' adaptation to life in Britain as well as the survival of their family businesses.

It would be simplistic and erroneous to understand children's labor participation in these families only in terms of economic rationality or in terms of parents' need for their children's language proficiency. In addition to their importance as workers in these take-away businesses, we need to explore the other motivations and meanings underlying children's labor participation, including children's own commitments and understandings of their work roles in their families. In the next chapter, I consider both the material and normative context in which children made sense of their labor participation.

4

Helping Out

THE CHINESE young people in this study reported that there was a widespread understanding and expectation that all family members should work in their take-away businesses. Their understandings of their "family work contracts" (FWC) were centered upon the belief that they should, in principle, help their parents in their take-away businesses. The majority of respondents were unequivocal in saying that children *should* help their parents in their shops: Twenty-five respondents (of forty-two) said that children should help out as much as possible; fifteen respondents thought that while children should help out, there should be limits to how much work children should perform. For instance, these fifteen respondents suggested that children's labor should not interfere with their schoolwork and social lives; also, some of these young people argued that children should not be forced to work, if they really hated it. Exceptionally, two respondents argued that children should not have to work at all in their family businesses. One of these respondents, Fai, reported that he did not feel obligated to help out and that the only reason he did so was because his father was very strict and authoritarian. However, Fai was very much the exception rather than the norm.

These family work contracts (FWCs) were not explicitly agreed "contracts" in the usual, legalistic sense. Nevertheless, the relations of production in these families, and the norms that governed these relations, constituted a different kind of contract. FWCs represented the inverse of a typical modern contract. That is, the duties involved in FWCs are diffuse, based upon trust, and not premised upon explicit consent to specific obligations (Fox, 1974:153).

Parents and children in very few families had actually discussed their respective expectations and concerns about working together. There were no clear and formal agreements about the terms of children's labor—an issue discussed in more detail in the next chapter. Nor did family work contracts evolve from conscious plans to adopt "rules" about all family members working in the take-away. Nevertheless, the children in these families suggested, in a variety of ways, that they were subject to a kind of binding and unspoken contract to help out.

Instead of being an enduring part of Chinese culture (though these contracts obviously draw upon Chinese cultural norms and traditions), these FWCs developed in the context of these families' experiences of working together under great economic and social pressure, as racialized minorities in Britain. Young peoples' beliefs and understandings about their FWCs were consistently elaborated in terms of: (a) the need to contribute to a family survival strategy; (b) helping out, and how it differed from the terms of formal employment; and (c) the recognition that children's work in take-away businesses reinforced their sense of Chinese identity in Britain.

A Family Survival Strategy

Even under auspicious conditions, migration is a jarring experience that pushes individuals and groups to acquire new knowledge as they negotiate survival and adjustment. Immigrants learn how they fit in the larger society through the contacts they establish in familiar environments. Whether youngsters sink or soar frequently depends on how they see themselves, their families and their communities. (Fernandez-Kelly and Schauffler, 1994:682)

Chinese young peoples' understandings of their FWCs were based upon a strong awareness and concern about family survival. In contrast with the norm of parents engaged in waged work in

Britain, shop ownership was commonly regarded as the culmination of a family survival strategy among many Chinese families in Britain. According to Paul, "We did accept the fact that this is how Chinese families cope if they was to immigrate to England. It was the only way. Like my mum and dad can't speak English. What can they do? The best way is to open a restaurant or take-away. I don't see any other way, to be honest, to survive. I accepted it completely." As Paul emphasized, his parents had few work options outside of the take-away. FWCs emerged out of a collective strategy in which every family member was expected to help out.

For families who were separated by staggered migration, a livelihood to which they could all contribute enabled them to unite together as a family, as in Kam's case:

M.S.: Were you happy to be united as a family?

Kam: Yeah. Because maybe you noticed before my family was separated for many years, and then we joined together in England, then we worked really hard for it [to start a business]. That's why we're so close to each other. We are not the only family; it is like this with other families over here. Closer than English families; this is different.

Therefore, working together in a family livelihood, especially in the aftermath of families being separated, was seen to be both the material and symbolic means by which families could unite, survive, and hopefully prosper. Furthermore, some individuals like Kam articulated the belief that their families were "closer than English families," as a result of their hardships and their collective efforts at survival. Although Kam may not have drawn as sharp a distinction between her family and English families running small businesses, she emphasized the centrality of immigration and family separation in shaping her and her family's appreciation of being together.

Many young people grew up with the knowledge that the survival of their family livelihoods depended upon their own labor participation, and they tended to feel a great deal of personal responsibility for contributing to their families' welfare. For instance, David completely accepted his parents' reliance upon him: "With family working, and children helping out, you save on labor costs, on wages. That's an asset, isn't it?". For Anna, survival was a key concern in childhood: "You always had certain responsibilities around the shop, and you were always aware of finances. When it's quiet [pause] I remember my sister and I used to talk, like this has been a really bad week. And you become kind of business orientated because you know that economically this is all your family has to survive." Given these families' very real concerns about meeting subsistence needs, emphasis was typically placed upon collective needs and aims over individual goals and desires.

In addition to concerns about survival, helping out was regarded as "the least we can do," according to many young people. Since working in the business was part of a collective strategy, it was expected and justified in terms of *equity:* Children felt that it would be wrong not to work, when their parents had to work very long and arduous hours in their businesses. According to Pue-lai, "Cause they [parents] always say you have to work to live. The shop is not only for me, you have to help me to earn as well. So we got the shop." As a result, many children, like Wai-sun, reported that they had an "equal responsibility" (with their parents) for the viability of their family livelihoods:

> I'm just as responsible as my parents really, cause it's a family business, we have it. It's not like oh, I'm just doing my job, and that is it, and I don't care about anything else. I care for it, and we really feel that it's our own business.

Racism and Family Support

This collective sense of responsibility for survival was keenly felt not only because of material survival pressures but also because of experiences of racism. In addition to racism at school, university, and in employment, young peoples' experiences of racism while working at the take-away counter were rife. According to

Stephen, "They'll [customers] say things like, 'You're in our country, chink, and you should be serving us.' Things like that. So generally, we tend to ignore that, to avoid trouble."

Some racial and drunken abuse was the norm for most families, and most young people tried to steel themselves to it over the years. Thirty-seven of the forty-two respondents considered racism to be a serious problem, and had a number of stories to tell. In addition to fights breaking out in their shops, these families' livelihoods were also threatened. According to Foon, who experienced many racist incidents in the take-away:

> The work itself isn't hard or difficult. It's just the duration of it, and the unsociable hours. None of the work's hard, it's not dirty. Some of the customers are difficult. If you've got rowdy customers, it's unpleasant for everyone. They take the mickey [teasing, but often with a hostile edge], and they call you all sorts of names. After the pubs shut, there will be a whole group of them; they've drunk too much, and they give you hassle. And it's murder, just those five minutes seem like a lifetime. . . . We have the odd times when like this guy came in with a rotweiler, yeah, and he said, "If you don't give me this for free, I'm gonna let this dog go." So we just gave it to him. There wasn't much that we could do. Things like that. You don't mess about with these people, you know? That is the bad aspect, obnoxious customers.

In another interview, Kam stressed that her family's vulnerability to racism and threats had ramifications for their personal safety, as well as for business survival:

> M.S.: Do you ever have difficulties with customers?
>
> Kam: Of course, you have. Some people do make trouble. Sometimes they just grab their food, and just run away, without paying. Sometimes they say, oh, I forgot my purse. Ask for credit. You can't really refuse.

M.S.: Did you ever give credit to regular customers?

Kam: We had, but they never come back. My parents keep saying, don't do any more credit, but they still do it. It's hard to refuse, you're still living in that area, you don't want [them] to break your window, your glass. To keep the peace.

I also found that young women who worked at the counter had to negotiate various forms of sexism and sexual harassment in addition to racist abuse. Many young women reported that they were treated as sexually available and pliant by certain male customers—these young women encountered male customers calling them "lotus flower" or "Suzy Wong". Despite the prevalence of racist encounters across the take-away counter, a number of young people also reported that their families had good relationships with some customers and were clearly proud of the fact that their businesses were established in their neighborhoods, especially in comparison to the plethora of new pizza and kebab businesses, which changed hands quite often.

Chinese young people were often protective of their parents, who were less able to counter verbal abuse, since many parents spoke little or no English. Some respondents reported that they tended to differ from their parents on how to respond to racism. While most parents tended to uphold the dictum "the customer is always right," most young people said that there had to be limits to serving abusive customers. However, according to Jacqui, even parents could be pushed too far, and fought back:

There was this one occasion: It was late in the evening, and my mum came out to serve this customer. This customer was the only one in the shop. It was about quarter to twelve, and he was verbally offensive—racially and sexually. He'd obviously had something to drink or was on something, and he was saying things like, "I'd like some cock chop suey." And my mum made out that she didn't know what he was saying, but she knew, and she was getting infuriated, and went back into the kitchen, pulled out a chopper, a big knife, and she went back, and said, with her accent and everything, "Would you like this!" and pulled out this knife, rammed it on the table. And the guy just looked at her, looked at the table, and just froze, turned white as a sheet, and walked out of the shop. That just gives you a smile at the end of the day. I'm sure she was pleased that she did that. My dad was in the kitchen, but she didn't say anything; she wanted to deal with this.

Nevertheless, respondents said that they understood their parents' very pragmatic motivations for not fighting back on most occasions. A number of young people reported that their protectiveness of their parents, as well as their collective anger at racist abuse, brought their families closer together in some respects. Thus racism (which is also discussed later in this chapter) had some fortifying, as well as debilitating, effects upon Chinese families; family members rallied together and protected one another (Joseph, 1981; Carby, 1982; Modood et al., 1994; Virdee, 1995).

This sense of shared responsibility and mutual support, against the background of business pressures and racism, meant that these young people saw their family work contracts in terms of familial *interdependence,* rather than just having to work for one's parents. The sense of mutual need and support developed, over the long-term, as families migrated, adjusted, and worked together—even for integral children, who performed a great deal of caring work for their parents. For instance, Jacqui, who was integral to her family business, reported, "The dependency, it was almost an equal dependency in many ways, between the parents and children, in the business. . . . My parents didn't speak much English when they first started out. We as children were dependent upon our parents because they had the business. It was a way of getting food on the table, clothes." According to Sai, "Yeah, because basically, I think we needed each other. My brother, his wife, and my parents, they really needed each other, cause that business, the second shop, we started it from scratch. So it was quite a big risk to start something afresh. And my brother and his wife needed a job. It took nearly a year to set up a business. So whether they like it or not, they were dependent upon each other. At the time, they couldn't afford to have new staff. They give each other security, they help each other." Therefore, most family members had no choice but to depend upon one another. It was in a context of collective material survival and social adaptation that family work contracts developed.

The Terms of Helping Out

The relatively widespread consensus that children should help out in their take-away businesses reflected the complex balance of both moral and material imperatives underlying these Chinese families' FWCs. Most respondents talked about the strength of family and family obligations in ways that suggested the powerful ideological pull of such terms and the potentially double-edged nature of family ties. As Mary noted, "With your family, you have to work extra hard, because it's your family, whereas if you're in nine-to-five, you don't kill yourself over it." Mary is articulating the view that because family relationships are somehow "special," in comparison with employment relations, more is expected of someone as a family member. One therefore goes beyond the call of duty, because working for one's family is infused with power-ful meanings (Rapp et al., 1979; Finch, 1989).[1]

In talking about helping out, many young people reported a constant tension between *wanting* to help out and feeling that they *had* to help out. As Pue-lai put it, "It's really hard to say pushed or not, but thinking, oh yeah, your father's earning, and you have to help as well, so I help." Some young people reported feeling a great deal of pressure to help out, particularly if they were integral to the viability of their family take-aways.

Annie struggled with the sense that helping out seemed to be "compulsory:" "'Thinking back on it now, I think, I had all this ac-cess to food, I could do what I wanted with it, I had a TV, and I think, what was so bad about it? I think it was because I had to be there, confined to that space, like being in prison, compulsory. That was what it was. I wasn't free, but I wasn't forced to work."

According to Colin: "It's family ties that come up, you know.

We'd all be quite happy not to do this. It's like a magnet, it just draws you. In a way, it isn't that bad. You do make some money, and it's fairly safe, but the emotion factor can be vindictive."

According to Sai, "It's family, I mean, you can never abandon your family, no matter how much you hate it. I mean, I hate it [the shop] an awful lot, but when it comes down to it, when they say, 'come home,' I will be home, whether I like it or not."

Kelly, too, articulated a sense of being bound to the family work contract: "Survival. They [her family] can't survive, I mean, without me. It's obligation really. Part of the family; you're meant to do this for the family. I mean, it's not like on a friendship basis. Yeah, that's no choice. I mean, if they ask you to do something, it's not as if you could say no, isn't it [laughs]? You can't say no. As Kelly notes, helping out for the family is "not like on a friendship basis." That is, family ties and obligations are perceived to be much more binding than most friendship or employment ties—they cannot be easily broken or denied.

These excerpts demonstrate that young people who believed that they should help out were not necessarily unconflicted about doing so. The ways in which Colin, Sai, and Kelly described their sense of obligation to help out indicated that they were somehow powerless, frustratingly, in shaking off the force of the magnet. Their sense of this familial magnet developed over time, as family members worked and lived together, experiencing the low points as well as the good times in their business. Although most young people did not feel solely negatively about working in their take-aways, the respondents above articulated complex and ambivalent feelings about helping out (an issue explored further in the next chapter), in ways that were representative of the entire sample.

The seeming nonnegotiability of helping out, as part of the FWC, stemmed, in large part, from the fact that most young people perceived that their families needed and expected their labor. At the same time, as long-standing participants in their family livelihoods, most of the children in these families believed in helping out; in this sense, they sanctioned the operation of this largely unspoken contract.

The Moral and the Material

A common way in which Chinese young people differentiated the norms and expectations regarding a FWC from formal employment was by referring to their labor participation as helping out, as opposed to waged employment. Family members did not contribute their labor as free workers who worked in the open labor market, but as family members. In comparison with the terms of formal employment, children in these families were subject to a more subtle and less formally prescribed contract, which stipulated employers' and employees' duties to each other. Helping out was what one respondent, Chris, called a "home ethic." As Alan Fox (1974:154) notes in *Beyond Contract:* "Thus the relationship between members of a family can hardly be said to be contractual, since there is no detailed listing of the number and duration of the rights and duties; there is usually the presumption that any particular member of the family will go far beyond his normal responsibilities in case of an emergency involving another member."

A number of analysts, in particular various feminist theorists, have argued that the public and private spheres provide two different principles of organization, with different value orientations attached to these spheres (Ferree, 1985; Cheal, 1991; Ribbens and Edwards, 1995). Olivia Harris (1981:146) has pointed out that norms based upon family and kinship obligations have been popularly regarded as constituting the antithesis of economic or market relations based upon monetary exchange—a view which suggests that there is something special and nonquantifiable about kin relationships. Also, analysts as disparate as Becker (1981) and Lasch (1977) have asserted the centrality of altruism in the functioning of households, in contrast with the outside world. Similar debates about the nature of kinship have been key within social anthropology. Bloch (1973) and Fortes (1969), among others, have broadly argued that there *is* something special about kinship obligations and ties, which distinguish them from other kinds of social obligations, in that kin will perform unconditional acts of assistance (what Fortes calls "sharing without reckoning"); that is, without considering if the assistance will be reciprocated.

By comparison, some analysts have argued that kin relationships, like other social relationships, are ultimately based on self-interest. Within such a perspective, support and assistance between kin can be explained by the expectation that both the giver and receiver will somehow gain from this exchange (either in the short or long term). That is, kin relationships do not have a distinctive moral character, and moral rules around kinship cannot be evaluated apart from the material circumstances of peoples' lives (Cohen, 1974). However, as Finch (1989:215) has pointed out, a key limitation with this view of kinship is that it may place an overly deterministic emphasis upon economic and material pressures, at the expense of the complexity of peoples' motivations.

In fact, the recognition of normative pressures to assist kin in various ways does not preclude the possibility that there may be economic and calculative aspects embedded within various forms of exchange within families. A number of anthropological studies have stressed the importance of both normative and material aspects of intergenerational exchange for family firms. For example, in his study of overseas Chinese family firms, Benedict (1968) argued that children's involvement in family firms was based upon "prestations" involving both obligations toward parents and the expectation that they would receive forms of assistance or eventually inherit their parents' businesses. Like the giving of a gift (Mauss, 1954; Corrigan, 1989), which involves not just an exchange of material commodities, but which also constitutes a moral transaction, the contribution of family labor is infused with complex meanings and social ties. Working for and with one's family has a twofold significance: Work for economic sustenance has an instrumental value, and work on the basis of family membership and obligations has a symbolic value. The ways in which Chinese young people spoke of helping out suggests that they conceived of their labor both in terms of their symbolic and material importance.

Nevertheless, a key way in which helping out was distinguished from formal employment was that it was not to be contingent upon remuneration. As a home ethic, helping out was generally seen to be unconditional, and based upon family ties. This understanding of helping out was manifest in most young peoples' attitudes toward being paid for their labor.

Young Peoples' Attitudes Toward Payment

Apart from a few individuals who worked full-time in their takeaways, few of the children in these twenty-five families were paid what could be called a wage—at least at current market rates. Most Chinese young people did not regard helping out as a part-time job. As Chan notes (1986:10), "Working for the family business is rather a duty and not a job; money given to the children is therefore not a wage but a reward or allowance."

Nevertheless, young people in five of the twenty-five families had either asked for money for helping out, or had asked for more money than they received. These children were exceptional in the sample in that they expected to be paid for their labor. Karen expressed this expectation most strongly:

> *Karen:* They [parents] give us some allowances. If they didn't, I wouldn't do it.
>
> *M.S.:* So you feel you should be paid?
>
> *Karen:* Even though I'm not employed. It's like slave labor, I reckon. It's really wrong because even if they pay 10, 20 [pounds], they [children] can be very happy as well. If you work for nothing, you just get annoyed and miserable.

Although Karen expected payment, she made it clear that she was not expecting the going market rate; rather, she pointed to the importance of a token wage. Furthermore, Karen's expectation of payment did not diminish feeling obligated to help out. For instance, later on in the interview, Karen stated, "We [she and her brother] feel we should help out because our mother works so hard, and we want to do something for her."

Unlike Karen, most respondents were acutely aware of business survival, and they tended to view payment as a perk rather than as a necessity or a right. These individuals reported that they did not and would not ask their parents for money, except for emergencies. For instance, Chris, age 17, said that *not* asking for money was part of an understanding in his family. He and his sister, aged 15, thought that they were initially given too much money: "We asked for a reduction. It was £20 before [weekly]. It's ridiculous. It was too much. And we're not really in that wealth strata, to hand out all this money. Be more realistic about how much money we have." [In recent years, the exchange rate has fluctuated between 1.5 to 1.7 dollars to each British pound.] Mindful of how financially stretched his parents were, Chris felt that accepting that much money from his parents would have been irresponsible—despite his appreciation of his parents' generosity.

Young people in seventeen of the twenty-five families had been paid some money throughout their childhood and teenage years, while children in eight families had never been paid on a regular basis. However, the amounts of payment reported were quite variable: While respondents in most families reported being paid 10 to 20 pounds weekly, those in a few families were paid as much as £80 per week, while they had still been in school. Some of these respondents reported that their payments had gradually increased as they grew older and more involved in shop work, but that the amounts they were paid could vary, depending upon how well the business did from week to week. Increased payments also reflected young peoples' need for pocket money and day-to-day expenses, such as transport, as well as the purchase of clothing and personal care items.

For the majority of young people, payment, however small, was regarded in a positive light, because it symbolized the recognition and appreciation of their labor:

M.S.: Did your parents offer you more, or did you negotiate that with them?

Anna: They offered us more. We never asked for more. Cause it was seen as a bonus, cause we worked anyway. And it was just like a little token gesture to buy yourself a record or something nice to read.

M.S.: Did you appreciate that token gesture?

Anna: Yeah, because it made us feel kind of valued, like we were a part. An integral part of that work unit. And that we weren't just doing it unappreciated. Like our labor meant something. . . . If the business did well, you might get an extra quid [pound]. You might get something nice to eat, and we'd celebrate. You were made to feel that any gain's our family's gain. It wasn't like my dad pocketed the extra.

Paul also noted that it was gratifying to feel that he had earned any money his parents offered him, given that he helped out in the take-away business: "Paying us was a nice way to do it; it meant that we weren't just putting out a hand and taking money from our parents. We were actually helping out as well. I felt sort of quite justified having taken it." Paul's sense of having earned this money, however, was not based upon a market calculus of his labor; rather, the offering and acceptance of payment for helping out was a mutual recognition of the material and symbolic value of his labor. Besides, as some children pointed out, *their* getting paid (as opposed to an employee) was all right, since it all "stayed in the family."

Unlike those who viewed payment positively, for young people in three families, payment for helping out seemed to be at odds with the way in which they differentiated helping out from waged employment. Getting paid for helping out could be contradictory for children who knew that the acceptance of payment diminished collective family resources (Parker, 1994). For instance, Laura reported that although her parents offered her and her siblings money for helping, she felt uncomfortable about accepting it: "It's because being a family business, it's part of our lives, and you don't think, it doesn't feel like real work, you know? It felt awkward, the idea of receiving a wage."

Ming, too, was not paid, and did not feel she should be: "I don't ask for money. I just feel, it's their [her parents'] money. I haven't done anything. O.K., I've worked for them, but I don't expect to get money in return. I think they've worked so hard and it's nothing compared to how they set off in the beginning, and why should I sit back and put my hand out for money?" Ming's reasoning reflected the importance placed upon fairness and "doing your own part" in a collective family strategy: Helping out was one way of "paying back" their parents for their hard work and sacrifices, which were seen to be made on behalf of their children. For these young people, getting paid for helping out seemed to contradict their understandings of their FWCs. That is, helping out could not, and should not, be quantifiable. As Ming put it: "They [parents] say that there's no price tag to family obligations."

In one case, receiving payment for helping out was regarded in quite negative terms because it could reinforce children's obligations to work in their family livelihoods. Annie, who disliked working in the take-away, saw payment as a bribe: "It was a tie. We provide a service, and she [mother] paid us off, and it's OK." Thus payment could be seen to legitimize, and to regulate children's labor participation, which was, ideally, offered willingly, impervious to calculations of material gain.

In spite of the fact that a few respondents were uncomfortable or disapproving about receiving payment for their labor, it was very difficult to insulate helping out completely from the commercial aspects of the take-away. For one, some children reported that it was difficult *not* to accept money, because money was one of the only things that parents could give to them. This was because most parents had little time and energy to take children on holidays and family outings. Respondents understood that receiving money from parents who offered it helped to assuage their parents' guilt about relying upon their help in the first place. Payment was a ritual that recognized children's contributions, and yet paying children also confirmed parents' status as providers and bosses.

As a recognition of and reward for children's labor contributions, payment did not fully commodify family relationships, and could still be consonant with most young peoples' understandings of their FWCs. Although most young people valued payment as a symbolic gesture of appreciation, most of them did not feel entitled to such payment. Therefore, a key way in which helping out was distinguished from employment was that it was labor which was performed out of good will, and it was not usually remunerated in terms of comparable market wages. With formal employment, earnings are usually the key reward for one's labor and earnings are provided in direct exchange for one's labor. When working with and for one's family, however, the provision of one's labor was supposed to be motivated by a sense of equity, family obligations, and the desire to maintain good family relationships.

Therefore, it is difficult to understand the complexities surrounding children's labor participation in small ethnic businesses (such as Chinese take-aways in Britain) primarily in terms of economic exchange. Such an analysis cannot adequately explain children's labor commitments to their family businesses, where the children are not paid or where they do not stand to gain materially from the performance of their labor (e.g., through inheritance or taking over the business).

Give-and-take

Although helping out was not supposed to be contingent upon monetary compensation for most young people, this did not preclude other forms of intergenerational exchange. Forms of exchange in the FWC were generally regarded in terms of nonexacting give-and-take over the long term. While children provided their labor, including caring work in many of these families, parents reportedly provided emotional support and pampering, in addition to forms of material support.

Maurice Bloch's (1973:83) distinction between long- and short-term exchange relationships is useful here: "the long-term relationships have a great tolerance of imbalance in the exchanges between individuals, while the shorter-term, less moral, relationships only tolerate shorter-term imbalance." Similarly, Sahlins (1965) distinguished between balanced reciprocity, which entailed direct and immediate forms of exchange, in contrast with generalized reciprocity, which was characterized by forms of exchange in the long term without any expectation of exact return. The expectation of balanced reciprocity was, in fact, seen as a denial of any close social relationship, such as kinship (Bloch, 1973).

Family work contracts, based upon family ties, tended to be understood in terms of nonexacting, generalized forms of reciprocity over the long term. Interestingly, the minority of young people working full-time in the take-away did not articulate different views of the FWC in comparison with those who only helped out on weekends or evenings. All six of these young people lived at home with their parents, but only three of them received a wage, which was between £200 and £300 (net) weekly, in addition to room and board. For instance, both Colin and Jack worked full-time in their take-aways, and Colin received £50 weekly, while Jack received free room and board but was not paid a wage (I was unable to determine if any of these wages were paid above board or under the counter): According to Jack, who seemed a bit defensive about admitting that he was not paid, "I mean, I think it works in a way. A lot of Western people don't think of it this way—unpaid work is [*pause*] but the way I look at it isn't that way, because I'm getting free boarding, all my meals cooked for me every day, and I'm getting pampered and well looked after anyway, so I can't complain. I'm getting money whenever I want. I just ask for it when I need it."

Jack's case was rather exceptional, not only because he did not receive a wage, but because he had suffered a very serious illness a few years ago, which had forced him to rely upon his parents for care. Although he had now recovered, he reported that he was "not a very independent person." Jack argued that his not being paid for working in his parents' take-away was not a problem, and made this point by contrasting his situation with how Western people might perceive such an arrangement—suggesting that Western children would have expected a real wage.[2] Despite the absence of a formal wage, Jack regarded his work role to be amply compensated by other forms of give-and-take. He did not see his work as unpaid, as in the usual dichotomy of paid/unpaid work, in which unpaid labor is devalued and unrecognized (with "women's" domestic housework and child care as the typical case of devalued unpaid labor). In another family, Richard worked full-time in the take-away and was paid £300 weekly. He had wanted to pursue another career but decided to help his parents in the family business. Therefore, being paid a real wage did not mean that the norms of the FWC did not apply.

Thus family work contracts, which were based upon generalized nonexacting forms of exchange, tended to be contrasted with a characterization of Western forms of exchange as more exacting and immediate. To the extent that FWCs were associated with Chinese families running take-away businesses in Britain, white British families, who typically had one or two parents as breadwinners, were seen to be more exacting (as one respondent put it, "tit-for-tat") in money matters. For instance, Mary observed, "We get English people in the shop who are couples, and they pay for their own meals, separately. Chinese would never do that."

Although Finch and Mason (1993) found that there was less reckoning between British parents and their adult children (in terms of various forms of exchange, such as monetary exchange), in comparison with other kin relationships, many of the families they studied also stressed the importance of "balancing responsibilities" between the giver and receiver of assistance. For many Chinese young people, one implication of helping out was that their family relationships and understandings of family were different, and "special," in relation to other British families. However, there is evidence that forms of material and emotional support also play an important role in white kin networks (see Willmott and Young, 1960; Firth et al., 1970; Pahl, 1984; Wilson and Pahl, 1988; Finch and Mason, 1993). It is therefore interesting that many Chinese respondents spoke of their family ties in ways that suggested that they were somehow different from white British families. This belief in their distinctiveness from other British families probably stemmed from these Chinese families' experiences of working together in a family livelihood, with the accompanying stresses of migration and racial discrimination.

Clearly, it was important to both parents and children that they were "giving and taking" in various ways. For example, while money for room and board was not officially recognized or accepted by parents (regardless of children's work status, whether in the take-away or in other waged work), a number of young people reported making occasional contributions by buying food and household items. Laura, who was 21 years old, worked full-time as a secretary but lived at home, and continued to help out, particularly on weekends: "I tried to give my mum some money for food and stuff like that, but she would have nothing to do with it. She'd say, 'Use that for your spending money.' She'll ask, 'How much are you getting?' and she'll say, 'You can't live off that.' And she'd just knock it back. And she'd come up with these Chinese phrases like: 'We still earn money, so we can help you out, but when we get old, you can help us out.'" Laura's mother refused the money Laura offered her, but instead noted that she would expect assistance from her daughter in old age.

In addition to forms of payment in some families, parents could offer other kinds of compensation and practical assistance. Like Jack, who was not paid, but who was pampered in various ways by his parents, Annie, who viewed payment negatively as a bribe (discussed earlier), pointed to forms of reciprocity between her and her parents: "A positive aspect of helping out was that because my parents relied upon the children, they would help us out at home when we needed it. If I needed some new shelves, my dad would fix it for me. A lot of giving and taking in that way. That was really nice. My mother would go out and take my clothes to the dry cleaners. Small things, but it's very thoughtful. So they weren't always taking from us all the time. It was more equal; they appreciate what we do." Both Jack and Annie believed that their parents' pampering of them indicated an appreciation of their children's labor.

Although most young people did not expect payment for helping out, and parents did not expect board money from their children, some children relied upon their parents for forms of material assistance. In addition to their local government grants, those who entered into higher education often needed some assistance from their parents for their daily expenses (although a few young people did not want their parents' assistance, as an assertion of independence, and/or due to concerns about their parents' financial vulnerability). It was sometimes understood that parents would offer financial assistance with children's higher education, or mortgages, or that children might inherit the business or the proceeds from it:

M.S.: Have your parents ever given you a wage?

Foon: No. I've never taken anything from mum and dad, and they've never given to me. A lot of my friends say, "Foon, you're waiting for a banker in years to come," you know what I mean? For all the work I'm doing, well, not work, I'm helping out.

M.S.: Well, it's work, isn't it?

Foon: Yeah, it's work, but I'm not getting paid for it. In years to come you might get one pay-off when they retire; obviously they can't take their money with them, you know? I've not asked. It's mutual, this thing, that you're gonna get [*pause*] it's understood. And now that I've got full-time work [outside the take-away], there's no need for that. You know, where you are today, that comes from your mum and dad. They feed you, they clothe you. And in terms of the house [a house shared with his brother], they funded a certain amount for a deposit. Maybe that's their way of saying, "For your years of work in the 80s," or whatever.

However, most young people did not verbalize any expectations about their parents offering material rewards or assistance in the future. In fact, because some of these businesses were doing poorly, some young people expressed concerns about their parents saving enough money to retire.

Therefore, while most young people reportedly believed in helping out, without expecting remuneration, they did value the various forms of material, practical, and emotional give-and-take between themselves and their parents. Although forms of payment or other material support were in recognition of children's labor participation, family work contracts were generally conceived of in terms of nonexacting forms of long-term exchange between family members.

Family Work Contracts and Chinese Cultural Identity

In addition to survival pressures and an understanding of the family obligations underlying the FWC, expectations that children should help out emerged in a context where there was an awareness that other Chinese children in Britain also helped out in their take-away businesses. As one respondent explained: "We all do it. It's not just me." According to Susan, "I think it's with most Chinese families who have shops. It's the same for them. . . . If they [other children] could put up with it, why can't I put up with it?" These young peoples' awareness that children's labor participation in take-away businesses was typical contributed to their sense of Chinese cultural identity in Britain.

Up to this point, much of the burgeoning British literature on cultural identity has been very abstract and has not considered immigrant adaptation or children's roles in family work strategies. Rather than conceiving of cultural identities in terms of a pre-given essence or a primordial sense of "original" culture, they are seen in terms of an ongoing process of "hybridity" (Bhabha, 1990a, 1990b) and the mixing of different cultural forms (Hewitt, 1986; Back, 1993).[3] This relatively new literature has stressed multiple and shifting points of identification, or "positionings" (Hall, 1989), which are formed within the context of postcolonial diasporas (Hall, 1991; Gilroy, 1993; Ang, 1994). In Britain, much of the literature on the second generation, particularly in relation to Asian young people, has situated and explored issues of young peoples' identities in relation to their parents' cultural practices and their ties (e.g., the idea of being between two cultures [Watson, 1977b]), if any, with their countries of ethnic origin (see Weinrich, 1979; Stopes-Roe and Cochrane, 1990; Drury, 1991; Brah, 1992; Knott and Khokher, 1993; Modood et al., 1994; Shaw, 1994). Moreover, much of the literature on young black people in Britain has stressed the centrality of racism for their lives and identity formation (Pryce, 1979; Cashmore and Troyna, 1982; Alexander, 1996).

Serving in the Take-away

Because of the prevalence of Chinese families running take-away businesses, working in the take-away signifies a particular social and economic status for Chinese people in British society. Not only do children provide labor in these businesses, and fulfill their family obligations by doing so, but these children also sell an ethnic food to the wider public. In exploring the cultural identities of young Chinese people in Britain, David Parker has portrayed the importance of working in the take-away for Chinese young peoples' senses of identity. There are a number of reasons why this is so. According to Parker (1995: 84–85): "First, the encounter with a mainly white clientele is racialized to begin with—the customers have come specifically to purchase Chinese food, an ethnically differentiated cuisine. The family is trading on the basis of cultural difference. . . . Working at the take-away counter can be seen as a metaphor for the place of young Chinese in Britain and the limited control they have over their own lives—their horizons in the short term confined to the world as viewed through the front window of their parents' shop."

As Parker has aptly put it, through selling Chinese food, these families trade upon cultural difference in Britain. As such, working in these take-away businesses is not only of practical importance, in terms of family survival and family obligations. For young people, working in the take-away evokes issues of what it means to be Chinese in Britain. One way in which their work in take-aways shaped their sense of identity was the "mixture of boredom and vulnerability [in the shop] which comes to dominate the lives of the majority of young Chinese people" (Parker, 1994:84). As Parker notes, young people sitting at the counter could feel very exposed to passersby and to traffic, who could see them through the large front windows. Also, serving customers could be harrowing and stressful: What young people most objected to was the colonialist tinge of white customers treating them as if they *should* serve them, with the implication that there was nothing else a Chinese person would or could do. Some young people, such as Lisa, who ventured into the "outside" world, found that people could be surprised to see her "out of context":

> *Lisa:* It wasn't until college that I realized that a lot of things that they'd [parents] said were home truths.
>
> *M.S.:* Like what?
>
> *Lisa:* Like, you know, people will always see you as Chinese. It was because they really hadn't seen an Oriental person from behind the counter walking out, freely, as it were. When I left home, I wanted to be as far away from home, so I wouldn't have to help out, to detach myself from everything. Only to find that I became more and more, not homesick, but traditional Chinese.

These young people employed various ways of coping with racial stereotyping (see Kuo, 1995, and Kibria, 1997, on Asian Americans) and of redefining a sense of Chinese identity. In response to the denigrating stereotypes foisted upon them by their customers, Chinese young people tried to conceive of the work they performed in their take-ways in a positive, rather than a negative, light. Furthermore, these young peoples' growing interest in various forms of Hong Kong popular culture, including films and music, was formative in shaping their sense of Chinese cultural identity in Britain (Parker, 1995). There is also evidence of young people in other British ethnic minority groups actively reshaping their cultural identities, as a result of racial exclusion and denigration.[4] For instance, in their discussion of young British Bangladeshis' growing allegiance to Islam, Gardner and Shukur (1994:162–63) have argued that Islam has been key in providing young Bangladeshis with a positive identity (see also Thompson, 1974; Jayaweera, 1993 on racism and the reinforcement of ethnic identity).

Defending the Family Work Contract

The sense of upholding a widespread Chinese practice in Britain—helping out as part of the FWC—was important in providing these young people with a sense of Chinese identity in Britain and of belonging to a Chinese community, even though some of these families had little contact with any such community. Some recent studies of ethnic minority young people have argued that their links with their ethnic communities can provide young people with both material and emotional advantages.[5] For example, in a study of Vietnamese youth in New Orleans, Zhou and Bankston (1994:821) found that "strong positive immigrant cultural orientations can serve as a form of social capital that promotes value conformity and constructive forms of behavior, which provide otherwise disadvantaged children with an adaptive advantage." In the case of Cuban Americans, they have retained a strong and positive sense of their Cuban origins through their use of the Spanish language in their homes (Perez, 1994). Their Cuban heritage is sustained by the strength of a Cuban enclave in Miami (see also Portes and Schauffler, 1996, and Waters, 1994). In fact, "one of the most effective antidotes against downward mobility is a sense of membership in a group with an undamaged collective identity" (Fernandez-Kelly and Schauffler, 1994:682). A positive and collective interpretation of helping out, which derived from a common Chinese experience in Britain, could be empowering, particularly because of racist and degrading stereotypes and images attributed to Chinese people working in take-aways, by both their customers and the wider (predominantly) white culture.

In addition to the desire to counter racial stereotypes, another factor that could explain why these young people attributed positive meanings to their FWCs, as emblems of Chinese cultural identity, was that many white customers were seen to be unsympathetic and lacking in understanding of Chinese peoples' situations in Britain. In fact, most Chinese young people actively defended their FWCs. They were keenly aware that while their work was normatively prescribed among Chinese families running take-aways in Britain, it was proscribed by British law and social norms. Many respondents noted that although most customers understood their labor participation in the take-away, they were also aware of legislation barring children under age 16 from working any substantial hours.

When asked about working in their family businesses, it often seemed that these Chinese young people assumed that I (and the wider public), as a non-Chinese researcher who did not grow up working in a take-away, disapproved of their labor participation. For instance, during the course of our interview, Kam, who was speaking about wanting to help her parents in their business, abruptly stopped, and asked, "Have you ever worked in a take-away?". It seemed that Kam was concerned about how I would understand her and her family's way of life. On a number of occasions, I had the strong sense that respondents had *prepared* to defend their work roles in the interviews. For instance, when asked if she thought that children should help their parents in a family business, Lisa replied, "I know you think, oh, the children shouldn't help. Maybe I think they should because I've been through it. Say you eat, you're there [in the shop], and naturally, you help your parents. Having your life at home, and having the shop, it's all the same thing. You have to be doing something constructively as well."

In another family, Jacqui's ambivalent rationalization of working in her family's take-away was typical: "I can't separate the shop from family life: Growing up in that environment, *I don't know what life is like without that business.* The fact that we had a take-away, and the fact that it was downstairs, so close, are such a part of my life. To have that removed, is quite a different concept. I just don't know what it would be like if my parents had gone out to work. I would feel guilty to say I actually hate working in the shop, partly because it's part of my life and I've sort of learnt from that" (my emphasis). Like Lisa, Jacqui's understanding of her labor participation was not just a defense of her own family, but a defense of an entire way of life for many Chinese families in Britain.

The perception that others lacked an understanding of their views and experiences, as Chinese people in Britain, could be very alienating for respondents. According to Mary, "Quite a few friends had birthday parties, always on Saturday evenings. We could never go because we had to help out in the shop. Some of my friends just couldn't understand it; they thought it was quite barbarous, actually. They don't understand how my family operates, that we were from a different world from them. Our fathers do not have a nine-to-five job, we don't have evenings and weekends free, holidays."

Chinese young peoples' cultural identities were thus heightened by the recognition that their family lives diverged greatly from those of most other Britons. As Rumbaut (1994:754) has observed, "Contextual dissonance [from the dominant culture] heightens the salience of ethnicity and of ethnic group boundaries, all the more when it is accompanied by disparagement and discrimination." Despite many individuals' feelings of vulnerability, exposure, and experiences of being stereotyped in offensive ways, they did not passively accept the imposed meanings of being Chinese. As Fernandez-Kelly and Schauffler (1994:663) have noted, "Some identities protect immigrants; others weaken them by transforming them into disadvantaged ethnic minorities."

Therefore, helping out, as part of a FWC, was not only crucial to the survival of these family businesses, but it also represented a widespread Chinese practice in Britain—a norm which enabled Chinese young people to interpret their labor in positive, rather than negative, ways. Since they encountered, in their view, ethnocentric disapproval of their labor participation in their family livelihoods, their support for their FWCs could be seen as a positive affirmation of their identities as Chinese people in Britain. In contrast with James Watson's observation from the late 1970s that "The Chinese caterers, including even the younger migrants, have not begun to redefine themselves as a consequence of exposure to British society and culture," I would argue, twenty years later, that helping out in their take-aways has been formative for Chinese young peoples' identities in Britain.

The ways in which young people spoke of helping out suggested that the combined force of material, emotional, and normative pressures to help out were great. That is, young people understood and experienced the expectation that they help out as a clearly prescribed norm. In other words, helping out was understood to be more "obligatory" than "permissive" (Firth et al., 1970). Although elements of these contracts are also likely to be relevant for small family enterprises more generally, the binding nature of these FWCs developed over time, in the context of both material and moral pressures arising from these families' experiences of migration and ethnic minority status. In comparison with "native" family businesses, these FWCs not only relied heavily upon various forms of children's labor, but they also developed in an often hostile social and business environment. However, there was nothing intrinsically and exclusively Chinese about the meanings embodied in these family work contracts. Rather than simply being an extension of traditional Chinese culture, these contracts emerged in a specific material and historical context. It is therefore possible that, given similar circumstances and group resources, such contracts may arise among other immigrant groups engaged in small, family-based ethnic businesses.

5

Upholding and Negotiating the Family Work Contract

CHINESE YOUNG peoples' consensus that children should help out in their parents' take-away businesses was central to the working of these family work contracts (FWCs). However, their stated beliefs in their FWCs did not necessarily mean that helping out was automatically or unproblematically achieved in these families. How children's labor is elicited and maintained cannot be explained solely by culturally based assumptions about "natural" feelings of affection or obligation between parents and children. Nor can we make simplistic assumptions about children's passivity and powerlessness in relation to their parents (Qvortrup, 1985).

Although these children worked under their parents' authority, their work could not be characterized simply in terms of being either voluntary or coerced labor participation. In their study of a wide range of family responsibilities in Britain, Finch and Mason (1993:80) have argued against the idea that there are "rules of obligation which people follow."[1] They argue that kin responsibilities have "negotiated" as well as normative elements—that people must work out what types of responsibilities they acknowledge. The idea of negotiation is interesting in relation to children working in ethnic businesses because it actually posits some tension in collective family endeavors, whereby individual and collective needs and goals must be worked out (see Wallace et al., 1994).[2]

Rather than being simply a given, upholding the FWC involved constant and ongoing forms of tending and reinforcement of the expectation that children should help out. Young peoples' experiences of working with their families were much more divided than has been suggested thus far in previous studies (e.g., Jackson and Garvey, 1974; 1975; Baxter, 1988). This was because for most young people, helping out could be a double-edged experience, as was the case for Jacqui: "The fact that you rely upon the family is a very bonding and secure experience. It can be stressful because your parents do rely on you, and sometimes you think it's a bit unfair on you, because they are putting pressure on you. The family became a source of guilt as well. If you didn't want to get involved, or you didn't want to help out—my parents laid on the guilt trip: 'This is the family, and this is how we survive.'"

For some daughters, as in the case of daughters in black British families described below, helping out could be a particularly ambivalent experience, given that they tended to perform much more domestic housework and childcare than their brothers: "There are contradictions and contradictory experiences for black girls who may, on the one hand, find themselves subject to quite considerable working demands as carers of younger siblings or as home workers whilst also deriving considerable support from their families in the face of white racism" (Hood-Williams, 1990:158).

Not surprisingly, guilt was a prevalent theme raised by virtually all the respondents, who reported that they felt guilty if they did not want to help out. This was particularly the case for integral children, whose parents relied upon them much more heavily than the parents of minor children. According to David, "It would be hard for me *not* to help. Cause basically by nature, I'm really helpful. If I'm not doing anything, I feel guilty. Cause I can do it. Yeah?" Not only did their parents work extremely long and arduous hours, but these young people knew that they should contribute their labor to a livelihood from which they themselves benefited.

The young people in most families reported that their parents regularly reinforced their expectations that children should help out—though to varying degrees of explicitness. One of the most common ways in which parents communicated such expectations was by either guilt-tripping children, or by citing traditional Chinese adages about children helping their parents.

Young people were often guilt-tripped about the sacrifices their parents had made for the benefit of their children, or parents would compare their children's labor commitments to those of other model Chinese children. One daughter, Pue-man, described a commonly used guilt-trip technique by her parents: "My mum's got a lot of friends with take-aways. She's always saying, whoever, whoever's son is working for his parents, and he's giving up his studying, and how they've sold the shop, and he's gone back to studying, and I think I'm not gonna waste my life like that. And sometimes she compares us to her friends' daughter: 'She's been working until she's 30.' And I said I'm not gonna be like her. She always compares us with people who have children who work."

Comparisons with other Chinese children, whether fictive or real, could be very effective in inducing guilt because, as I discussed in the previous chapter, helping out was not only a home ethic, but also a recognized norm among Chinese people running take-aways in Britain. According to Anna, "We also picked up a lot by looking at other families. And you see other children doing exactly the same. It was exactly the norm, and sometimes if you got a bit rebellious, your parents would actually say, 'Look at so and so; they manage.' And it was a great pressure."

Some parents invoked notions of parental sacrifice and filial piety to reinforce their expectations that children should help out. As Lisa explained: "My parents guilt-trip us. 'Your father and me have worked very hard, and throughout our lives we've worked hard for you,' and it's a good thing and a bad thing because the three of us have all gone to college. And my brother's planning on going as well, and they see this as an achievement, but it can also backfire on you. Because they say, we've spent a lot of our time and energy so that you can go to college, and refer it back to helping in the shop. Usually, it runs on the line of 'We've done all this for you.'"

Such forms of guilt-tripping were relatively explicit ways for parents to communicate their expectations to their children. In addition to the theme of parental sacrifices, expectations that children should help out were articulated on the basis of fairness and the collective sharing of labor, which were key values embodied in the FWC. However, in two exceptional cases, parents who expected their children to help out were seen to have either failed in contributing their fair share of labor or to have engaged in illegitimate tactics of persuasion. For instance, daughters in two families reported that their parents had not upheld their part of the FWC: Helen reported that she had to work extra hard in the shop to compensate for her father's irresponsibility. Not only did he leave much of the hard (labor-intensive) work to his wife, but he also spent a great deal of money on drink and gambling. Another daughter, Sui, reported that her parents pressured her to help out by engaging in "emotional blackmail": "It was quite emotional, and plus, it was, like, your duty [pause] emotional blackmail, basically. 'If you don't help, my back will be [pause] I can't take it anymore,' my mum would say. Or, 'If we were to hire someone else, we wouldn't have enough money for all the things, the car, the bills.'" Sui reported feeling angry about how much she had had to work: "I was quite stupid, actually. I thought I was really, really stupid; they always said that they can't cope without the family working. Suddenly when I grew a bit older, and looking at it from the outside, when I wasn't tied up and involved, I thought that they could easily have gotten someone part-time to help in the shop, and um, kept us, the children, out of the busy working [routine]."

Although both of these young women believed that children should help out, they felt that their parents had relied too heavily upon them, and that they had abused their parental authority to ensure their children's hard work. These parents were seen to have failed as responsible and caring parents. Furthermore, these parents had effectively violated the implicit workings of the FWC. Such a contract was based upon an understanding of give-and-take by *both* parents and children.

The few families in which parents reportedly exerted little pressure on their children were those where children were minor workers. Some mothers of minor children reported that they were reluctant to push their children because they could not pressure their children without potentially negative ramifications for parent-child relationships. According to one mother, Susana, "Sometimes my husband, he say, 'You spoil them, they're not working enough. They're not doing school work, they're watching TV.' Well, I think, well, that's their life. I don't want to get blamed later on. If they don't have freedom, or whatever. At 16 or 17, they should be able to make some decisions themselves."

When asked if she would like her children to help out more, Pauline, another "liberal" mother of three minor children, replied: "Well, they're not committed. There's no point in pushing. They would be unhappy. They're unhappy, we're unhappy, so what's the point? Other families, the children work a lot, but then they suffer, so what's the point? They have their own lives. Otherwise, if anything happen to their studies, they blame you."

Clearly, these mothers prioritized the happiness of their children, as well as their relationships with their children, and were unwilling to enforce their FWCs at any cost. Even though these parents did not regularly articulate their expectations that their children should help out, minor children were clear that their parents still wanted them to help out. When asked about how they discerned this expectation, one respondent typically replied, "Oh, you can just tell, that they expect it." In fact, both of the "liberal" mothers above conceded that they would be pleased if their children helped out more. This implicit and widespread sense that their parents expected them to help out was tied to young peoples' understandings of their FWCs as a widespread norm for Chinese families running take-aways in Britain.

In comparison with the parents of integral and supplementary children, parents of minor children had more latitude regarding the degree to which they relied upon their children. The parents of minor children did not rely upon their children for caring labor. Neither Susana nor Pauline wanted to push their children into helping out because they had decided that doing so was not worth the consequences—making their children unhappy or resentful toward them. In addition to reinforcing the expectation that their children help out, and thus ensure the viability of the family business, parents' stated expectations of their children were also seen by some young people to be a means of reinforcing their children's sense of Chinese identity in Britain. As discussed in the last chapter, the belief in helping out contributed to a sense of Chinese identity in Britain. Therefore, for many parents, who were reportedly concerned about how "Westernized" their children were becoming, their stated expectations of their children served a dual purpose.

Reconciling the Two Ideals of Family and Identity

In addition to the potentially oppressive nature of parents' expectations, young peoples' ambivalence about their FWCs stemmed from their acute awareness of their families diverging from Western norms of family and work—an ideal which did not involve children in a family livelihood or children performing an array of caring work on a day-to-day basis. These young people tended to experience tensions between two polarized *ideals* of family and identity—one Chinese and one British. Despite the critical dismissal of the notion of being "between two cultures" (a notion elaborated by Watson, 1977, among others), I found that this idea, or very similar elaborations of it, was articulated by many of the young people in this study.[3] This is hardly surprising, since, as Rumbaut (1994:754) has observed, in relation to immigrant children in the U.S., "Youths see and compare themselves in relation to those around them, based on their social similarity or dissimilarity with the reference groups that most directly affect their experiences." In fact, most of these young people tended to see themselves as being informed by *both* Chinese and British cultures (discussed in more detail in the next chapter). Similarly, Drury's (1991) study of the ethnic practices and attitudes of Sikh girls, and Knott and Khokher's (1993) study of Muslim girls' religious practices, found that Asian girls in Britain negotiated complex senses of identity.

A common source of tension that arose in upholding FWCs was the need for young people to subordinate their own needs and desires to collective, family needs (see also Auernheimer,

1990, for Turkish young people in Germany). For instance, many of the respondents in the sample, especially those who were integral to their family businesses, struggled with the fact that they had very limited social lives. This was particularly the case on weekends, when most social activities, such as parties and dates, were planned by their peers. Because of time constraints and their need to be at their shops, their Chinese friends or partners sometimes joined in helping out, so that this labor was performed in what was partly a socializing context. Given that weekend nights were usually the busiest of the week, working together in the shop was one way of spending time together; after closing hours, some young people went out to late-night clubs or restaurants where they could congregate with other Chinese people in the same situation. In this respect, the rhythms of their social lives were very distinct from those of their non-Chinese peers.

However, children's socialization seems to have been an important factor in shaping the degree to which young people experienced tensions in relation to helping out. The majority (thirty-one of forty-two) of the Chinese young people in this study were born in Britain, while ten were born in Hong Kong, and one in Yemen. However, of the thirty-one young people born in Britain, five of them were sent back to Hong Kong and partly raised there, before returning to Britain. Individuals born and raised predominantly in Hong Kong and those born and raised in Britain (or brought to Britain by primary school age) tended to have different expectations about family and work. In her study of Chinese immigrant children in New York City, Sung (1987:173) found that, "There may be two distinct sets of children [within families], one older and reared in China, another younger and born in the U.S."

Children born and raised in Hong Kong, who were in the minority, tended to have strikingly similar views about helping out: Not only did many say that they "did not mind," but they also said that they had expected to work in Britain with their parents. Some of them had witnessed and experienced poverty in the New Territories, where they had grown up. Children raised in Hong Kong tended to report much less tension around upholding the FWC because they had been more accustomed to children working in Hong Kong (Easey, 1979). Nor did these young people articulate concerns about the implications of helping out for their cultural identities. When asked how they had felt about working in their businesses, the following respondents, all of whom spent their childhoods in Hong Kong, replied:

Yee-ling: It was what you had to do to survive, if you're poor. It's not a matter of liking it or disliking it. Put it this way. If you're poor, you just have to learn [a new trade]. We worked every night. You had to.

Peter: Because my family was poor in Hong Kong, we know what it's like to be poor. Even from a young age, we never minded hard work.

Pue-lai: It's not fair or unfair. You still have to work [to survive].

By stressing their concerns about material survival, children raised in Hong Kong, like Fai, tended to be extremely pragmatic and fatalistic in their views about working: "We all [he and his siblings] just did it [helped out], so to me, everybody did it. That's all I knew, at an early age. It's not like I had a dream life before that and suddenly I had to do that. . . . I never did go out on weekends, so I don't really know; weekends were the busiest days of the shop, and you was there, and that was it."

In contrast, children who were partially or wholly socialized in Britain (who referred to themselves as BBCs, British-born Chinese) tended to report more ambivalence and difficulties associated with helping out, especially in terms of their families' atypical family and work lives in Britain. For instance, some BBCs found the merging of their family and work lives, which was common in most Chinese families running take-aways in Britain, problematic. In Colin's case, he disliked customers being able to see his family's sitting room, which he considered to be his family's private space, from the front of the shop (the counter). Another example of private space being intruded upon by work was that some families had telephone lines for take-away orders in their living quarters—in sitting rooms and even bedrooms in some cases. Some boundaries between work and home life, and of time-out, was an expectation articulated more by BBCs than by young people primarily socialized in Hong Kong.

Typically, BBCs also reported that as they had grown up, they had resented their parents at times, not only for relying upon them or for putting pressure on them to help out, but for not being like other parents. Such feelings could be especially intense for BBCs who were integral children, like Anna: "It was difficult coming to terms with the fact that they were not like other parents. Talk to them, get advice, take you on holiday, etc. But they always had your best interests at heart. You had to realize their constraints, and that they didn't fit the ideal of parents."

While the money from helping out was seen by some young people to be a nice "bonus," it could never replace the leisure, freedom, or "normal" family life that some BBCs wanted. As Colin put it, "They [his parents] tried their best, but there was no bedtime story, you know?"

Although most young people actively defended their FWCs (including BBCs), as a way of life, some of these young people were still coming to terms with negative senses of identity (in relation to the take-away) that they had internalized. A number of BBCs differentiated their attitudes and experiences of helping out in terms of "before" and "now," referring to their work experiences as adolescents and as young adults. In fact, many respondents noted that it was not surprising that issues of cultural identity had come to the fore during their adolescence (Erikson, 1968). Quite commonly, they reported that they had been much more negative or conflicted or both about working in the take-away in their early teens than they were now. According to Jacqui:

Throughout my childhood and adolescence, I questioned why certain things were the way they were. My own identity came into question, and I questioned how living above a shop could be normal. Normal is like what I saw on the telly, or my friends.

It was quite a bizarre thing coming home to a shop. But beyond that, the fact that I was Chinese-British, and living a sort of typical background to what the British see the Chinese as being, was quite a problem for me at one stage, partly because I saw myself as being British, and tried to push away my Chinese identity. . . . I remember one time, I was about 16, and I went to this girl's birthday party, and her house was really nice, obviously middle class, her father had a business, self-employed. I remember having a lift home, and I was the last one to be dropped off, and I saw all their houses, and it was really strange seeing all these really nice houses, and then he dropped me off, and mine was above a shop. Nowadays, I'm quite open about saying that I've lived in a Chinese take-away all my life, but it can be a disadvantage with some people, who back off.

In another family, hearing stories about her parents' own childhoods and families in Hong Kong helped Laura to come to terms with her uneasy feelings about the differences between her family and what she imagined to be the "normal" British family: "My dad usually tells us about his background, and it's great to know a bit of their history because then you understand why they do certain things. Especially when you're living in England, especially when you're young, you're always comparing your family to my friends' families. My family, and why they reacted in a certain way, doing things a certain way."

Therefore, while most young people spoke strongly and supportively about their FWCs in principle, in practice, many of the BBCs had to work actively at reconciling such a belief with more ambivalent feelings about helping out, much of which were related to the negotiation of their cultural identities.

Challenging and Negotiating the Family Work Contract

Given the ambivalence and tension that many Chinese young people experienced in the course of upholding their family work contracts, as well as the pressure they encountered from their parents, some of them challenged or rebelled against their FWCs in various ways. However, only sixteen (of forty-two) young people (all BBCs) reported that they had openly challenged or argued with their parents about helping out (children within families could differ in terms of the ways in which they worked out tensions around their labor participation—an issue which is explored more fully in the next chapter). For instance, Anna reported that, during her teen years, she had gradually grown more angry about having to work in her family's take-away: "The only time I walked out was when I'd asked for the night off specifically, and my parents had not given me that time, because it was particularly busy, and I just said, 'I'm going', and I walked out. When I'd come back, my father had locked me out. I spent the night out, and then I moved in with my partner for a little while."

Leaving home after arguments with parents were, however, very rare. Indeed, most of the children in these families did not openly resist or challenge the expectation that they help out. As was illustrated by Anna's experience, in which she was locked out of the house for disobeying her parents, there were clearly limits to how much children could rebel, given their parents' ultimate authority over them—at least while they remained in school and lived at home. Like Sung (1987:188), who found that Chinese children in New York were reluctant to go against their parents' wishes, some young people simply did not want to or feel able to confront their parents. As Sue, a BBC, put it, "I suppose we resisted in the heart, but how often can a child actually confront their parents openly? I've hardly done that at all. Once or a few times." Moreover, parental approval and a desire to maintain a "good" reputation, not only within the family but also within Chinese social networks, was an important incentive to help out. According to Sui: "In that sense [working hard], I had quite a lot of respect, because I was able to help out, and they can't say, 'Oh, my daughter's no good.' Because I did help out and everything, in the ways they wanted."

Young people who were reluctant to "moan" or argue openly with their parents could, however, challenge or resist their FWCs in other ways. For instance, one way in which two individuals resisted was by refusing payment from their parents. This was done with the knowledge that payment was one of the few ways in which parents could reciprocate and express their appreciation toward their children. For instance, Annie was quite clear about how refusing payment would make her mother feel: "My mother, she used to pay us before, when we were younger. She used to say at the end of the evening, 'Now here's 10 pounds.' And that would get rid of her own guilt [*pause*] because she doesn't like to see her own children working. I eventually stopped taking the money because I wanted her to feel guilty for giving me money cause that's the only thing she had on me, and I wanted to show her, 'Look, I'm working for you, but I'm not getting paid for it. This is just for you.' And I want her to feel guilty about it so that she'll sell the shop."

Refusing money for the work they performed was a potent way for children to communicate resistance or unhappiness with working in the business. By doing so, children effectively stripped their parents of a key way of paying back their children for their labor. As Annie pointed out, refusal to accept payment meant that parents had no way of assuaging any guilt they may have felt about relying upon their children. Here, Annie's refusal to accept payment for helping out was also a means of guilt-tripping her parents.

Another way in which some young people resisted helping out was by not being readily available to help out; as a result, they made parents explicitly ask for their help. Most commonly, such tactics included being home late to open up the shop, or being "incompetent" in various ways. By refusing, either consciously or subconsciously, to learn certain tasks, such as cooking, some young people effectively limited the degree to which their parents could rely upon them in the shop. In this way, their parents were encouraged to think that they were "hopeless," and were discouraged from requesting help.

Limitations to Challenging the Family Work Contract

Despite the evident tensions that arose as a result of upholding their FWCs, many young people were ultimately confronted with a number of factors that discouraged them from resisting or challenging their FWCs in ways which actually went beyond the occasional complaint or "moan." For one, most young people reported that despite the fact that their parents could pressure them to help out, they knew their parents wanted the best for them. As Alfred Chan (1986:6) points out in his study of Chinese young peoples' employment in Britain, "Parents, especially those running a small family business, were faced with a dilemma. On the one hand they sincerely wished their children to do well in school, as some put it, 'Education is free, our kids have a chance we never had.' At the same time they sometimes felt that the economic well-being of the family had to come first: 'I know he is going to take exams. But what can I do? We can't close for a few days, all the customers will have disappeared when we open again" (see also Pang, 1993:150).

A number of young people said that they were aware of their parents' own ambivalence about their children helping out, particularly when parents knew that children's labor took time away from their studies. With the exception of the two daughters who felt that their parents had worked them too hard, most young people reported no evidence of parents being anything but quite eager for them to do well at school—in contrast with Jackson and Garvey's (1974, 1975) findings. However, it was sometimes frustrating for children because their parents simply did not understand what was involved in studying for major exams or applying for university. While wanting the best for their children, parents who had little or no education were not always able to appreciate the difficulties of juggling both studies and helping out, as Sue found out:

M.S.: You said you found it difficult when school work built up.

Sue: Definitely so. That was particularly when O-levels [secondary school examinations] came up, when I was 16. It's very traditional in a family business to say, especially parents, 'Work hard, we don't want you to follow in our footsteps. We only followed this work, long hours, hard work, because we don't have proper qualifications. If you have, then you can leave it.' So this was indoctrinated into us, but at the same time, we still had to help out. It is contradictory. It's family obligation. You should do it. Without this business, there's no way you could continue on with schooling.

Thus young people were constantly confronted by the fact that although helping out took time away from their studies, the well-being of their family take-aways was also ultimately in their interest.

In addition to the knowledge that their parents wanted the best for them, some children were concerned *not* to challenge parental authority. As discussed in chapter 3, children, particularly integral children in these families, knew that they were crucial to the viability of their take-away businesses, and they were aware of how their parents' reliance upon their children might be difficult for them, in terms of maintaining parental authority and respect (Alvarez, *New York Times*, October 1, 1995). Khan's (1977:86) study of Pakistanis in the north of England observed that intergenerational relationships could be destabilized by the processes of migration (see also Min, 1998): "The traditional hierarchy of authority and respect within the family is frequently upset by the migration process and the ability of younger members to use the social skills of the wider society."

Such an observation was applicable to the Chinese families in this study. Chinese children in these families felt that they had to be delicate about the ways in which they attempted to challenge their FWCs, keeping in mind parent-child hierarchies and parents' potentially mixed feelings about relying upon them. Most young people were anxious not to exacerbate the discomfort they (and their parents, they imagined) experienced from their parents' heavy reliance, even dependence, upon them. According to Annie, "I know that my mother is very proud. And for her to ask me to help her was really like, coming down, on a different level." Here, Annie reveals that she did not want to make it any more difficult for her parents to ask for help. Yet, as discussed earlier in the chapter, Annie had refused to accept payment so that she could guilt-trip her mother. These two different excerpts illustrate the very contradictory and ambivalent feelings that many young people had about helping out and their parents' reliance upon them.

Perhaps most importantly, the fact that many parents depended upon their children for various forms of shop and caring work made it very difficult to resist helping out. According to Jacqui, a BBC, "We would argue about how much work we were doing with our parents, but nothing would ever be resolved because there's an element of dependency which is always there. So you can never just . . . [balk or refuse to work]."

Most children did not see their parents in wholly authoritative positions, because of the degree to which their parents relied upon them. Also, the tendency to see their parents and themselves as sharing a common predicament—survival, adaptation, and racism—rather than seeing themselves in opposition to their parents, was instrumental in dampening frustration or overt resistance to helping out:

> M.S.: Did you or any of your siblings ever try to talk to your parents about working less?
>
> Yee-ling: Um, not really. They were very understanding persons. If we had exams coming up, they would easily let us go, but apart from that you knew they were working hard. That's why we tried to help as much as possible. We didn't like it, let's put it this way [laughs], but it's something you have to do anyway.

When Yee-Ling says that "it's something you have to do anyway," she stresses her entire family's lack of choice regarding the matter of helping out or not, and points to her parents' hard work and her family's precarious economic situation. Thus Yee-Ling's strong sense that her own well-being and interests were inextricable from her family's collective well-being could mitigate individual "gripes" about helping out. Rather than simply blame their parents for relying upon them, many Chinese young people who were ambivalent about helping out tended to stress their families' situations. The shop and the way of life it entailed were not seen to be of their parents' choosing, as immigrants.

In fact, as oppressive as being guilt-tripped by their parents could be, this did not seem to vitiate children's sense of obligation to help out. This was because, despite some young peoples' anger toward their parents for guilt-trips, they ultimately believed in the legitimacy of their parents' expectations of them. For instance, according to Kelly, "You know, she [mother] kind of suckers me up, and I'll agree in the end [*pause*] it kind of hurts my feelings, but in the end, I'm just talking to myself, really." Yet a few minutes later in the same interview, I asked:

M.S.: Have you or your siblings ever tried to get them [parents] to hire someone?

Kelly: No [*laughs*]. I don't know, um [*pause*] if the family can do it, why don't they do it? I mean, it's gonna cost you to hire someone. I mean, half your profit's gonna go, when the family can do it.

Again, this excerpt exemplifies the deeply contradictory feelings many young people articulated about helping out. Although they found the expectation that they should help out (as well as the fact that they were needed) oppressive, their parents' reliance upon them made eminent sense, given the economic and social constraints faced by most of their parents. A number of respondents also noted that there had been some positive aspects of having to work from a young age—they had learned how to be responsible and learned business and interpersonal skills. According to these young people, although working in the shop had meant pressure and sacrificing social lives, it had also prepared them for adulthood and had fostered "competence."

Even in the two cases discussed earlier, in which the daughters felt exploited by one or both parents, neither Helen nor Sui fundamentally objected to or questioned helping out as part of a FWC. One way in which Helen and Sui rationalized their parents' treatment of them was by using knowledge of their parents' difficult life experiences as a frame of reference for their own. For instance, Sui expressed empathy for her father: "It's quite funny. My dad can be quite charming when he wants to. If his English, and also time had permitted, he would have really loved the social aspect, he would have enjoyed life much, much more, instead of getting quite cooped up and feeling quite closed in [in the take-away]. It was quite suffocating."

Despite her anger toward her parents for working her so hard, Sui continued to help out, as expected by her parents, and recast her own experience and understanding of her work role in terms of what she imagined her father's experiences to have been. From her perspective, equity and fairness had been violated in the FWC, but her parents also suffered unhappy lives, and this seemed to be a mitigating factor in her anger toward them. Thus, rather than openly challenge or confront parents about perceived inequities in the FWC, these young women chose to cope with their difficult situations by trying to contain their anger and frustration and by depersonalizing their situations as much as possible. According to Helen, "I think I've never looked back and resented it because it [helping out] would always have been an essential part of surviving."

My findings about various factors militating against children openly challenging their parents are supported by some recent literature on second-generation immigrants in Britain, which has de-emphasized the notion of intergenerational conflict between parents and children. For instance, Drury (1991) found scant evidence of overt conflict between parents' and children's attitudes and cultural practices, and identified various categories of children's "maintenance" and "non-adherence" to Sikh traditions, rather than a total acceptance or rejection of them. Similarly, Bhachu (1985:171) has argued that, "At present, there is a remarkable fit between the expectations of the East African Sikh parental generation and that of the youth, a fit brought about by making internal changes in the system."

Rather than stressing "fit" between parents and children, I would argue that children in these Chinese families had to work out the tensions inherent in upholding their FWCs. In doing so, neither the notion of rebellion nor compliance captures the ways in which these children negotiated these tensions. Despite the mixed feelings around helping out, and some young peoples' wish at one point or another to cut back or withdraw their labor, it was very difficult for them to openly discuss such feelings with their parents. Openly negotiating with parents about their work roles was difficult because in the majority of families communication between parents and children tended to be limited.

Discussion: "Not the Done Thing"

As discussed in chapter 3, children in most families had been gradually incorporated into their take-away businesses at a relatively young age, and most of them had not actually discussed the issue of helping out as part of a FWC. Because most parents and children had never discussed the terms of their labor participation, children in these families had no baseline agreement to refer to in negotiating their work roles. Rather, as I argued in the last chapter, such an understanding that they should help out had gradually developed over time in a context where family and work lives were merged. This made the open discussion of changes in labor participation awkward and without precedent. Even the minority of children who had been incorporated into their family businesses when they were older, and who had been told or asked to help out by their parents, reported that they had had few further discussions of their work roles over time.

Exceptionally, in one family, Jacqui and her three siblings, who were integral children, approached their parents collectively, and asked for reduced work hours and a part-time employee. This was an unusual case, not only because these children were explicitly trying to rework the terms of the FWC, but also because they approached their parents collectively, rather than on an individual basis. One reason why Jacqui and her siblings opted for an open discussion with their parents was that their parents were reportedly responsive to the idea of a "family conference" (Finch and Mason, 1993:65). Therefore, approaching their parents collectively was recognized as a legitimate way of making their case.

Although in the minority, respondents from six families reported that their families had very open communication; such a characterization was also linked with reports of harmonious family relationships. Of these six families, young people in two of the three families with minor children reported that their parents communicated with them and understood them and that their parents were less traditional than most Chinese parents. Most Chinese young people considered a lack of discussion between parents and children to be a typical characteristic of Chinese families in Britain. According to Foon:

> It's difficult to communicate sometimes because we do so little. It's really strange. . . . We talk to each other, but it's not how an English family would talk. "How you doing?" "How was your day?" you know? There was a bit of that, I suppose, but mum and dad came from a generation where they didn't have that, they had to learn the hard way, they didn't have no comfort in the house, you know. They was working when they were 10 or 11. To the [English] guy next door, that [communication] might be straightforward, but to my mum and dad, it isn't. They don't know how to question their kids, or find out certain things, you know? My mum's better [at communicating].

Like most young people who reported a dearth of communication with their parents, Laura expressed a desire to be able to talk with her parents: "I'd like to be able to talk to my parents about things [*pause*] yeah, a lot of personal things. She [mother] doesn't really share her personal feelings; I suppose that in her own family, which was so big, she was the second oldest [of eight], so she hasn't really known that kind of relationship with her own parents. I'd like to talk to her about personal things, but I don't know how."

One mother, Susana, also noted the difficulties of limited communication, not only between parents and children, but also between spouses: "Especially with the Chinese family, they don't used to have that kind of communication, to talk your expectations, to express. And all the time the husband thinking, 'I'm working hard, so what you want out from me?' And the wife thinking, 'I'm doing everything.'"

The young people in nineteen of the twenty-five families reported that there was little communication with their parents, but many of these interviewees also reported that they were able to talk with their mothers much more easily than their fathers. There were a number of factors that could hinder open discussion in these families, including language disparities and the stresses involved in running, and largely living in, a take-away.

Language Disparities

In a few families, communication between parents and children was obstructed by language disparities, particularly in cases where parents only spoke Cantonese (the language of urban Hong Kong and Kwangtung province) or Hakka (a dialect of the rural New Territories), while children primarily spoke English (see Taylor, 1987).[4] In such cases, parents and children had difficulty conversing because they did not possess a common language. Also, there could be language disparities among siblings within families, so that some children were better able to converse with parents than others. For instance, in one family, the mother was bilingual in English and Cantonese, but the father only spoke Cantonese:

M.S.: Do you talk with your parents in Cantonese?

Colin: Well, unfortunately, I only talk to my dad in small talk. We don't ever converse. If he's really pissed off about something, he'll try in English. Same with mum, when she's angry. Makes sure I understand it. I do find there is a language problem. My Cantonese is very basic. Simon's [brother] Cantonese is slightly better than mine.

Of the forty-two young people in this study, four reportedly spoke only English, while thirty-eight were reportedly bilingual. Although a majority of respondents considered themselves to be bilingual, the BBCs reported that they were more fluent in English than in Cantonese or Hakka, while those born and raised in Hong Kong were more fluent in a Chinese dialect than in English (as is evidenced in some of the interview excerpts). BBCs often stressed that their knowledge of a Chinese dialect was colloquial and that they did not feel able to carry on an "intellectual" or "complicated" conversation in these dialects.[5] Although contact with a concentration of co-ethnics and a vibrant economic and cultural community have been said to be key to "home language retention" by second-generation immigrants (Portes and Schauffler, 1996), the language limitations of many Chinese parents may also have necessitated some retention of a Chinese dialect by children in these families.

Apart from the four respondents who spoke only English, most respondents spoke Cantonese or Hakka with their parents, and spoke English (or a combination of English and Cantonese or Hakka) with their siblings. Many young people observed that their parents had had little interest in learning English, especially given the little amount of time they could spare from their shops—it was, according to Chris, "not the done thing" among Chinese parents. More commonly, children in the majority of families had, at some point, attended Chinese language schools on the weekends.

In some families, staggered family migration also contributed to barriers in communication between parents and children, particularly between fathers and their children. Studies of other ethnic minority groups in Britain reveal similar difficulties. For instance, Pryce's (1979) study of West Indians in Bristol illustrated that West Indian children who were separated from one or both parents by staggered migration felt that they did not know their parents, upon family consolidation in Britain. In one Chinese family, Sai remembered meeting her father when she came to Britain when she was 7 years old. She had been raised by her uncle and grandmother in Hong Kong:[6] "It's a long gap, and because of that long gap, I think in a way, it affects my relationship with my dad, because I was 7, but it wasn't until I was about 10 that I saw more of him [because her father moved around the country for jobs]. So my relationship between me and my dad, sister, and brother are not so close. It's not a close relationship; he's just our father, and we have to respect him because of that."

Stress and Conflict in the Shop

Many respondents also reported that communication between family members was greatly hindered by the lifestyle entailed by the take-away. Because so much of family life revolved around working in the take-away, it was difficult for families to preserve family time separate from the shop. For instance, most families had difficulty in having a sit-down meal when they could talk. Evening meals were often rushed, during shop hours. On a few occasions when I ate lunch or an evening meal with these families, we often stood around the kitchen with bowls of quickly prepared food. It was fairly common for family members to eat in the kitchen, but their meals were usually interrupted by customers. As a result, there was often a rota for eating, and meals were usually a casual affair:

> *M.S.:* Is it difficult to find time to eat together?
>
> *Kelly:* Oh, yeah. Really only on Sundays. My mum's at the shop most of the time, and me and my brother just cook for ourselves [when at their house], individually. Just English meals. I mean, the meal time's not that important, really, for my family. We don't have to be home for lunch, or have to be home for dinner. Me and my brother, if we did eat together, it would be really funny. He'd be sitting opposite me; it would be really funny. It would be awkward; we'd probably start laughing, I don't know.

For families who did work together in the shop, particularly when it was busy, there was not much time for conversation, unless it was about shop matters, such as passing on orders. Furthermore, for some young people, spending a lot of time together as a family, without much outside stimulation, did not facilitate talk. According to Sui, "In one sense, we're closer, in a sense, because we needed each other. On the other hand, um, because of us working all the time, I think we were generally bored of each other, and there was no outside stimulation. I couldn't say, 'I was at somebody's house the other day, and . . .' There was nothing to talk about. Nothing, really. Insular, extremely so. I hated it. All the other Chinese families are like that."

Another reason why discussion among family members was difficult was because working together could entail intense pressures upon family relationships, particularly when subject to financial worries and racist hostility from their customers. A key factor that reportedly contributed to family tensions and conflict was that many parents suffered from a great deal of stress stemming from financial worries, and experienced conflicts about how to run their businesses. Respondents from two families also reported that their mothers had suffered long periods of depression, due, they felt, to the social isolation, stress, and monotony of their daily lives. In two other families, fathers reportedly suffered from alcoholism. Needless to say, the incidence of mental illness and alcoholism could have been under-reported, given the sensitivity surrounding these issues.

Young people in about half of the families also reported that tension and conflict between their parents, and more broadly in all family relationships, could make working in the shop very upsetting and draining (see Light and Bonacich, 1988: 431). According to Helen, "It's o.k. [working in the take-away], but I just don't like the fact that they argue every day. Because of the strain, it makes them argue more. Over money, over petty things. I think it's the stress that builds up that makes them argue. I don't really mind going home after college and help. It's hard work, but I can take it. It was the atmosphere that really made me so emotionally distressed."

These respondents made it clear that they understood why working together contributed to conflicts in their families. While they tended to see such tensions as an inevitable consequence of running a family business (Rosenblatt et al., 1985), these young people stressed the claustrophobic nature of a livelihood in which family members worked in close proximity with each other every day. Such a lifestyle, in which they and their parents were tied down to their shops, and unable to go out and socialize, compounded the pressures and stress involved in working together.

Negotiating Work Roles with Siblings

Given the difficulties of talking with their parents about their work roles, some young people reported that they engaged in more explicit negotiations of their labor with their siblings. Not only was it easier to talk with siblings, but through negotiations with them, some individuals were able to achieve some flexibility and control over their work schedules. It seemed fairly common for siblings to arrange a work schedule. In this way, parents were not seen to be simply laying down the law about helping out. Siblings could be responsible for working out a schedule from week to week. For instance, they might agree to switch nights on a weekend if one had an exam or a party. In some cases, a nightly schedule could be shared between siblings as well. Such an arrangement was described by Yee-Ling, who divided her work with her brother:

> *Yee-Ling:* How I worked it out with my brother was that either he worked the first three hours [pause] instead of working from 5:00 [p.m.] to 12:00 [a.m.], I'd work the first three hours, then he'd work the next three hours, then we could get some sleep or watch TV, otherwise we couldn't have any of that. But Fridays, everyone had to work.
>
> *M.S.:* Did you have trouble negotiating hours with your brother?
>
> *Yee-Ling:* It was stressful, but we didn't have much options. We don't have a choice to say we don't want to work, or we won't work. We can't do that. So actually by splitting the hours, it was one of the most appropriate options to us. Otherwise, we'd have to work there full-time.

The schedule that Yee-ling and her brother worked out was seen as a helpful way of creating some choice within the larger set of constraints that required their labor participation. Although it was generally understood that parents expected their children to help out, parents did not always have to be involved in the day-to-day negotiations of labor supply. By having to negotiate work schedules among themselves, children, in addition to parents, exerted pressure upon each other to uphold their FWCs.

In addition to the factors discouraging open discussion and negotiation concerning children's labor participation, it seemed that one unspoken convention of the FWC was that it should be implicit and that parents and children should not *have* to discuss the expectation that all family members should work. In fact, such discussion may have been taboo in some families; by explicitly raising such issues, children may have felt that they were calling into question their commitments to their FWCs.

The Transition to Leaving Home

A lack of open discussion about children's work roles eventually posed difficulties in many of these twenty-five families because pressures to negotiate and to reorganize children's labor participation came into relief as children started to leave home. It was often at this critical juncture that their labor participation, and the operation of family work contracts more generally, came into question by them and their parents. Also, the "exiting" of children from families sometimes engendered, for the first time, questions about the future viability and continuation of their businesses—an issue I explore in chapter 7. As has been noted in other studies of migration, household economic strategies are dynamic and must constantly adjust over the course of the life cycle (see Massey et al. 1987).

The "normal" Western timetable for children leaving home and establishing their independence is not easily applicable to the Chinese families in this study.[7] According to Gill Jones (1992), the transition from dependence to independence for young people in Britain is stratified by class. I would argue that this process may also be mediated by ethnicity in Britain. In the case of Chinese children in families running take-aways, the transition to independence has been even more blurred and gradual a process, given their centrality to their family businesses. Historians adopting a life course perspective on Western families have argued that, because of the difficult economic circumstances faced by many American families in the late nineteenth century, family and individual needs had to be coordinated to a considerable degree (Hareven, 1982; Elder, 1985). For example, children might postpone certain transitions in their lives, such as marriage or leaving home, in order to match family needs at particular times. By coordinating the needs of both the family and individual family members, families were able to maximize their resources.[8] Though situated in a very different historical and social context, Chinese children who wanted to leave home were also subject to pressures to coordinate their plans and needs with those of their families (Salaff, 1981).

The exiting of children from home, and any subsequent modifications in their work roles, was most commonly triggered by children entering into higher education or full-time outside employment. In comparison with employment and higher education, marriage was not usually the initial trigger for withdrawing from FWCs, since marriage usually followed young peoples' entrance into employment or higher education. The departure of children from these families sometimes resulted in families hiring employees again, after a number of years when they had been without them. Relying upon employees was sometimes the only available option, if children were either no longer available or willing to work in the shop.

Entrance into full-time employment and higher education, particularly if this meant living away from home, often signalled the first opportunity for young people to disengage from their FWCs. Leaving home in pursuit of an outside job or higher education created an opening for young people to revise or curtail their labor participation because such pursuits were usually sanctioned, particularly if they were of a professional nature. However, children who entered into higher education or full-time employment did not necessarily curtail their work roles in their family shops. Actual co-residence with the family household was not necessarily a prerequisite for the continuation of an individual's labor participation. Not surprisingly, however, children who lived significant distances from their take-aways were no longer able to contribute their labor, or contribute as regularly as before.

A number of respondents reported choosing places of higher education that either enabled them to live at home or made weekend commuting viable, so they would be able to continue helping out. Although full-time higher education could be very demanding, most students had much more flexible schedules than children who were in full-time outside employment, and they felt that there were few excuses not to help out, except when there were exams and papers approaching. For instance, Lisa, who was in her second year of university, came home every weekend: "I go home weekends for Friday evenings, Saturday days, and I'm back in London by Sunday afternoon. It's not that much time, actually. It passes a lot more quickly than it used to." Lisa reported that her parents implicitly expected her to come home on weekends to help out. Nevertheless, Lisa reported that her parents' expectations of her were reasonable, especially since they did not impinge upon Lisa's study time. Susan, who also attended university in London, commuted two hours (each way) almost every weekend to help out. Going back home was important for Susan, who felt that her parents were very supportive of her obtaining higher education:[9] "Basically, they keep telling us that they want us to get a good education because they don't want us to work like they do, because it can be very difficult. They just want what's best for us, which I suppose is just natural with any parent."

A number of factors combined in determining whether or not children entering other pursuits would continue to help out or not, but those who made clean breaks from their FWCs were in the minority. A commonly reported way of thinking of these transitions was that helping out entailed a separate activity from pursuing higher education or an outside career. This reasoning echoed the way young people differentiated the relations of production in employment from those in their FWCs, in which their FWCs were understood in terms of ongoing long-term commitments associated with family membership and a sense of Chinese identity in Britain.

Although many young peoples' attitudes toward helping out did not significantly change, their entrance into higher education or outside employment often entailed uncertainty and adaptations in these families. As with communication more generally, many parents had not signaled their expectations of children's labor commitments, even after children had taken outside employment or pursued higher education. As a result, many respondents reported that they interpreted their parents' lack of encouragement to lessen or withdraw their labor to mean that their parents still wanted them to help out. In fact, most respondents reported that there had been little or no planning by their parents in response to children leaving home. As a result, young people leaving home tended to negotiate their departures, and any corresponding changes in their labor commitments, in rather different ways. In turn, their departures tended to engender varied responses and forms of adaptation by their parents and siblings.

Pue-ling: An Unexpected Departure

In a few families, the departure of an older child greatly destabilized or even jeopardized the continuing viability of the take-away, especially if the family had been completely unprepared for the departure. Pue-lai, age 22, was the second of four children who were supplementary to their family livelihoods. She and her older sister Pue-ling, age 23, had spent their early childhood years in Hong Kong, while their two younger siblings had been born and raised in Britain. Pue-lai and her elder sister had grown up helping out regularly for their parents, while their younger sister and brother had worked considerably less than they had. A few years ago, the eldest child, Pue-ling, went to Hong Kong with her mother on a vacation, and did not return to Britain. Pue-ling's refusal to return home was extremely upsetting for her entire family:

> *Pue-lai:* Since she [Pue-ling] left, it's had a massive big change. Yeah. My mum start disliking us, because she [older sister] just left. She went with my mum to Hong Kong, but she don't want to come back. She don't want to work in a take-away. She knows she comes back, she has to work. She wants to live her own life; get a job and live her own life.
>
> *M.S.:* So your parents were upset?
>
> *Pue-lai:* My dad was upset because she just left and don't tell us. My dad says that she can come back and tell me, just work for a while, and tell me she wants to work in Hong Kong, and let her go. She's got no responsibility left for my dad. But my mum, she moans, for months and months. Now she calmed down.
>
> *M.S.:* So your mother was moaning because your sister wasn't working there anymore?
>
> *Pue-lai:* Yes. Now my sister left, she [mother] have to work really

hard. She [mother] was always saying if you leave, all the sisters and brother start thinking to leave. Who's gonna work in the take-away? You gonna leave these two old grans to work in the take-away?

M.S.: Was it hard for you when your sister left?

Pue-lai: I missed her, and [was] angry at the same time. Like, she leaves, and she don't care who's working hard. But now, she phones and says, "I bet you're working every day, you must be tired." But I'm thinking, is it worth to say you're working hard, when you know I'm working hard. Cause you leave, I have to work even harder. See?

Therefore, explaining individuals' continuing labor commitments involved more than understanding a particular individual's sense of obligation or commitment to the FWC. In Pue-lai's case, her continuing commitment to helping out had to be understood, in part, in terms of the pressing practical need to compensate for the loss of her sister's labor. Not only did Pue-ling's departure leave her family with the problem of replacing her labor, but it also left Pue-lai and her family feeling abandoned and somewhat deceived. The unexpected nature of her sister's departure impressed upon Pue-lai her sister's desperation to leave home. Clearly, such a departure indicated that Pue-ling could not face the thought of actually negotiating her departure openly with her family; instead, she made sure that negotiation was not even possible. Although Pue-lai was not unsympathetic with her sister's desire to lead her own life, she felt resentful about the fact that her sister's seemingly impetuous decision meant much more work for her. Since her sister's departure, Pue-lai was under a great deal of work pressure. She lived at home and helped out every night. She had an extremely taxing schedule: She worked full-time in a photo lab, from 7:00 a.m. until 3:00 or 4:00 in the afternoon. As soon as she came home, she went straight to the shop and worked there most evenings until closing.

Some families experienced more tensions and difficulties in adjusting to older children's departures from home than others. Much of how families made this adjustment was shaped by not only the way in which children left home but also how remaining children negotiated ways of continuing to uphold their FWCs. Unlike Pue-ling's family, Jacqui and her siblings made a concerted effort to discuss the implications of older children leaving home.

Jacqui and Sarah: Discussions around Equity

In Jacqui's family, the four integral children were very close in age, particularly the three eldest, who were all daughters: Sarah, age 23, Jacqui, age 22, Lisa, age 21, and Alex, age 18. All were born and raised in Britain. Given how close in age they were, Jacqui's family was in a state of almost constant flux for a number of years, as they adjusted to the departure of various children. Although their parents had encouraged them to attend university, Jacqui and her parents had not discussed what would happen when their children started to leave home. They had not prepared for the transitions their family would undergo, even when these impending changes were known about in advance.

Sarah and Jacqui, the two eldest children, left home the same year, in 1988, to pursue higher education. They lived sufficiently far away from home so that they went home only on occasional weekends to help out. This left a great deal of responsibility for Lisa, who remained home until 1989, when she too left home for university. At the time of interview (1992), Alex, too, was on the brink of leaving for university. For this family, the departure of children involved a great deal of change in both the parents' and children's lives. Jacqui explained that she and Sarah had been concerned about "loading down" Lisa when they first left home: "Me and Sarah left home the same year. Um, I think my parents didn't realize the potential of having your children leave. And a lot of the slack went on Lisa, because she was a year younger, and she had another year. And she worked really hard, and we tried to find more help, and it was on and off—people would come and go. It created a lot of friction between Lisa and my parents because they didn't see how much pressure Lisa was under, and had underestimated how much work Sarah and I had contributed. After three or four months, they hired someone, but it was very much on and off. There was a high turnover rate."

The three eldest children in the family had recently finished university at the time of the interviews, and only one sibling, Alex, remained at home. According to Jacqui, "Alex has to do more now. He has no choice, really. Because the part-time workers were so erratic, whether we'd have one or not get one, we never knew." The youngest child, Alex, made a significant transition in the degree to which he helped out as his sisters left home. His three sisters explicitly communicated their expectations to him that he should take on more work.

> *M.S.:* What's going to happen when Alex leaves?

> *Jacqui:* Um, they're gonna get some part-time work, I think. But the business is not as it used to be, because of the recession and everything. And it's become more of a local business because there's so many Chinese take-aways opening up around the area. And in many ways, they don't have the same pressure to get as much money in regards to putting us through college. So the pressures's off a little with respect to how much money they need to turn over.

Although Alex's upcoming departure from home posed yet another adjustment for his parents, as Jacqui noted, some financial pressure would be eased by that time. Alex's departure signaled a new phase in their parents' lives, when no children would be at home. In this case, which was rather exceptional, siblings discussed the implications of children leaving home for the continuing viability of the shop and for those children who would remain at home. Jacqui and her sisters took it upon themselves to address the adaptations that would be required because they realized that their parents were unlikely to do so. As a result of their discussions and concern for siblings remaining at home, Jacqui and Sarah felt that they had acted responsibly, although they had withdrawn most of their labor.

Ann: Negotiating a Gradual Departure

Some young people like Pue-ling left home without warning, but it was more common to pave the way gradually for departures—

particularly if an individual was a key provider of caring labor and work in the take-away. Such individuals knew that it would be difficult for their families to replace them and the reassurance their parents gained from their presence.

Ann, who was 24 years old, was the eldest of three children, who were born and raised in Britain. She and her siblings were integral to the business. At the time of the interviews, Ann had worked in the shop full-time for the past six years. Her parents had relied upon her for many years, and she lived above the shop with them. Her brothers Tom, age 23, and Paul, age 22, were both pursuing graduate degrees, and lived away from home. Ann explained that although she had not intended to run a take-away business, she had never been interested in studying, so it had seemed sensible that she stay at home and manage the shop while her brothers pursued their careers. According to Ann, her brothers were conscientious about coming home on occasional weekends to help out.

While Ann stressed that she had not been pressured into staying at home, she indicated that in the past few years, she had become increasingly hopeful of leaving home and starting her own career. However, this was a very difficult issue for her because she knew that her parents relied upon her a great deal. Furthermore, she effectively freed her brothers of a greater responsibility to the FWC (see Salaff, 1981).

After our first interview, Ann was offered a job in Hong Kong, and she revealed that she was eager to take it. Ann, however, was concerned about the ramifications of leaving home for her family and for the future viability of the business: "I was talking to Paul on the phone, and I told him that if I go, he'd probably have to come home more on weekends and look after mum and dad. He encouraged me and said, 'I support you completely.' He said I should go, and I was glad because I wasn't sure if he would have given me a mouthful. But he said that I'd been there for years, working, and that I shouldn't worry about him, he'd be fine." Paul's support for Ann to leave home was crucial to her, and enabled her to exit from their FWC. Paul's encouragement vindicated Ann's desire to leave home: He communicated to her that she had more than done her share of work over the years. Despite this, Ann knew that her parents' endorsement of her leaving was, at best, half-hearted:

M.S.: Have your parents encouraged you to take the job in Hong Kong?

Ann: Yeah. But deep down I think they want me to stay until the shop's sold, but they haven't said so. It's hard making the break. I feel really guilty.

In an interview with Paul, which occurred shortly after Ann left for Hong Kong, Paul revealed his ambivalence about Ann leaving home, although he felt that he could not, for her sake, reveal this to her:

Paul: She's always been with my mum and dad, and the shop [*pause*] she was the sort of manager of the shop. And I'd say that my dad and mum were very dependent upon her, completely. Even if Ann went to Hong Kong and say that I was willing to work in the shop, it would be quite different. She's been there so long, on a permanent basis, so it's quite different. But now she's gone to Hong Kong. When she left for Hong Kong, my dad and mum felt very sort of, not unhappy, but felt different. Very different, without her in the shop and the house. I think they didn't sleep that well, as well.

M.S.: I spoke to her on the phone before she left and she said that she was torn about leaving.

Paul: I actually supported her to leave. Because I feel that she's been in the shop so long, and I don't see her working in a takeaway forever, that that's not a very good prospect for the future. I'd like to see her going out to meet different people, and [*pause*] but in a way, I feel that it was a shame, because the business, the family business, was doing quite well. And basically, I think it needed her to sort of continue.

M.S.: So it sounds like you feel mixed about Ann leaving.

Paul: I wanted her to leave because I think that's what's best for her. She can't stay there all her life. . . . When I was at university, I do see Ann, and I look at Ann, and I think it's quite sad, quite unwise, and when we were at university, she was prepared to work, she was prepared to sacrifice.

In this family, Ann's hope to leave home and start a new career forced her family to consider the implications of staying on at the take-away for Ann's future and well-being. It also put into question the continuing viability of the take-away, which her parents and her brothers wanted to continue running. Although Ann's desire for a career was problematic for the continuation of their family livelihood, her family also wanted Ann to be happy in pursuing her own life.

Ann's departure from home was negotiated gradually, through her discussions with Paul, rather than engendered by a clear-cut decision or event. Although Ann had a good relationship with her parents, she negotiated her departure much more explicitly with her brother Paul, than with her parents. In fact, Paul also spoke to his parents about Ann leaving, and made it clear to them that he thought the move would be good for her, in order to give her moral support. Without Paul's support and approval, it would have been extremely difficult for Ann to leave at all. Therefore, the way in which an individual left home made a difference in how families responded, and in how one was perceived. Leaving in what was regarded as a considerate manner, as in Ann's case, was not seen as breaking with the FWC and ensured that Ann stayed on good terms with her family.

Letting Go

As indicated in the above cases, young peoples' feelings of liberation upon leaving home could be tempered in a number of ways. Without the explicit blessing and encouragement of parents and siblings to leave home, and without the knowledge that their departures would not endanger the shop's future viability or result in burdening siblings who remained at home, leaving home could not be an entirely positive experience.

Although Sui did find her time away at university quite exhilarating and liberating, she knew that her family still relied upon her from time to time: "We all tried to get away. It [the shop] was such a restriction on our lives. We all thought, 'Whoopee, we're going now'. But home was still near enough for us to come back on weekends if we wanted to, or if we were needed to, rather." Wong was more emphatic about the need to leave the shop and start his own life, despite the difficulties of leaving behind parents who relied a great deal upon him and his siblings:

> *M.S.:* So you were quite excited to leave, and felt fully justified?
>
> *Wong:* It wasn't a case of justification. It was a case of feeling that I *had* to do it. You know, it wasn't like, 'Hey, I've been working for you for the last eighteen years, and I've earned the right to go.' It wasn't like that. There wasn't any feeling of being owed anything, because it's all part and parcel of being a Chinese kid in a typical Chinese family where the parents own a take-away, so there's no dues or anything. It was something I felt I had to do.

Most young people, like Wong, did not try to justify their departures, in terms of feeling entitled to withdraw from their FWCs. Rather, leaving home was talked about as a strong *need* that had to be fulfilled. Some BBCs, like Anna, also realized that rather than simply representing a rebellion against her parents, leaving home and disengaging from the FWC were fundamentally about working out their identities: "I knew I would have to go, because I was getting very unhappy, and we'd row about a lot over different things. I'd become much more irritable. I'd become much more aggressive toward customers. I became very resentful of my time, and not being able to put my time into my study. But I don't think that [pause] my rebellion against them was much more a rejection of my culture." Like Anna, BBCs who had been integral to their family livelihoods needed to pursue their own lives and to come to terms with being Chinese (and what it meant) in Britain *independent* of (though not rejecting) the Chinese take-away.

Unlike individuals who had decided that they had to leave home, some young people found it extremely difficult to let go at all. According to Foon, who worked full-time outside, and who also helped out in the shop in the evenings, "Well, let's see. It's difficult to let go. I haven't got the courage to do that. It's gotta come from them [his parents]. Things might have been really different if Wong or I said something ten years ago: 'Look mum, you're gonna have to find someone else.' But could you do it?"

Not only did some young people feel unable to tell their parents that they wanted or needed to withdraw their labor, but paradoxically, they could also feel anxious about curtailing such a long-term commitment, which had developed over time. Howard Becker's (1960) discussion of the notion of commitment attempted to explain indidviduals' consistent lines of activity over time. Using the analogy of a side bet, which is similar to economists' notion of opportunity cost, Becker noted that some lines of activity were difficult to curtail because individuals could become very invested in that commitment. However, Becker acknowledged that his theory was weakened by a neglect of "an analysis of the system of values"—for instance, as embodied in these FWCs. Such values were integral to an understanding of why someone acted in a consistent fashion over time. The economic rationality informing Becker's theorizing of commitment can explain only so much. Becker's analysis did not consider the emotional and normative dimensions of withdrawing from a family livelihood, particularly if parents were very reliant upon their children.

Despite the pressures of feeling relied upon by their parents, letting go for some children could also be a frightening and emotionally charged experience because they had grown accustomed to their parents relying upon them. In an exceptional case, a daughter had very mixed feelings about her parents becoming more independent *of her*. Laura, who was an integral child, had been out of the country for four months, and during that time, her mother had joined a Chinese women's group that met twice a week: "When I got back, I really noticed that she wasn't at home. I know this sounds bad, but sometimes I felt sort of resentment that she wasn't home, and I could go out with her and do a bit of shopping. Because when I left home, I felt really guilty leaving home, and uh, then coming home, I'll be home for mum, and she wasn't there. She doesn't really need me, really."

Although Laura was pleased about her mother's initiative and resourcefulness in joining the group, she worried a great deal about her parents' ability to cope without her. In addition, she seemed to feel somewhat uneasy about the idea of not being as central or necessary to the FWC as she had been in the past. Thus leaving home and letting go meant different things to different people, and some found this process much more conflicted and protracted than others.

Children leaving home was a critical juncture in these families' lives, because their departures often revealed that their family work contracts not only needed reinforcing and tending, but that FWCs were vulnerable and subject to some instability. A key difficulty of negotiating or challenging the FWC was the perception that there were no clear rules about the appropriate limits or boundaries concerning children's commitments to their FWCs. Although the expectation that Chinese children should help out was widely recognized, there was no clear consensus about the right thing to do, when it came to disengaging from the FWC—apart from the view that leaving home unexpectedly and "loading down" younger siblings were regarded as irresponsible acts. In fact, the ways in which these young people worked out tensions and ambivalence around helping out, and the ways in which they left home, revealed that despite a widespread consensus that helping out was important and meaningful, their commitments to their FWCs were negotiated in different ways by individual children. The ways in which individuals worked out their labor commitments were partly circumscribed by their siblings' actions. In the next chapter, we will examine how individual children positioned themselves in relation to the FWC.

6

Siblings' Labor Commitments and Family Reputations

IN ADDITION to the fact that the negotiation of children's labor tended to differ among families, individual children within families could experience or exhibit differential degrees of commitment to the family work contract (FWC). While the family is a shared environment, Frank Sulloway (1996) has argued that the family comprises a series of distinct micro-environments in which siblings experience it in different ways. Because some children exhibited more committed behavior than others in many of these families, the dynamics of FWCs ultimately could not be understood without examining individual children's labor contributions (Song, 1997b). How did some children come to be more committed to their FWCs than others, and how were siblings' differential commitments understood in these families? Although disparities in siblings' labor participation could be shaped by gender and birth order, not all differences could be explained in these terms, particularly as young people left school and pursued distinct life paths. In some families, younger children were reported to be more committed than their older siblings, and in some cases, sons were reported to be more committed than daughters.

It was clear in the course of interviews that rather than suddenly arising when young people started leaving home, issues of equity and differential labor commitments between siblings had developed much more gradually over time—over the course of these families' relationships and histories. As Finch and Mason note (1993:26): "Responsibilities toward parents or children are not negotiated in a vacuum when a need arises, but are built upon a history of the relationship between parent and child, into which the biography of each gets incorporated and gives significance to the form which responsibilities might take."

I interviewed two children (siblings) in seventeen of the twenty-five families so that I could compare siblings' understandings of and commitments to helping out. I asked respondents to compare their labor participation with those of their siblings, in terms of how much work they had performed over the years, taking into account labor performed in the take-away (shop work), caring work, and domestic housework. In asking this question, I wanted to gain a sense of how siblings understood their own and their siblings' commitments to their FWCs, rather than simply discern who had actually worked more than others. In particular, I was interested in exploring the implications of differential labor commitments for individual siblings, family relationships, and the workings of FWCs.

In the seventeen families in which I interviewed two siblings, there was a high degree of agreement in their assessment of their own and their sibling's labor participation. Although respondents usually started talking about their respective work roles, they tended to equate differences in labor participation with disparities in commitments to the FWC. The siblings interviewed in thirteen of the seventeen families reported disparities in labor participation between themselves and other siblings, while the siblings in the other four families reported that they and their siblings had shared similar or relatively equitable work roles. Of course, reports stressing similarity or sameness among siblings did not necessarily mean that these siblings actually shared work responsibilities more equitably than those who reported differences (Song, 1998). What mattered, however, was that for those siblings who reported disparities, these differences were seen to be significant.

In the case of two of the three families with minor workers, siblings stressed similar experiences because their work roles had been very limited all along. As Theresa explained, "None of us did very much, so I can't really compare"—a sentiment confirmed by her brother, Stephen: "We've done more or less the same. One of us volunteers to help out, and there's no argument about it. Someone will go and help out. Maybe Tom might be a bit difficult about it. . . . But we're pretty equal. Between us, the age difference between us is small; there's only a year between us. So you could say, we can more or less be treated as equals. So you don't put more pressure on the eldest or give the youngest one nothing to do."

Conversely, the integral children in two families stressed similarity in siblings' work roles because they had all worked hard growing up—no one had been spared. In fact, some of the respondents stressing sameness resisted comparison altogether. For instance, Helen replied, "I don't like to compare. We don't count who does what. We help each other." Her sister Rita also replied, "I think she [Helen] did her bit and I did mine. It's difficult to say who's done more because I've done a lot in the earlier stage, then I was away studying for two years, and she was in the shop. Can't really compare the commitments."

In Helen's and Rita's case, it was implied that a very close and supportive relationship between these sisters precluded comparison, or "counting who does what." Moreover, it was also implied that to compare their relative commitments to helping out would have been divisive and at odds with their understandings of their FWCs—that you don't count who does what.[1] However, cases such as Helen's and Rita's were rather exceptional in the sample because most sibling sets emphasized differences rather than similarities in their labor commitments. Since reported disparities in labor commitments seemed to be the source of some tension and controversy in these families, I focused upon how young people understood and attributed meanings to these perceived disparities.

Among siblings reporting disparities in labor commitments, some siblings could be quite competitive about how much responsibility each had exercised over the years. For example, Tina, age 19, and Kelly, age 18, both claimed to have done more than the other:

M.S.: Would you say that you and Tina, then, have done similar amounts of work?

Kelly: Um, my sister really is the favorite of the family, so she can go and even watch the TV and not get shouted at. But if I go in, it's like "Come on, we need your help out here."

M.S.: So you think you've done more than her?

Kelly: Well, I think I did more work than her. People do say I work longer hours than her.

Interestingly, in her interview, Tina said, "Out of the four children, from my point of view, I think I've done the most, growing up through the years. Then my sister second, then my little brother, then eldest brother. I don't think it's anything to do with the male/female [arguing that gender did not explain why she and her sister performed more work than their brothers]."

In Tina's and Kelly's case, each of them asserted that she had done more work than the other. From Kelly's point of view, perceived disparities in labor participation between her and Tina were shaped by the fact that her parents reportedly favored her sister over her. Clearly, Kelly was hurt by her belief that Tina got special treatment as "the favorite of the family." As Allat (1996:139) has noted in her study of children's understandings of parenting, "The value of fairness is jealously guarded by children, and parental dispensation of it is closely monitored since it intimately reflects a child's relative status." Therefore, rather than being a uniform blueprint to be followed, the operation of FWCs could vary from family to family (despite the common values and meanings underlying these contracts), according to factors such as the balance of responsibility among siblings.

In another family, Lisa's (age 20) explanation for why she ranked herself above her sister June (age 22) was that they had performed quite distinct work roles while growing up. Lisa had primarily worked in the kitchen, and June at the counter. According to Lisa: "Even though June is older than me, I tended to tell her how to do things. I had more family responsibility than she did. On the shop front, I naturally had more responsibility because basically for her, her job involved just standing in the front, and maybe answering the phone, whereas I'm on the more difficult demanding side, actually cooking and doing what people think is a quite hard labor job."

I was struck by the conviction with which Lisa disparaged her sister's work role. Lisa's reasoning for why she had more family responsibility than June rested upon her insistence that she performed qualitatively more difficult and demanding work than June did at the counter. This was an interesting characterization of counter work, because some young people saw working in the front as particularly stressful, in terms of dealing with customers (see Parker, 1994). In contrast with Lisa, June reported, quite unequivocally, that she had contributed the most labor over time and that she had the strongest sense of "family duty" of all her siblings: "If I argue with my parents, then eventually, I will go around to their way of thinking, or I'll do it, whereas my sisters and brother don't." June felt she had been the most committed, not only because of the sheer amount of work she had performed in the shop, but also because she saw herself as most obedient to her parents' wishes.

Clearly, the meanings and the implications of these perceived disparities in siblings' labor participation went beyond issues of fairness and of sharing work equitably in these families. In fact, these examples suggest that one's family reputation and recognition of one's commitments to helping out were of great personal importance to these young people. Both of the sibling sets discussed above illustrate that in addition to a favorable family reputation, these young people vied for their parents' affection and approval.

"Good" and "Bad" Family Reputations

Young peoples' interpretations of differences in siblings' labor commitments were centrally based upon the individual reputations of siblings within families. As Finch and Mason (1993:149) note, "Reputations, we shall argue, are the means by which the moral identity of each individual gets built up, consolidated and modified over time, and gets carried from one situation to another." Although the reputations of individuals could change, they argue that the shared images of individual family members tend to be stable over time.

In families where young people reported differences in siblings' labor participation, polarized reputations as "good" or "bad" children were widely shared among family members. "Good" reputations were associated with helping out and an unwavering commitment to the FWC, while "bad" reputations were associated with irresponsible behavior, selfishness, or resistance to helping out. As relative terms, the attribution of a good or bad reputation was not determined by any fixed or formulaic record or act of commitment across these families. Both good and bad reputations were elaborated in terms of behaviors and attitudes toward helping out, that developed over time. One's reputation as a "good" child developed vis-à-vis siblings who had reputations for being troublesome or less committed. Equally, a "bad" child may not have had such a reputation without a sibling who was seen to be more committed to helping out.

Young people who saw themselves as the most committed children in their families clearly wanted to see themselves (and be known) as "good" and responsible members of their families. For instance, Ming reported that before her elder sister left for Hong Kong, her own work role had been limited in comparison with her sister's. But in the years that followed her sister's departure, Ming's work role increased, and she now claimed that she had "overtaken" her sister.

Securing a good reputation mattered a great deal to these young people because not only did they take pride in it, but those who claimed the moral high ground as committed children could be in a position to judge and criticize siblings whom they perceived to be irresponsible or uncommitted. In addition to demonstrating polarized family reputations between siblings, the dynamics around claiming the moral high ground and criticizing "bad" siblings can be illustrated in the following family.

Annie and Shirley

In one family, reported differences in labor commitments between four siblings were the source of a great deal of tension. All four children in this family, who were supplementary workers, were two years apart in age, and all were born and raised in Britain: Andrew, age 28, Shirley, age 26, Kathy, age 24, and Annie, age 22. The two siblings who were interviewed, Annie and Shirley, had a very close relationship. Shirley, who worked as a secretary, was married and had a young baby. Annie was in her first year of university. They considered each other their best friends and seemed to have formed an "alliance" of sorts within their family (Segalen, 1984), which was based upon their shared sense of being committed to helping out. They considered themselves to be equally committed, in relation to their other siblings. The disparities in labor participation were seen by both respondents as problematic because, Andrew and Kathy, according to Annie and Shirley, had not done their "fair share."

Both Shirley and Annie reported that despite the fact that all the children in their family had disliked working in the shop, *they* had felt obliged to help out: They had all grown up with the shop, and they had found the lifestyle and hard work difficult. Most of all, they disliked the fact that their lives had revolved around their shop so much. Despite their own ambivalent feelings about upholding the FWC, both Shirley and Annie reported that of the four children, they had been much more "responsible" and "committed" than Andrew or Kathy:

Shirley: Andrew left first, but not to move away, but he was studying, and so he didn't actually move away from the family, but he stopped work at the shop, and that caused big problems, and when I left, it was even worse. My sisters had to take a night each. That was really hard. It was hard for them because sometimes my mother was ill. She was ill quite a bit. Stressed out, came and went. My brother refused to come back to the shop, ever.

M.S.: Why was that?

Shirley: He hated it, he hated it more than all of us.

M.S.: Did that cause a lot of tension between him and the parents?

Shirley: No, it caused a lot of tension between us [siblings] and him. We thought that he let the family down. He wasn't doing his part. When my mother was ill, he didn't come back to help. When he moved off, and stopped working in the shop, he actually broke away from the family. He didn't have a lot of responsibility toward the family. I think he'd had enough. He wanted out. He never came back. . . . What we used to say, we've had this discussion before—Me, Annie, and mum—we have similar characteristics. We did it; we didn't like doing the work, but we did it because we're helping each other. We were very bonded, even now we're close. My brother's emigration elsewhere hasn't really affected mum as deeply as he'd expected. I think he was very disappointed; had we [she and Annie] moved, it would have been more of a blow to her [mother].

M.S.: So Kathy doesn't do much either?

Shirley: Yeah. She and my brother were able not to attend work. They were able to do it without guilt. We hated it, but we felt we had to come back. She'd [the mother] always count on us being there, whereas with my brother and Kathy, you don't know. I think they shut themselves off to any feeling of it; they hated it so much. No matter what my mother did, they shut themselves off, shut their emotions off.

This case illustrates that the noted differences between the reportedly "good" children (Annie and Shirley) and the "bad" children (Andew and Kathy) mattered in various ways: According to the two sisters, Andrew's and Kathy's reported failure to uphold the FWC had very negative consequences for Annie and Shirley in terms of greater work responsibility. Andrew's and Kathy's "irresponsibility" also mattered because it was seen to represent moral failings on their parts—Andrew was seen to have violated the

FWC by withdrawing his labor altogether, while Kathy was seen to be resistant to helping out. According to this narrative, these "bad" siblings had stopped caring, and had failed their families. Furthermore, Annie's and Shirley's reputations as good children were linked with their closeness with their mother; their mother's reliance upon them (as opposed to the reportedly negligible effect of Andrew's departure upon his mother) was valued, even though it stemmed from inequities in siblings' labor commitments.

Despite the strength of beliefs around the FWC, this did not preclude the possibility that individual children might not honor the contract. This has also been shown in the case of some young Vietnamese Americans adopting individualistic, rather than collective, approaches to their families' economic activities (Kibria, 1994).

Despite the two sisters' resentments toward their other siblings, whom they saw as irresponsible and not committed, Annie also realized that she had "selfish" motivations for fostering her reputation as a "good," committed child: "I saw a counselor in college last year. I was having some silly problems, and when I was talking, I poured out all these things. I was really angry cleaning out this storage, in my parents' attic, thinking why am I doing this, and not anyone else? My counselor talked to me, and made me realize that I was doing it because I wanted favoritism, that I wanted to be the good child. And that I could help them out, I'm making myself out to be great."

Based upon Annie's and Shirley's case, a great deal was at stake in the determination of good and bad family reputations: If the withdrawal of one's labor was seen to be irresponsible or selfish, as in Andrew's case, doing so was regarded as tantamount to breaking away from the family. Andrew's family membership was actually jeopardized by his sisters' perception that he had run away from his responsibilities. However, as Annie conceded, striving for a reputation as a good child was not necessarily motivated by purely altruistic motives. Some children sought parental approval and special relationships with their parents, and were gratified by being able to occupy the moral high ground in relation to their "bad" siblings.

Although some committed children, like Annie, had insights

into their complex motivations for wanting good reputations, they were generally less interested in talking about or explaining why they themselves were committed to helping out, than in explaining why their siblings were "bad." Perhaps one reason why most young people had much clearer understandings of "bad" siblings' behavior was that "good" children were widely seen to be the ideal associated with upholding family work contracts. In this sense, "good" children simply fulfilled the perceived Chinese norm in Britain. Family stories (and those circulating in Chinese networks and communities) about supposedly bad or irresponsible children constructed these children as deviating from this idealized norm. Such children were seen by their families to have either broken or challenged their FWCs.

Escapees, Rebels, and Traitors

As was the case with "good" children, children in these families usually gained "bad" reputations as a result of consistent lines of behavior over time. However, in some cases, children who had regularly helped out could suddenly gain a bad reputation, due to an unexpected withdrawal from the FWC, as in the case of Andrew (discussed above) or Pue-ling (discussed in the last chapter). Young people like Andrew were seen as escapees, who refused to return to work in their take-aways or to the caring labor their parents relied upon. Andrew was seen to have escaped from the FWC in a dishonorable way because he had allegedly relinquished responsibility without consideration of how his departure would affect his family.

While siblings with bad reputations could face censure and moral disapproval (see also Pang, 1993:145), there tended to be differing degrees to which they were judged or criticized by their families, depending upon the way in which they challenged or broke away from their FWCs. For instance, being unable to provide assistance, as opposed to being able but unwilling, was one important factor that distinguished legitimate from illegitimate excuses in a variety of exchanges between kin (Finch and Mason, 1993:98). Similarly, escaping from the FWC, by completely and suddenly withdrawing one's labor participation, was widely regarded as an illegitimate act—in contrast with Ann's negotiated withdrawal of her labor (discussed in chapter 5), which was supported by her brother Paul and her parents. However, there were other ways in which bad siblings were understood to have challenged their FWCs.

Sai: A Rebel

In one family, Sai reported that she was the rebel in her family. Sai, who was 25 years old, was the youngest of three children, and there was a considerable age difference between Sai and her brother and sister, who were aged 34 and 38, respectively. Although all three children were born in Hong Kong, Sai was only 7 years old when she came to Britain, in contrast with her siblings, who were already young adults by that time.

As discussed in the last chapter, young people who were predominantly raised in Britain experienced much more tension around helping out than those raised in Hong Kong. According to Sai, she was seen by her siblings and her parents as a rebel, because she disliked working in the shop, and complained about helping out. Nevertheless, she still felt compelled to help out. She did not want to abandon the take-away entirely, for she still felt a great deal of loyalty toward her family and wanted to maintain good ties with them. As a result, while she continued to help out, she also persisted in arguing with her family about how much they expected her to work.

Despite the genuine anguish that the conflicts with her family caused, Sai also seemed to be somewhat proud of her position as a rebel. For instance, she saw herself as a principled protector of her nephews and nieces:

> My mum asks my niece to translate something on the news, and my niece can't translate it. I did tell my mum that it's not as easy as that. Don't put pressure on my niece, because I'm very protective toward them. I have said this to my brother: If I see you pressurizing them to help out, and I think it's too much, I will report you to the authorities. And I will. Because I feel so strongly about it. . . . And I can see exactly what's com-

ing, especially for my eldest niece. And I will report them. They wouldn't take away the children. They'd get warned, and I think that would be enough to scare him.

For Sai, maintaining her reputation as a rebel in her family enabled her to reconcile her ambivalent feelings about helping out with continuing to work with her family. By being a rebel, Sai felt that she was able to maintain her integrity because she could express her strong feelings about helping out without withdrawing her labor.

Thus, being a rebel could be experienced positively to the extent that it was a way of asserting individual beliefs and individual identities within their families. For Sai, her rebel identity countered her family's characterization of her as a moaning and somewhat spoiled child. Rather than families simply foisting "bad" reputations upon them, some children actually fostered their reputations as bad children, as in Sai's case. By limiting her involvement in her family's business, and by protecting her niece from helping out, Sai was not only negotiating her labor participation with her family, but she was also negotiating her own identity in her family. Furthermore, her "bad" reputation enabled her to keep a certain amount of distance from the take-away business, and provided her with some room for maneuvering within the FWC.

Jenny: A Traitor

One exceptional case in this study involved a daughter (who was not a respondent), Jenny, age 28, who acquired a "bad" reputation, due to a single act of betrayal. Jenny was the eldest of four children, all of whom were born and raised in Britain. As the eldest child, Jenny was particularly integral to the business; she had been indispensable at the counter when the shop first opened, because her parents did not speak enough English. Jenny came to be regarded as a traitor by her family when she told her teacher that she was having difficulties with working in the shop and keeping up with schoolwork.

Jenny reportedly had a heavier workload than her younger brothers and sister. One day, some years ago, they were visited by social workers who warned them about the amount of work Jenny was doing. According to Laura, the younger sister, everyone was in shock, because no one had known about Jenny's distress up to that point—Jenny had burst into tears upon the social workers' arrival. Jenny and her siblings had to translate the social workers' warning for their parents. According to Laura, "I'll always remember my brother saying, 'I just can't understand why Jenny had to tell her teacher.'" According to both siblings, it was unclear whether or not Jenny knew that her disclosure to her teacher would result in a formal warning (I was unable to interview Jenny about her interpretation of events). Although both siblings were reportedly sympathetic with the situation that Jenny had been in, they agreed that Jenny had violated family trust and solidarity by talking with her teacher.

However, from Laura's perspective, Jenny, as a daughter and as the oldest child, had been expected to work more than her younger siblings: "He [Laura's older brother] was helping out as well, but not as much as her. It's funny, but this is how I see it. The boys were more protected in a sense. Um, you can see that in the way my mum has the girls do the counter work, even though we don't like it. My brothers, they don't like it, but they could stay in the kitchen. And I always hated counter work; I mean, now, I'm o.k. about it. But I had a real hard time about it before, and being in public." Although Laura was more understanding about her older sister's predicament, because she believed that her brothers had been privileged as sons, she still shared her family's consensus that her sister had unforgivably broken ranks in that situation.

Jenny's work role did diminish after this incident, although she remained a key worker. Ever since that incident, they reported, Jenny was never seen in the same way again, by the family. Her outsider status was compounded later on by her marriage to a white English man when she turned 19. Her family saw her marriage as an attempt to leave home. At the time of interview, Jenny lived in a northern city, and did not have much contact with her family. When she did come for visits, Laura reported that Jenny had lost much of her Chinese language facility. In spite of the fact that Jenny's act of betrayal was seen to be precipitated by the difficult circumstances she was in, she was never fully forgiven by her family.

Although many families manifested similar patterns in attributing "bad" family reputations to individual children who had failed to uphold their FWCs, these cases demonstrated that there could be some variability in the kinds of bad reputations attributed to certain siblings. Reputations of rebels were, on the whole, not as negative as those of escapees or traitors. Rebels were seen to be oppositional and selfish, but they had not actually abandoned or betrayed their families; they caused trouble, but they still remained committed to their families by helping out. They continuously engaged in negotiations or forms of resistance that allowed them to express their unhappiness or ambivalence about upholding the FWC. Because escapees fled their families, the withdrawal of their labor effectively precluded discussion or other forms of negotiation. Escapees such as Andrew tended to make clean breaks. However, these kinds of clean breaks were relatively rare in most families.

Polarized Cultural Identities

Although young people who were attributed bad reputations by their families could be judged in somewhat different ways, most "bad" reputations tended to be associated with a certain type of cultural identity. In general, "good" children who were committed to helping out were seen to be more Chinese than "bad" children, who were seen as more Western or (white) British.[2] For instance, in one family, Paul considered himself to be more Western than his older brother and sister and noted, "I was the naughty boy of the family. I had the more sort of English way of thinking or whatever. We call it 'selfish' in Chinese." Such polarized (and idealized) notions of Chinese and British cultural identities were linked with the characterization of Chinese families in Britain as possessing a more collective, rather than individualistic, orientation compared with most British families. In fact, most young people who were born and raised in Britain tended to see themselves as being informed by both Chinese and British cultures. The recognition of this complexity, however, did not preclude the development of polarized ideal-typical cultural identities between siblings.

Other studies of immigrant families have found similar

dynamics in the differential identities adopted by or attributed to youths. For instance, in a psychological study of second-generation Italians (from the 1930s) in the United States, Italian youths adopted a range of identities that indicated their attachments to or distance from their Italian ethnicity (Child, 1943, in Rumbaut, 1994). Also, a study of Mexican American young people found that within families, some siblings were quite anglicized, while others identified strongly as Mexican gang members (Vigil, 1988). However, none of these studies has discussed the performance of family labor as an important marker of cultural identity—albeit a less commonly identified marker of cultural identity, in comparison with language abilities or other cultural practices (Song, 1997b).

Colin and Simon

In one family, Simon, age 17, and Colin, age 20, grew up in Britain as minor workers in their family. Although there was not a huge disparity in the amount of work performed by them (because their work roles were already limited in the shop), Simon was reported to be "the more reliable one," according to Simon, Colin, and their mother. They all agreed that in the occasional event that they were needed in the shop, Simon was much more likely to be "available" and "cooperative" than Colin was, who had a "bad" reputation in this respect.

Simon made it clear that he did not resent Colin for avoiding work in the take-away, because Simon himself felt that his own role had been very limited. Nevertheless, when asked why Simon was more committed to helping out than Colin was, Simon explained that Colin's aversion to working in the take-away had to do with Colin's attitudes toward being Chinese: "He's a white man. He has black and white friends, but not Chinese friends. And now he lives in [a town where Colin has just moved]. It's all white. There isn't even a Chinese take-away down there." Here, Simon implicitly links a Chinese identity with working in his family's take-away business and suggests that Colin has engaged in various disidentifying strategies (Goffman, 1963) to diassociate himself, as a Chinese person, from the take-away. Compared with Colin, Simon reported feeling much more Chinese than his brother: Not only did he not mind the take-away in the way that Colin did, but he also spoke better Cantonese, and he also had Chinese friends.

When I asked Colin about his work role in comparison to Simon's, Colin seemed aware of and did not refute Simon's depiction of him as having a bad reputation and a more Western identity in his family. Cognizant of their respective reputations in their families, Colin confirmed Simon's view that Colin did not want to be associated with the take-away: "I don't know if I should say this, but have you thought about the people who work in McDonald's? It's just things like, you look down on people who work at McDonald's. Uh, because you look at them as people who don't really have anything left. You look at them, and think, what are you doing here? I don't like customers seeing me in that way, serving someone."

As Colin explained, in the course of the interview, his aversion to serving customers stemmed from the habitual linking of Chinese people with take-aways, as well as from his belief that working in a take-away was a menial job.

In some families, differences in commitments to helping out (and their associated cultural identities) could be understood in terms of differences in socialization. In families where some siblings were raised in Hong Kong, while others were raised in Britain, the different socialization among siblings could mitigate blame attributed to "bad" Westernized siblings. However, in cases where siblings experienced similar upbringings, as did Colin and Simon, children who were perceived to be resisting the FWC and who were more Western than their siblings were seen to have deliberately *chosen* such reputations and identities. In such families, individuals with "bad" reputations for being relatively Western, in relation to their siblings, could be subject to strong disapproval from their families. This was the case with David's reputation as an "English" person in his family, below.

David: Limited Ethnic Options?

Two sisters, Anna, age 24, and Mary, age 26, reported that one of their two brothers, David, age 29, was effectively a pariah in their family. All four children were BBCs, and had provided key forms of caring and shop labor as integral children. The basis for his outsider status was his long-standing refusal to help out in the family shop. According to his sisters, as soon as David turned 16, he moved away to a nearby town and started working as an auto mechanic, and he wanted nothing more to do with the take-away.[3]

As with Simon's explanation of why Colin rejected any association with the take-away, both Anna and Mary believed that the reason why David distanced himself from his family and the FWC centered on David's cultural identity: According to his sisters, David didn't like being Chinese. Because helping out in the take-away largely symbolized Chinese identity in Britain, David reportedly wished to distance himself from this association and this way of life. Anna and Mary claimed that David's cultural identity was effectively English; David was described as being "individualistic" and "selfish." According to Mary,

Every time he comes home, mum and dad say, "You're becoming more and more English." And he is. David is cut off from Chinese society totally in [x]. He's actually living with an English woman in [x]. His Chinese is quite poor. He has trouble communicating with friends of my parents. He thinks like an English person now. You know how, for instance, it sounds terrible saying this about my brother, but if we all went to Chinatown one day, you offer to pay, and you fight to pay the bill, basically. That's what the Chinese do. One day, it was mum and dad's birthday. I said, let's go halves and share the bill, and he says, "Well I suppose so, I'm a bit broke." And I said, "listen, we've got to do something," and some English people are like that, you know. One of my dad's friends came and joined us, and after the meal, David says, "I'm not paying for him. I don't know him." Well, that's just typical of an English person. You pay for yours and I pay for mine. I said, "Forget it David, I'll pay for the meal." I'm not quibbling over who's eaten what, and who you know and who you don't know. It's dad's friend.

Since David was not interviewed, we do not know if he would agree with such an assessment of himself. However, according to his sisters, his reputation for being English was widely shared in their family.

What David's siblings objected to was not only the fact that he had broken with the FWC but also their perception that he was trying to deny altogether his Chinese identity and heritage. David's behavior was especially upsetting to his sisters because no matter how hard he tried to be "just English," his sisters believed that he could not and should not push away his Chinese identity. According to his sisters, David would not be accepted as an English person by white English people; he would always be seen, first and foremost, as Chinese, regardless of any lifestyle he adopted.

That is, his sisters believed that David exercised little control over his ethnicity in Britain. In her exploration of white ethnicity in the United States, Mary Waters (1990) has argued that ethnicity for white Americans is largely symbolic (see Gans, 1979), meaning that ethnicity is purely individualistic and without real social costs. As such, ethnicity can actually be an "option" (see also Alba, 1988 and Zenner, 1988 for a discussion of Italian American and Jewish American ethnicity, respectively). That is, ethnicity is not something that influences white Americans' lives unless they want it to. Ethnicity is invoked selectively by white Americans in order to feel 'special' (Waters, 1990). However, Waters notes that for ethnic minorities (such as Chinese people in Britain), ethnicity is not an option, as it is for white people, given their distinctive physical attributes and cultural practices and the fact that they are racialized. According to Waters (1990:160), "all ethnicities are not equal, all are not symbolic, costless, and voluntary." For racial minorities, their cultural identities, and their daily lives more generally, are fundamentally shaped by their race or national origin. Waters' analysis is helpful in illustrating the limited "choice" that these Chinese young people in Britain were able to exercise, in relation to their cultural identities. As Chinese people, they were almost always linked in peoples' minds with the take-away, reflecting this group's heavy concentration in this economic niche (see Chung, 1990).

In fact, there is evidence that even long-settled and relatively assimilated ethnic minorities must constantly contend with *imposed* ethnicities and racial categories by the white majority. For instance, Mia Tuan's (1995:34) study of third-and fourth-generation ("multigeneration") Americans of Japanese and Chinese origin found that most did not feel accepted as "real" Americans; this was one of the reasons why Asian Americans still saw themelves as "ethnics":[4]

> While partially motivated by the currently favorable climate towards ethnic self-awareness, foods, festivals, music, and clothing, Asian ethnics do not feel it is an option to do away with ethnic distinctions and identify themselves as unhyphenated Americans. They believe the label, American, is reserved for describing white ethnics and would not be appropriate or acceptable for describing themselves. This belief is based on personal experiences with prejudice, discrimination, and stereotyping as well as a general perception that Asian Americans are understood by the wider society as a population composed of recent immigrants.

Similarly, the Chinese young people I interviewed, and in particular those who were born and raised in Britain, reported that they were not seen as British by the majority of the white British population—despite the emergence of Chinese people who also identify as British, or more locally, as Scottish or Liverpudlian. A number of respondents also reported that some customers were surprised to hear them speaking "such good English," thus confirming Tuan's (1995) observation that many white Britons, like white Americans' indiscriminately viewed Chinese people in Britain as recent immigrants.

As Nagel (1994:152) has argued, rather than being simply a matter of personal choice, the construction of ethnic identity is the result of *both* structure and agency—"a dialectic played out by ethnic groups and the larger society." Although ethnic minority individuals cannot fully control the ways in which they are ethnically constructed by others, they can, as Roger Hewitt (1992:34) puts it, adopt "the interiorised sense of self and belonging," which may be at odds with other peoples' labeling of them. If we are to believe Anna's and Mary's characterization of David's identity, it would seem that David has responded to the "cost" of his ethnicity (the imposition of negative and racialized associations with the take-away) by distancing himself as much as possible from it. However, his sisters believed that this disidentifying strategy was largely ineffective.

Despite her characterization of David as an English person, Mary acknowledged the actual complexity of her own cultural identity. For instance, Mary reported that she was "quite Westernized," compared with "traditional Chinese" people, but that "it [her sense of identity] depended on the situation" (see Wallman, 1978). While Mary conceived of her own cultural identity in terms of partial and situational identifications with both British and Chinese cultures and practices, she spoke of David's identity as being wholly English. Anna, too, spoke of her identity in nonfixed terms: "At the time, I just thought it [the take-away] was all shit, and I wanted time, and everything was a constraint. And I was very anti-shop. There was something really humiliating at the time about, 'Yeah, my dad's got a take-away', and everyone would say, 'Oh, yeah', but now I actually take great pride in saying, 'Yeah, my dad's in catering, and it's something we're good at. And it's something we've fallen into, out of necessity.' So there are positive things about working together as a family, and I think we're more solid." Although Anna used to be embarrassed about her family's reliance upon a take-away business, she had come to terms with the shop, by imbuing the FWC with positive meanings associated with family solidarity. Despite the fact that she had experienced some very negative feelings about helping out in the past, Anna was not as sympathetic to David's reported aversion to the take-away.

Like Mary and Anna, most young people in the study acknowledged the complexity of their own cultural identities. In reality, their identities were not static and were not effectively captured by dichotomous either-or categories such as Chinese or British (or English). Although being of Chinese heritage does not preclude the possibility of also being British, some analysts have noted that dominant notions of Britishness have been predicated upon being white, which constitutes the norm and the "center" (Frankenberg, 1993). For instance, Paul Gilroy (1987) has argued that in Britain, from a white majority perspective, being British and being black have tended to be seen as mutually exclusive identities. I found that most Chinese young people in this study regarded themselves as neither wholly assimilated (as "Western") nor wholly Chinese. As is conveyed by the notion of "hybridity" (Bhabha, 1990b) and in writings on the diasporic experience (Ang, 1994) and a "global melange" of cultures (Pieterse, 1995), people can experience partial and wide-ranging forms of identification, rather than a wholly unitary sense of identity (Hall, 1991; Song and Parker, 1995).

The apparent contradiction of some young people conceiving of their own identities in complex and fragmented ways, while understanding their "bad" siblings' identities in more crude terms (in terms of fixed and uncomplicated identities), can be explained by the fact that those with "bad" (Western) reputations tended to be demonized in their families. The actual or potential attribution of a "bad" reputation, and the consequences of it, seemed to be used in these families to reinforce the expectation that all children contribute their labor—although the attribution of bad reputations did not seem calculated in the way that some parents knowingly guilt-tripped their children.

Nevertheless, the threat of a bad reputation did not necessarily mean that all children complied with this expectation. The motivations for "bad" children distancing themselves from their takeaways, and by extension, their Chinese identities, were complex and could not be easily be explained by "rational," functionalist explanations for the maintenance of ethnicity (e.g., Patterson, 1975). The "cost" of withdrawing one's labor was a "bad" reputation, unless there were mitigating circumstances, such as having to move far away from home for an esteemed profession or respectable career, or marked differences in socialization between siblings. Withdrawals from the FWC that were seen to be attempts to opt out of being Chinese were especially condemned. Those with a "bad" family reputation, like David, endangered their family membership: Not helping out on "illegitimate" grounds was tantamount to a rejection of family and a rejection of Chinese cultural identity. As David's case demonstrated, rather than simply assuming that parents were the key enforcers of the FWC, siblings could also be instrumental in the process of sanctioning children who withdrew from the FWC.

Committed by Choice?

Many young people, therefore, relied upon relatively clear-cut and polarized family reputations (good versus bad) and cultural identities (Chinese versus English) in their understandings of siblings' differential labor commitments. Unlike "bad" children, whose rebellions or escapes were seen as fairly clear-cut actions taken by them, the extent to which "good" children had "chosen" to be committed to their FWCs was more difficult for young people to explain. Gaining a reputation in a family for being a good committed child seems to have involved a complex confluence of events and circumstances involving both siblings and parents. While siblings' accounts tended to concur on the respective family reputations of individual children, these accounts were much less clear about *how* some siblings had come to be more committed than others.

Young people who found themselves more committed to helping out than their siblings made sense of the positions they occupied in their families in different ways, particularly by pointing to various degrees of choice and control that individuals exercised in relation to the FWC. While a few siblings reported that they had chosen to be a "good" child in their families, the majority of such children understood their committed status to have developed in a context of circumscribed parameters of choice in which a number of circumstances and events had structured their labor commitments in their families.

Only two of the respondents who saw themselves as good, committed children in their families reported that they had made a choice to commit themselves to working in their take-away businesses. As illustrated in the two cases below, making such a choice, however, did not necessarily mean that they had wanted (at least unambiguously) to be especially committed to upholding their FWCs.

David

David, age 23, was the middle child in a family of three children, who were all born and raised in Britain: his older sister Susan, age 24, had recently married at the time of interview, and his brother Philip, age 17, was studying for A-levels (British exams for university entrance). David worked full-time outside and also helped out in the shop in the evenings. As an integral child in his family, David reported that he had grown up doing much more housework, shop work, and caring work, than either of his siblings:

M.S.: Would you say that your attitude toward working in the shop is different from that of your sister and brother?

David: Yeah.

M.S.: Are they less accepting of it?

David: My sister doesn't really want to do it. My brother definitely doesn't want to do it.

M.S.: Does he actually resist?

David: Hmmm [pause] not resist. He won't say, "I'm not doing it." He'll just like, he won't be there. When the shop's open, he's somewhere else, or watching TV upstairs, playing with the dog downstairs.

M.S.: So would you say that you have helped out more than the others?

David: Yeah. But I wouldn't bear any grudges against them [siblings]. That's what I want to do, and let me get on with it. You know? If I set my sights on doing something, I'll do it. . . . There was [an] opportunity to leave, opportunity to consider.

David stressed his choice and agency by noting that he had had an "opportunity to leave, opportunity to consider"; he was far from forced into such a commitment. David also explained his strong labor commitment in terms of his very close relationship with his parents: "I get on with them [parents] more [than his siblings]. I've been with them all my life."

Although David said that he did not "bear any grudges" about his siblings being less committed than he was, later in the interview, he criticized his sister for being "lazy":

M.S.: It sounds like you did a lot of the housework growing up.

David: Yeah. I loved it. I used to come home from school, after watching all the children's programs, I had nothing to do, and it wasn't dinner time yet. There was dust on the TV. Dust it, then start on the carpet, then my room. . . . My sister's damn lazy. She does it like once a year.

Therefore, although David claimed that he had effectively decided to take on the most responsibility in terms of helping out in his family's business, this decision came about in a context in which he valued and fostered a special relationship with his parents and in which his "good" reputation developed alongside two siblings who showed little interest in the business. His sister and brother, he felt, simply could not be relied upon to "be there" for his parents.

Furthermore, David seemed to be proud of the fact that he was "more Chinese" than his siblings. For example, David claimed that he spoke better Chinese than his siblings and that he was more involved in Chinese community networks than either his brother or sister. Helping out was central to David's maintenance of his Chinese identity and was therefore an important incentive for him to remain committed to the FWC. Therefore, a number of considerations shaped David's "choice" to be a committed child in his family.

Richard

At the time of interview, Richard, age 24, effectively managed his parents' take-away business. Richard had started working in his parents' shop, full-time, when he was 18 years old. He was absolutely integral to the business:

M.S.: Did you always have a strong sense of your parents needing your help?

Richard: Yes. He [father] actually said that. He said to me that he would need a lot of my help if he started the business. He warned me. If you don't succeed in what you're doing, I don't want you blaming me, he said. I said, OK, I'll do it. I wanted him to do it, since he was always working for someone else, managing.

Exceptionally, Richard and his father had actually discussed the implications of shop ownership for Richard's life and his future career. Richard, whose parents spoke very little English, decided to work for his parents, full-time, so that the shop could get started. When his parents asked him if he would work with them, Richard knew that, in theory, he had a choice, and that he hadn't been forced to accept the position. Richard tended to describe his commitment to the take-away in terms of a clear agreement between his father and himself. For instance, when Richard was asked if he ever resented working in the shop, he replied, "No, because we talked it over, and we agreed to it. So when the hard bits came, you didn't want to complain because you made that decision, and you live with it." Nevertheless, Richard's choice to work for his parents and to relegate his own aspirations in graphic design were shaped by other considerations as well:

M.S.: Have you felt a lot of pressure from them [parents] to help?

Richard: Indirectly, there's a lot of pressure on me. Yes. You feel obliged to do it sometimes. But it's [pause] when it comes down to it, it's your decision. You could have said no, I'll have nothing to do with it.

M.S.: Could you imagine having said that?

Richard: I would [could], but I don't think things would have worked out that good. It would have distanced us much more, especially with my dad. I didn't want to do [create] [pause] more conflict between us. I think it's one of the few times I've conformed to what they wanted to do.

At the time of interview, Richard had already been working full-time for his parents for six years. Although the agreement he entered into with his parents before business start-up stipulated that he would be able to pursue his own career after the first few years when the shop had become established, Richard still did not feel that he could withdraw from the FWC. It was implicit that his leaving would be potentially upsetting for his father, despite their initially negotiated terms.

As Richard observed, despite his choice to manage the business, "Indirectly, there's a lot of pressure on me." In addition to his explicit agreement to work for his parents, his sense of obligation was still very much predicated upon an implicit understanding between him and his parents—that it was important to his parents that he helped them in their venture, and that it was common for Chinese children to participate in such family ventures in Britain.

Furthermore, Richard was "targetted" by his parents in a way that his younger sister, Karen (his only sibling), age 18, had not been. Karen had not been included in the discussions between Richard and his parents, regarding the wisdom of opening a shop. The fact that she was not included in the discussions suggested that neither her parents nor her older brother expected her to be a central worker in the business. Karen primarily helped out on weekends. Karen was six years younger than Richard and had very little interest in getting involved in the shop.

Richard explained that one reason Karen was less committed to the business was that she had a very different upbringing from his own: Richard was born and partly raised in Hong Kong by his grandparents when his parents emigrated; while Karen was born and raised in Britain. According to Richard, he and Karen had very different attitudes toward the shop and to helping out:

> I've always thought my sister's a bit naive in a lot of things. She just has her own life. Maybe she wasn't through the bad times, because when she was born, my dad was comfortable, say, and she was born here. When I was in Hong Kong, I was 8 or 9. I realized that the family wasn't rolling in it, as such. That's why my parents had to go. It sort of makes you grab a little bit more. So Karen doesn't know. *It's not her fault.* Brought up in England, as well, so more easy-going. My grandparents were stricter with me. (My emphasis)

Based on their different socialization experiences in Hong Kong and Britain, Richard implied that Karen's more negative feelings about helping out were understandable, and stemmed from a more Western mindset about family and individual needs. In addition to differences in socialization, the fact that Richard was considerably older than Karen seemed to mitigate any sense of inequity he may have felt about their respective labor commitments.

Richard had a strong sense of his own agency and consent regarding his commitment to his FWC. Nevertheless, his decision to commit himself to the take-away was made in the context of his parents' implicit pressures and expectations of him. In addition to feeling needed, a key consideration in not leaving the business and pursuing his own career was Richard's hope of improving his relationship with his father, whom he did not want to disappoint. The cost of giving up his design career, it seems, was not as heavy as the potential cost of damaging his relationship with his father. Furthermore, Richard's choice to commit to the business was partly structured by the fact that his younger sister did not want to get involved with the business.

Ultimately, respondents who said that they chose to be committed reported that they had accepted responsibility for their own lives, even if they might resent their siblings or parents from time to time. Claiming that they had chosen to commit could also have been one way of rationalizing and justifying their respective positions in their families. It is important to see David's and Richard's decisions to commit themselves in terms of ongoing processes and family issues over the long term. Although David and Richard believed that they had made a choice about committing to their FWCs, their choices were clearly shaped by their siblings' weaker commitments, their cultural identities, and their desire to maintain special relationships with their parents.

Child of Circumstance?

More commonly, young people who found themselves more committed to helping out than their siblings did not think that they had made a clear-cut choice about the matter. Rather, they spoke of having "drifted" (Lewis and Meredith, 1988) into that position over time. Similarly, Finch and Mason (1993:74) found that there were many examples of people who could not "reconstruct a consciously formulated strategy, or identify a point in time when there was an overt agreement" in situations where they had accepted responsibility for helping a relative. Becker (1960:38) also notes that commitments are not necessarily made consciously or deliberately. "The person becomes aware that he is committed only at some point of change and seems to have made the commitment without realizing it." This process of drifting into a commitment is illustrated in the following cases.

Colin

In one family, Colin, age 26, and his only other sibling, Peter, age 25, were both born in Hong Kong, and had come to Britain when they were 9 and 8 years old, respectively. Colin had studied graphic design, but had given up his pursuit in this field when it became clear that his parents needed him full-time in their take-away.

> *M.S.:* You see your mum as keeping the business going?
>
> *Colin:* Oh, definitely. I'm not sure now—I think it's possibly *me*. I still want to go and find a job, but there's so much work involved in here [the take-away]; you put so much work into it, you don't want to waste it. It's very difficult.
>
> *M.S.:* Do your parents know that you'd rather not be working in the shop?
>
> *Colin:* Oh, yeah. They know that. You spend so many years getting your qualification, getting your job, then give up. . . . I give it up for here, when this shop opened. My brother can't do it. His high qualifications; but, uh, he's ignored them [his parents]. He's much more harsher than I am.
>
> *M.S.:* You mean he wasn't willing to make that sacrifice?
>
> *Colin:* Well, he just ignored you. So, what are you gonna do?
>
> *M.S.:* When you came here and gave up your job as a graphic designer, did your parents ask you to do that?
>
> *Colin:* Uh, well, they waited a bit. It wasn't like they said, "come

down," in that way. I suppose [pause] I don't know how it happens really. You're expected to come down.

Interestingly, there were a number of similarities in this case with Richard's case, discussed earlier. However, unlike Richard, who had explicitly discussed the matter with his parents and who said that he had made a choice, Colin reported that he had gradually and implicitly become the "obvious candidate" to work in the business. This was because his brother Peter was seen by Colin, as well as his parents, as having a promising professional future; Peter was in the final stages of completing a doctorate.

Unlike his brother, Colin reported that he had never done well academically. He understood that Peter could not spare too much time in the business. Nevertheless, Colin did not understand his position as the committed child solely in terms of his poor academic record. In fact, Colin suggested that one reason why he was in his current predicament was that Peter had been "harsher" in response to his parents' implicit request for help in the business. Colin saw himself as a more yielding and responsible person than his brother. Therefore, Colin understood his position in relation to the FWC in terms of circumstances over which he had little control—namely, his brother's refusal to do more for the business and his own relatively poor qualifications in relation to his brother. Like Richard, however, Colin recognized that now that he found himself invested in the running of the business, it was increasingly difficult for him to break away and establish his own career.

For both Richard and Colin, their parents had been involved in relying disproportionately on some children over others. Children's differential willingness to help out sometimes provided parents with a "structure for negotiations" (Finch and Mason, 1993:159). Some parents reportedly targeted their "good" reliable children, as opposed to their "bad" ones. According to Annie, "What their [parents'] tactic was, it was easy to pressure the people that did work. Say there are four children, and there are two that don't really work, and two that do. It's difficult to tell the children that don't work to work. Because they would be faced with all this negative feedback, but if they told me and Shirley to work, then we would feel guilty, and we would just do it."

By targeting, I do not mean a deliberate, conscious decision to rely upon any one child. It would not be surprising if parents relied more heavily upon children who were willing to help out. As Annie pointed out, doing so required much less energy and strain for parents. Rather than trying to equalize their children's commitments to the FWC, some parents could unwittingly exacerbate inequities in siblings' labor particpation. Annie reported this to be the case with her mother: "Because Andrew and Kathy hated working in the shop so much, my mum would try to butter me up, so I would do it. It used to bug me so much, even though I could see why she did it." Therefore, when parents' efforts to elicit a labor commitment failed with one child, it could have the effect of increasing parents' expectations of their other "good" children.

A commonly expressed view among respondents who reportedly drifted into being committed children was a *fatalism* about their positions. These respondents often expressed that "someone had to do it," that is, be committed, and stressed the sets of circumstances and events that had structured their positions in their families—without wholly renouncing some agency and responsibility for their reputations as "good" children. Although most young people who had good reputations stressed they had not actively chosen to be in that position, their siblings did not always agree with such a view. In the following family, there was disagreement between the two interviewed siblings about how and why one had come to be much more committed to the FWC than the other.

Wong and Foon

Wong, age 27, and Foon, age 25, were both born in Hong Kong and came to Britain when they were 7 and 5 years old, respectively. Their sister, Helen, age 15, was born in Britain. Both Wong and Foon, who were integral children, started working in their family shop from a young age. As children, they had both performed a great deal of caring work, as well as shop work, while Helen had been relatively protected from working in the shop, both by her parents and her brothers. Both brothers said that they wanted to shield their sister from what they had been through.

Despite the fact that they had contributed similar amounts of labor growing up, Wong withdrew his labor when he decided to go to university in the Midlands. It was too far away for him to come back on weekends and help out. Wong's departure for university was a key transition point for his family. His withdrawal from the FWC was not a surprise to his family, for it accorded with his reputation for being relatively Western, particularly in comparison with Foon, who was seen to be the more committed child. Foon was bitter and somewhat resentful about Wong leaving: "Wong actually went to university, but he knew I was at home to look after things. He had the time of his life, that's why most of his friends are English, not Chinese." Foon saw himself as a more responsible person, and he explained this in terms of his steadfast commitment to helping out and in terms of his strong sense of Chinese cultural identity. In contrast, as the more "Western" sibling, Wong was seen to have been selfish in going to university far away. According to Foon, Wong had capitalized upon the fact that he knew Foon would stay home and continue to help out.

Although the two brothers clearly had an amicable relationship and agreed that Foon had been more committed to helping out over the years, they had different understandings of how and why Foon had become the more committed child. According to Foon, Wong was *able* to leave because Foon stayed at home with his parents. As a result, Foon considered himself to be a "child of circumstance." He had not actually chosen to remain committed to the FWC of his own volition. Rather, Foon's own decision about attending a university, which came up two years after Wong left for university, was shaped by the fact that Wong was not available at home. Foon's decision to live at home and attend a nearby university reflected his difficulty with leaving home and withdrawing his help. Foon also reported that his parents had implicitly held on to him, although Foon was having difficulty in juggling both his course work and helping out in the evenings. "I didn't actually say to my parents, 'Look, I can't cope.' Because I could cope, but I just wanted to let go. So nothing changed. They knew I was unhappy, but they weren't able to make that decision for me. They wouldn't be put on the spot and say, 'Foon, you don't have to help anymore.' They didn't offer it, and sometimes I'm bitter toward them that they didn't offer any sort of support, you know?" From Foon's point of view, his ability to leave home was circumscribed by Wong's departure and his parents' reliance upon him as the "good" child.

However, Wong interpreted Foon's commitment to their FWC differently. Rather than interpret Foon's commitment in a positive light, as an altruistic act or in terms of Foon being a victim of circumstance, Wong derided Foon's commitment by depicting it as an act of cowardice and a lack of conviction:

> I'd always had my mind on leaving. I'm not [*pause*] my view on all of this isn't like Foon. I'm not a good boy that he is, like being responsible. It was something I've always felt—that I've got to get on with my life. I had to leave. Foon is someone who I think is living his life at the expense of the take-away. When he went to university, he went to a really local place, so that he could still commute. Well, commute's the wrong word. Catch the bus home to go to college, which almost made it seem like going to school. And by doing that, he didn't force my parents to face that decision: Look, our kids are growing up, they're going about their lives, hey, we can't keep this going. But he wasn't prepared to do that, being the good boy.

Interestingly, Wong did not blame his parents for continuing to rely upon Foon because, from his point of view, his parents had not targetted any one child. According to Wong, Foon had *chosen* to stay behind, and he himself was to blame for not being able to let go. Therefore, Wong tended to de-emphasize his own actions and reputation as a "bad" child in his understanding of what had happened. From his point of view, it was each individual's responsibility to negotiate his or her own position in relation to the family work contract. In Wong's case, leaving home was seen to be necessary for his own self-respect and individual growth. However, Wong's independence and insistence upon leading his own life, he reported, were regarded as selfish actions by his parents, as well as by Foon.

It is likely that the family reputations of Wong and Foon, which had developed over time, were instrumental in shaping the behaviors of these brothers. Wong's decision to leave home was partly based upon his belief that Foon would stay behind and continue helping out; this knowledge made it easier for Wong to leave. Likewise, Foon's difficulty in letting go stemmed partly from the fact that he had maintained a reputation as the "good boy" for so long. Not only would withdrawing his labor have been difficult for his parents, but it would also have required an adjustment in the way he perceived himself.

Renegotiating the Family Work Contract

Although the reputations of individual siblings developed gradually and tended to be stable, this did not mean that "good" and "bad" children couldn't rework their positions in relation to the FWC, especially as the needs and circumstances of their families and businesses changed over time. For instance, Anna and Mary reported that, in contrast with their brother David, who had rejected the FWC (discussed above), Mary had a reputation for being the most committed child in her family. According to Anna, Mary was the "dutiful" and self-sacrificing child, because she lived with her parents, and did a tremendous amount of caring work and shop work: "She's crucial to my family's survival. She's far outdone everyone. Initially because of age, my two brothers were crucial. My dad had a lot of hopes on them; in a lot of ways, they let him down. They went and did different things. My sister has always been around. She's always been the dutiful one of the family—total respect for my parents, despite knowing what their faults are. She may moan when we're one to one." Mary was aware of her "good" family reputation, and valued it. Nevertheless, Mary also found her position as the good child rather oppressive—a position she thought she had drifted into, rather than chosen.

Two years after David's departure from home, and his withdrawal from their FWC, John, the eldest child, also left home after a serious argument with his parents. As a result, he too acquired a "bad" reputation in their family. Anna, the fourth child, left soon after John to go to a university in London. This left Mary as the only child remaining and working at home. Mary had a full-time job at the university, which she found very fulfilling, but she also helped out most evenings in the shop, after work. Mary revealed that she had felt left behind by her siblings: "And they all left. I resented them for it. It made me feel like, why didn't I do it first. At least one of them would. . . . You see, the last person to go, won't go, because they won't get stuck with it. You can't all go, and leave your parents. I was too slow, basically. I never thought everyone would just leave home. It just happened. John and Anna went within about a year of each other. It happened so suddenly."

Anna's interpretation of what happened reinforced Mary's assertion that her siblings' departures had structured Mary's decision to stay at home: "Had she had that choice to leave, I would have been left with no choice, which would have meant that I would have been stuck with the family. We couldn't have all gone away; and I wouldn't have left if my sister left. It's not a happy life for her." Unlike Wong, who interpreted Foon's commitment to the FWC negatively, Anna valorized Mary's commitment and self-sacrifice. From Anna's point of view, she and her brothers were partly accountable for their sister's position (as the committed child) in their family.

However, as in the case of many other committed children, Mary did indicate that she had, at one level, chosen to stay at home. One of the reasons why Mary felt unable to let go, in addition to the fact that she was the only child remaining at home, was that she did not want to lose her "special" relationship with her parents: "What I did benefit was, I was closer to my parents than any of the other three were, for the last five or six years of my life. To me, it's a good thing, me and mum could go shopping, and have a good time. She never said bad things about me. She'd never have a go at me. Because I was doing everything for them. I did benefit from that. And I had a really good relationship with my parents, and I loved it."

Nevertheless, Mary became increasingly anxious to gain her independence and move into her own flat. A major turning point occurred last year, when her older brother John returned home after many years away from his family. Mary was instrumental in his return. John had been unemployed, and had been having misgivings about his long-term estrangement from his parents. Mary managed to persuade John to return home. When John returned, he started to work full-time in the shop, with the understanding that he would eventually take over the business when his parents retired. In fact, John's return signaled his reinstatement with his family. According to Anna, "John spent time out [of the FWC], and he really didn't care about the family. So he's done a big turnaround, and he's learned to value the family again".

By persuading John to return home, and by encouraging her parents to take him back, Mary was then able to renegotiate her own position in relation to the FWC, vis-à-vis her parents, as well as her siblings. Before John's return, Mary reported that she had been resigned to staying with her parents; she could not see herself leaving them on their own. By our second interview together, Mary had just moved out of her parents' home, to a flat nearby, and she had reduced her work in the shop to three nights a week. She had also insisted upon receiving the same wage as their part-time worker. Mary's negotiated wage increase signaled a formalization of her work relationship with her parents (to one more like employer and employee).

Mary's new-found freedom was gradual. One of her concerted efforts, since leaving home, was to encourage her parents to do things for themselves: "It's time I have to think of myself. Sounds selfish [laughs]. I will never leave mum and dad, and if they need me, I'll be there, but I don't want them to depend on me. Since I've been away, they [have] started to become a little bit more independent. . . . I still type letters for him when he needs them done. I still do his books, the accounts, and I still go home and do them." Despite her growing independence, and the fact that she renegotiated the terms and boundaries of her commitment to her family, Mary made it clear she was still committed to her parents and to the FWC, albeit in a way that demarcated her responsibilities toward the FWC more clearly and formally.

This case illustrated that the status of either the bad or good child was not necessarily static or exclusive to one child. In this family, John, who had had a bad reputation for many years, gradually gained a better reputation after returning home and working in the family business. Furthermore, the eventual switch between Mary and John as the child living with their parents came about through both parent-child negotiations between Mary and her parents as well as sibling negotiations between Mary and her brother. Nevertheless, children's individual reputations as "good" or "bad" children were generally stable over time, and significant changes in the familial responsibilities between siblings was relatively rare.

The potential attribution of "bad" reputations by both parents and siblings in these families could be used to assert the expectation that everyone uphold the FWC. Nevertheless, it would be erroneous to assume that families unilaterally imposed a good or bad reputation onto a child. Rather, some children actively fostered reputations, for instance as an extremely committed child, or as a rebel who took pride in challenging the FWC. Even siblings with similar upbringings could negotiate their labor commitments and, by extension, their senses of identity, in disparate ways. This suggests that individual children within families exercised some degree of agency and choice regarding the degree to which they were committed to helping out.

Because there seemed to be no clear guidelines about the limits to children's labor commitments, individual children had to negotiate their positions in relation to their FWCs through a variety of ways. Such disparities among siblings illustrate the importance of disaggregating the experiences of children within families and point to the need to examine sibling dynamics and relationships, in addition to parent-child relationships, in studies of immigrant family strategies.

Furthermore, the motivations for fostering "good" or "bad" reputations are complex and depend upon each individual's priorities. Just as being the committed child did not necessarily mean all sacrifice, being an escapee or rebel did not necessarily mean that such individuals felt negatively about themselves; such bad reputations enabled some young people to adopt a desirable and distinctive identity in their families. Also, being "bad" could provide individuals with some freedom from being subject to their FWCs, despite the moral censure they had to endure. For some "good" children, withdrawing their labor commitments could be difficult, given that they had derived a positive moral identity in their families, and had been able to maintain especially close relationships with their parents.

The complex motivations underlying the formation of "good" Chinese and "bad" Western cultural identities suggest that rational, materialist explanations for the maintenance of ethnicity and ethnic ties (e.g., Patterson, 1975) cannot explain individual disparities in ethnic allegiance, particularly in the context of family relationships. These young peoples' cultural identities were shaped not only by their socialization in Britain or Hong Kong but also by their experiences of helping out in a family work contract. This finding complements the abstract poststructuralist theorizing on identity, which has emphasized "hybridity" (e.g., Bhabha, 1994) and open, multiple forms of identification, by situating the formation of young peoples' identities more concretely within family relationships and the everyday experiences of work. In addition to common "markers" of cultural identity, such as language proficiency and adherence to cultural practices, we need to pay more attention to forms of economic activity, such as the performance of family labor, for the formation of individuals' cultural identities.

7

Looking to the Future

AT THE TIME of interviews, many of the families in this study were faced with a number of possibilities concerning the future of their businesses: Would someone take over the business? Would it be sold? Did the children in these families want the takeaway to continue? According to the young people in two-thirds of the twenty-five families, their parents did not want their children to stay in the catering industry and wanted them (both sons and daughters) to obtain higher education and professional qualifications instead. This finding accords with Freeborne (1980) and Chan (1986), who found that most Chinese parents wanted their children to pursue careers as doctors, lawyers, and accountants—*san-si,* considered the top three professions.

The minority of parents who wanted their take-away businesses to continue via their children reportedly believed that self-employment was the best work option for their children, and they were said to be skeptical about waged work. Anna said this of her father: "He was always saying he never wanted to work for anyone. . . . He'd had a dream of being his own boss in that he knew he could never work for anyone English. It was always about getting enough money to sustain yourself and becoming a family; and to have that as the basis for your family, and not depend upon a wage. He's constantly telling us that if you don't have your own business, it doesn't matter where you are in terms of your career ladder, you will never be free. It's autonomy. He'd been dictated to all his life."

174

In families where parents wanted their children to take over the business, it was the norm for a son, rather than a daughter, to succeed his parents' business (Greenhalgh, 1994). Although many daughters did work considerably in their families' take-aways, they were not usually encouraged to take over the business, unless there were no sons willing to do so. In this respect, business succession in Chinese take-aways is gendered, as is also the case in many Western family enterprises (see Bertaux and Bertaux-Wiame, 1981; Hutson, 1987). For instance, in English family farms, children's interest in taking over their parents' farms was found to be gendered (Wallace et al., 1994); unlike many sons, who were keen to be farmers, few daughters wanted to be farmers (even if they enjoyed their work), seeing farming as a male preserve.

Moving away from the Take-away

None of the Chinese young people, regardless of sex, viewed take-away business ownership to be an unalloyed privilege or a desirable career. The Chinese young people in this study had no wish to take over their parents' businesses or to start take-aways of their own (see also Chan, 1986:8). All the young people in this study reported that they would prefer to move away from their parents' reliance upon take-away businesses.

Although the take-away had provided their parents with a viable livelihood and the means of raising their families in Britain, these young people reported that being reliant upon catering represented a serious barrier to Chinese people being accepted into more mainstream forms of employment. According to David Parker (1994:633), "The generation that arrived and grew up here in the last twenty years is increasingly viewing the counter as a hurdle to be jumped as they work on it to secure their escape." Such a sentiment is similar to the reported attitudes of West Indian female school leavers who wanted to avoid marginalization in working-class manual jobs, which their mothers had occupied in the labor market (Dex, 1983:66). Second-generation Greek Cypriot women in Britain have also consciously moved away from their mothers' primary areas of work within the Greek Cypriot ethnic economy—clothing manufacturing—into clerical jobs, banking, hairdressing, and travel agencies, expressing a preference for work in the broader labor market (Josephides, 1988). Ladbury's (1984:124) research on Turkish Cypriots in Britain also found that the second generation relied upon the Turkish Cypriot ethnic economy for employment, "but only after they had failed in their own attempts to find a job independently of their ethnic network." Like these other youths, the Chinese young people in this study expressed that they wanted to make it outside of the Chinese ethnic catering economy.

A commonly reported reason for not wanting to run a take-away was that it entailed a very difficult and demanding lifestyle—a finding that accords with Pang (1993:254), who argued that the younger generation Chinese wanted more from their jobs than their parents, who "possessed pragmatic and materialistic attitudes to work and life in Britain." As in the case of French bakers, whose children disdained the long and confining hours of running a bakery (Bertaux and Bertaux-Wiame, 1981), Chinese young people, including both British-born Chinese (BBCs) and individuals raised in Hong Kong, reported that they would prefer waged work rather than the long, arduous hours and the risks involved in running a take-away.

Furthermore, the prospect of taking over often entailed not only running the business, but also looking after (and sometimes living with) elderly parents. Another commonly reported reason for not wanting to run a take-away business was that most young people did not want the stress and conflict entailed in running a family business to impact upon their relationships with their own partners or children:

> *Sarah:* Working together as a family was very tense. If I am honest, it was very tense, and at times it could be fun or what have you, but it taught me that I would never go into business with family or friends. Never.

> *Pue-lai:* If you give it [the business] to me, I don't want it. Don't

give me one penny from it. My mum told my elder sister, you want to get married, get married to people who run a take-away, you can have my take-away. My mum also said that to me. I say no, if he's a cook, I prefer he go out and work for someone else. Cause I know if we have a take-away, sooner or later you get arguments. I don't want to work with my husband in the same place. You got experience from your parents, you see.

Some respondents tended to view Chinese take-away businesses as undesirable "immigrant jobs" (Gans, 1992:182). When asked how she would feel about owning a take-away business herself, Jacqui replied, "That's one of the last things I would want to do. I know how much hard work it involves, and the responsibilities are enormous, even though it's a good way of making money, I suppose. It's a very hard way. It can be turbulent as well. The first generation would say that having your own business and a secure income every week is one of the ultimate aims of their lives. The fact that the second generation have the opportunity of finding out what's happening in Britain as a whole, going to college, a lot of them are venturing outside of take-aways." While Jacqui saw take-away ownership as the only option for her parents, as a second generation Chinese person, she did not feel confined to that niche. In the United States, most children of recent immigrant business owners rarely remain within the ethnic economy. For example, the children of Korean business owners have aimed instead for higher education and professional occupations (Min, 1996b).

A Racially Stigmatized Niche

Some young people were much more contemptuous about staying in the take-away business than Jacqui. According to Sui, "Any self-respecting person would have to get out [of catering]." Some respondents expressed the view that take-away ownership, despite potentially good earnings, was low-status work. Annie remarked, "Working in a take-away is for really unintelligent people. It's the lowest of the low!" Her sister Shirley added, "There's no respect in that job. I used to think, when I hear young people say they're going to start a restaurant business, I cringe. I really cringe. It's almost like a defeat. Use your intellect. You lower yourself to doing it, washing dishes." These young peoples' negative attitudes toward the take-away and restaurant business fundamentally stemmed from their sometimes harrowing experiences with customers and their awareness of stereotypes automatically linking Chinese people with take-aways and the performance of menial labor.

Such attitudes about running take-away businesses tend to contrast with findings from other qualitative studies of small family businesses in Britain that are not part of a racialized economic niche. In their study of eighty-seven family-owned businesses, Scase and Goffee (1980b) found that fathers wanted their children to continue the tradition of entrepreneurship, rather than pursue careers within large-scale bureaucratic organizations. This finding accords with some literature on French and English family farms, in which not only an economic livelihood but also *family heritage* is at stake in passing on the business to children (Lem, 1988; Pile, 1991). For instance, despite some intergenerational conflict about whether or not children will take over the family enterprise, the children on family farms also tended to subscribe to the importance of continuing the farm as a symbol of the family (Lem, 1988; Wallace et al., 1994). In her study of French family farms, Lem (1988:515) observed that, "Children submit to the authority of parents, often subscribing as much as their parents to the ideology of family continuity as the identity of the family is so bound up with the entity of the farm. The integrity of the family as a unit is linked to the farm as a unit of production." Western farm families and other families engaged in traditional small businesses tended to regard their livelihoods as a way of life, and could exert considerable pressure upon their children to continue in these occupations (Thompson, 1995).

Compared with the literature on family farms or "native" small businesses, running a Chinese take-away business was regarded as racially stigmatizing. Unlike the unambiguously positive social identities and strong sense of heritage held by family farmers, which were also strengthened by regionally specific ties with the land, Chinese people running take-aways in Britain had to contend with degrading racialized images of themselves. Cognizant of racist stigmas and of the widespread expectation that Chinese people "belonged" in catering, Wong was very opposed to Chinese young people staying in the Chinese catering industry:

Wong: I'm very scornful of Chinese contemporaries [who have stayed in the take-away business].

M.S.: Why are you scornful of them?

Wong: Because I think we all had a chance to make a life for ourselves, and yet, you know, we're supposed to be the next generation, but by doing what you're doing, you're just perpetuating the Chinese take-away thing. It's a very easy option. It's very convenient.

While young peoples' support, in principle, for their family work contracts, could be understood as a defense of their family livelihoods and as a positive assertion of Chinese cultural identity in Britain, these young people did not want to stay within the catering industry. Nor did they, as the next generation of Chinese in Britain, want to be associated automatically with the take-away. Similarly, a study of Japanese American ethnic economies found that third-generation Japanese Americans (sansei) were even less likely to stay in their Japanese ethnic economy than members of the second-generation (nisei). As Bonacich and Modell (1980:140) suggest, "The structure of opportunities outside and within the ethnic economy changed historically, and perceptions of these changes affected choices made by nisei preparing to enter the labor market."

Chinese young peoples' support for their family work contracts (FWCs) was based upon their understandings of their parents' situations as disadvantaged immigrants who had relied upon them for English language mediation and other forms of caring work. Although these young people believed that family-run businesses, such as take-aways, were the best available option for their parents, they did not want to perpetuate a livelihood that had been the culmination of an immigrant survival strategy. Despite these young peoples' desire to leave the catering business, obtaining desirable outside employment could not be taken for granted.

Barriers and Opportunities in Outside Employment

To date, there has been relatively little research on the employment patterns of Chinese people in Britain, but a few recent studies have addressed their wider labor market opportunities (see Chan, 1986; Pang, 1993; Cheng, 1994; Modood et al., 1997). The dearth of studies on Chinese young peoples' employment may be partly due to the fact that many BBCs are still in full-time studies in Britain, making speculation about their labor market experiences somewhat premature (Cheng, 1994).[1] Although I cannot provide a comprehensive review of the literature on Chinese young peoples' educational and employment opportunities in Britain, this background is important in understanding why some individuals have continued to rely upon the Chinese catering sector.

While the picture is now rather mixed, there is considerable evidence that many ethnic minority young people in Britain are disadvantaged in the labor market. In the 1980s, the unemployment rates of West Indian, Pakistani and Bangladeshi young people were more than twice that of their white counterparts (Drew and Fosam, 1994). Brennan and McGeevor (1990) found that although Asian and African Caribbean students applied to more jobs than their white counterparts, they had more difficulty in obtaining jobs and were more likely to be employed in the public and voluntary sector, rather than the private sector. However, Iganski and Payne (1996) found that, despite continuing discrimination, there has been some occupational mobility for Asian and African-Caribbean people (the study excludes the Chinese), in relation to the white population (see also T. Jones, 1993). In fact, a recent national survey of 5,196 ethnic minorities in Britain reveals a great deal of ethnic diversity in areas such as educational attainment and employment: "On many measures of education, employment, income, housing, and health, there is a two- or three-way split, with Chinese, African Asian [Asians who migrated from East

Africa] and sometimes Indian people in a similar position to whites, Caribbeans some way behind, and Pakistanis and Bangladeshis a long way behind them" (Modood et al. 1977:10). Not surprisingly, it was found that far fewer ethnic minority women than men occupied top professional and managerial jobs (Modood et al. 1997:103). Overall, the proportion of women in such jobs was about half that of ethnic minority men in Britain. Interestingly, however, 30 percent of the Chinese women in this national survey (as opposed to 16 percent of white women in the study) held professional- or managerial-level posts.

Chinese Young People in the Labor Market

Evidence on the Chinese is inconclusive at this point, but in a study of the occupations of 16–30 year-old British Chinese, Pang (1993) found that there was a propensity for young Chinese adults to be situated in *either* the professions or the Chinese catering industry. Although most Chinese young people in this study perceived their labor market opportunities to be better than those of their parents, they still tended to perceive racial discrimination and stereotyping as major barriers in obtaining higher-level professional positions. While few of the fourteen individuals in full-time outside employment reported serious difficulties in obtaining employment for which they were qualified, most of them believed that being Chinese put them at a disadvantage in the job market in relation to white applicants with similar qualifications. Many of the five young people who were looking for work at the time of interview had recently completed various forms of higher education. Like those already in outside employment, they too believed that their ethnicity would, in general, put them at a disadvantage in the wider labor market.

Work experience in the take-away was not seen to enhance their attractiveness to potential employers, who didn't always see such work as "real" work. As Pue-lai explained, "I want to work outside because I want to get some experience. So, like, I don't want to rely on the shop. I want to start my career. But if I keep sticking to the take-away, I won't get a career. Cause I'm coming onto 21. They'll ask me, what's your first job? You don't have no first job. If you say, 'I work in my family's take-away,' that's your family's business. That's not a first job at all. What experience you got? Uh, cooking. Serving customers, doing the accounts."

Given the dominant image of Chinese people as quiet and hard-working, some respondents also reported that such positive stereotypes could be double-edged because, as in the case of Asian Americans (Kibria, 1997), Chinese people in Britain were perceived as being stolid and somewhat uncreative. Chinese women were also faced with employers' and colleagues' sexist and patronizing treatment of them as passive and "cute." According to Sui,

> After secretarial college I went to work at a firm typing. At first I found it quite exciting. I thought, I've found what I've wanted to do. It was different, working in a different setting, and you could wear skirts, look nice [laughs]. And after a while, I got very disillusioned because I looked extremely young, compared with others, and people didn't treat me as if I had, they were always calling, "little Sue," and "isn't she cute." and it got on my nerves. I was very competent. I was more than competent. And so I was really pissed off, and I thought, I could be as good as you, so I decided to go to university.

In a study of Chinese youth's employment prospects in Britain, Chan (1986) found, in accordance with the Government's Swann Report (G.B. Parliament, 1985a), that the main difficulty hindering Chinese young peoples' employment was educational under-achievement, much of which was explained by difficulties with the English language. Not surprisingly, young people who had been partly or primarily schooled in Hong Kong might have difficulties with spoken and written English. The following young people, who were partly raised in Hong Kong, reported limited English language skills and an ongoing effort to retain their English—an effort exacerbated by the fact that they had little contact with English-speaking people outside of the take-away:

Pue-lai: I choose this course [design] because first my English is not really good, so it's not worth it to go to English courses or higher educational course. I can't get English into my head, you see.

Fai: If you'd spoken to me one year ago, before I went to college . . . Cause I was losing it [English], that was another reason why I picked a course. Cause I was finding my English was getting really terrible. I wasn't communicating in English with anyone. Just the orders, and I don't talk to the customers as such. I really should do, but because of limited staff, you serve and just go in [the kitchen]. And with friends, we speak Cantonese-English, a mixture.

Jobs in design or in the sciences were regarded as more promising, since they would be less disadvantaged than in work requiring substantial verbal or written interaction and consultation with English-speaking colleagues and clients. As with young people of African Caribbean and Asian origin, who tended to be excluded from the government training schemes that were most likely to lead to permanent employment (Brown, 1992), Chan (1986) found that Chinese young people reported getting very little career advice in their schools.

As a result, ten of the forty-two respondents expressed an interest in going to Hong Kong to secure employment—even after it reverted back to China in 1997—given their perceptions of both overt and latent discrimination in obtaining work in Britain. According to David, "We [he and his friends] was talking the other night about me going to Hong Kong. There are lots of opportunitites over there and my friend has gone over; he's found work over there. And he's told me to come over as well. . . . They [people in Hong Kong] seem to be a bit more aware. Not so laid back, it's an exciting place. That's the way I see it."

In this study, young people in eight of the twenty-five families already had another sibling who had moved to Hong Kong for employment. Not only did these respondents believe that their employment prospects were better there, but they also said that they preferred the way of life in Hong Kong, in which they were not marginalized as ethnic minorities. Therefore, a move to Hong Kong was not solely motivated by concerns about finding employment. Going to Hong Kong also entailed a redefinition of home for some, from Britain to Hong Kong—a place important for the formation of Chinese young peoples' cultural identities in Britain (Parker, 1995). In the case of BBCs, young peoples' awareness of their diasporic identities, and their interest in finding their roots, shaped their desire to live and work in Hong Kong.

A Safety Net to Unemployment?

Although these young people did not want to run take-away businesses themselves, the shop was seen by some as a useful safety net against unemployment, because it was perceived to be the best employment option that some young people possessed (cf. Pang, 1993). As discussed in chapter 3, six of the forty-two young people in this study worked full-time in their take-aways at the time of interviews. None of these young people (two daughters and four sons) had other outside employment. Apart from their sense of obligation to remain committed to their businesses (as discussed in the last chapter), three of these six respondents either reported that they did not possess the qualifications to get other kinds of employment or believed that they would be unable to compete with their white counterparts; this was especially the case for individuals who had been born and raised in Hong Kong and, who saw working in their take-aways as their best employment option. For instance, Fai and one of his older brothers took over his parents' take-away business and ran it as a partnership:

> M.S.: How did you get involved in running the business with your brother?
>
> Fai: I drifted, I suppose. Me brother couldn't have run it on his own, and it was a offer of, just take it [from his father], and see where you go from there, or go out and find work, which I suppose, because I didn't do well in the A-levels [university en-

trance exams], I felt I didn't have much chance. Probably I could get work, yes, no problem, but not something where I could go somewhere from that. That type of grades, there's only so high you can get with [pause] so I thought I will take my chances [with the shop].

M.S.: So you never actually tried getting an outside job?

Fai: No.

M.S.: What about your other older brother?

Fai: He'd already done his degree, and he wanted [pause] he was at university at the time, and I suppose me father thought there was sort of a future for him. He's in Hong Kong, with computer programming.

Fai indicated that he had taken over the shop with his brother, not because he felt obligated to do so, but because he had felt that shop ownership was his best employment option, given his grades. Fai's case is also illustrative of how he, rather than his older brother, had been targetted by his father, to take over the business—not because Fai was known to be more keen on shop ownership but because Fai's job options were more limited by his poor educational qualifications.

Not all young people who had been raised in Hong Kong were necessarily disadvantaged, but for those who arrived in Britain in their teen years, outside work was seen to be an unrealistic prospect. Although they may have hoped for professional careers, their employment opportunities were hurt by limited English language fluency or lack of qualifications or both. For instance, Sai reported that her brother worked full-time in their take-away because of his limited English language and education: "One thing I was very lucky in was that work [in the take-away] never interfered with my school work. Never. When I was studying for my A-levels, at times it could be really busy, they [parents] always say homework first, so I was very lucky, compared with some of my friends. They wanted me to get an education, and if they had it their way, they wouldn't want my brother to be in the same business. They would prefer my brother. . . . But by the time he came here [to Britain, as a young adult], it was too late, it was the only thing he could do. For my brother, it was the only choice." The case of Japanese Americans also showed that less educated second-generation individuals were much more likely to remain in the ethnic economy than their better-educated counterparts (Bonacich and Modell, 1980).

Given most young peoples' desire to leave the catering industry, those who worked full-time in their family take-away businesses did so more by default than by an active wish to stay in the Chinese catering industry. As Annie Phizacklea (1988:21) has suggested, ethnic enterprise may be seen, to a certain extent, as a form of disguised unemployment, at least for the second generation. Nevertheless, overly bleak assessments about second-generation immigrants simply reproducing the "minority working class" (see Castles et al., 1984) are too static and disregard the mixed picture that is emerging.

Selling the Shop?

Aside from the few families in which sons had effectively taken over their parents' businesses, most families in this study had to consider the prospect of their businesses eventually being sold. The young people in most of these families (apart from the three families who had recently sold their businesses at the time of interview) reported that they were uncertain about what would happen to their businesses in the future. As discussed earlier, most respondents wanted to explore outside employment and did not conceive of their take-aways in terms of full-time careers.

The uncertainty surrounding the future of most families' businesses seemed to point to the eventual inevitability of selling up. Resolving the future of their businesses was important to these young people because they would not feel that they were released from their FWCs until their take-aways were sold; as long as their parents had their take-aways, integral children in particular felt obliged to help out. Although these young people could still feel compelled to perform caring work for their parents, even after their businesses had been sold, they would no longer feel such a strong sense of responsibility for ensuring the viability of their family livelihoods.

Triggers to Selling Up

The factors and circumstances surrounding the selling of a business could differ among these families. However, one factor that could trigger the sale of the take-away was parents' ill health and physical injuries. Illnesses and injuries associated with repetitive, labor-intensive work in the take-away were common, particularly given the long hours and stress associated with such work. This work required a great deal of standing, lifting, and the use of heavy woks. Young people in sixteen of the twenty-five families reported significant health problems of either one or both parents, including injured arm and shoulder joints (from using the wok), as well as back problems (from lifting and standing for long periods in the kitchen). A few parents also reportedly suffered repetitive strain injuries in their hands, due to the long years of labor-intensive cutting and chopping in the kitchen.

Another impetus for selling the business was that, at the time of interview, some parents (many of whom were in their fifties and sixties) were relatively elderly for such back-breaking and labor-intensive work. So aging, itself, took a toll on some parents' ability to continue working in their take-aways. Most commonly, parents simply slowed down; they were unable to work as quickly or such long hours as they grew older. Despite the pervasiveness of parents' health problems in families running take-aways, few parents actually reduced their work roles over time, aside from acute incidents when a parent was hospitalized. Even parents who were relatively young could be tired of the take-away trade. For instance, one mother, Susana, who was in her early forties, reported that she did not want to be tied down to the shop anymore: "I mean, I never planned to be in the shop for thirty years or something. . . . So now that the boys are grown up, I think it's time we don't need to have a shop."

In most families, however, selling the shop either came about, or was seen to be likely, due to a convergence of various factors rather than one single factor, such as parents' ill health. This can be illustrated in the case of two (of the three) families who had recently sold their businesses. For instance, Ming, age 19, was one of three daughters who had been integral in her family; none of them had been interested in taking over the business. Ming's parents wanted their daughters to have professional careers, and encouraged their entrance into higher education. It was therefore understood between the parents and children that the shop would eventually be sold; when this would happen, however, was not specified. However, Ming's father experienced a serious arm and shoulder injury, which made it impossible for him to handle a wok and this precipitated the selling of the shop prematurely.

Because Ming's family still needed an income, her mother started to work in a friend's take-away. Ming reported that even now, when she went home from university, she sometimes took her mother's shift at the take-away. Although helping her mother in her new take-away job was only occasional, this was an exceptional case because the selling of the family shop usually meant that children no longer had to help out in their take-aways. However, like other integral children, Ming's parents continued to rely upon her for various forms of caring labor, and her knowledge of her parents' precarious financial situation meant that she still wanted to help out. Therefore, not all families were in a position to sell their businesses, even if they wanted to—a few families had debts and did not always have savings which they could live on.[2] Although it had been understood that none of the children would take over their business, Ming's family had to sell up before they felt ready to do so.

In another family that had just sold the shop after running it for eight years, Helen and her sister had been supplementary workers in their family livelihood, and they had grown up working most evenings in the shop. Neither daughter had any interest in taking over the business. They had started to pursue their own careers and had had increasing difficulty in finding time to help out in recent years. These sisters' desire to sell the shop also stemmed from the fact that there had been a great deal of conflict in the course of working together. Business had been bad, and their father was reportedly fed up with the shop. Therefore, the two sisters' gradual distancing from their FWC was only one reason why their parents eventually sold their business. Unlike Ming's case, once their business was sold, Helen and her sister were essentially freed from looking after their parents because not only did their father speak some English but their parents also went to Hong Kong for an indefinite visit. Although both Ming's and Helen's families owned homes separate from their businesses, families who lived above their shops (and who did not own other property) faced the dilemma of finding other housing.

In the three families who had already sold their businesses, both parents and children had effectively concurred about the need to close their businesses, although parents' and children's motivations for doing so may have differed. These families had reached a point where the costs, both financial and social, of keeping the business going, seemed to outweigh the benefits. However, coming to such a consensus about selling up was rarely a simple or straightforward process in most families. As discussed in chapter 5, it was relatively unusual for these families to have discussed or planned for the future of their businesses.

Kam's family, however, was exceptional in this respect for she reported that she and her parents had always planned to run their take-away business for a limited number of years. She and her siblings were privy to her parents' future plans for their take-away. Despite the fact that this family had only had the shop for five years (Kam's parents had worked as waged workers in Chinese restaurants and take-aways for twenty-five years before shop ownership), Kam reported that they planned to sell the shop in the near future: "They're in their fifties. It's time to retire. Those jobs is too hard. They are so tired, and that's why I'm looking after them. I do most of the housework." Unlike other families who were under duress to sell up, due to financial difficulties, Kam's family planned to close their business because it had served their needs and because they no longer wanted such a difficult and arduous lifestyle. Her parents could afford to sell their business because they had lived carefully and saved over the years. Although it was not yet certain when they would sell the shop, there was reportedly a family consensus that the shop would be sold for neither the parents nor the children wanted any of the children to take over. Such open planning by this family effectively precluded tensions and difficulties around ensuring the continuation of the business and the perpetuation of the FWC. Kam's knowledge that her family's take-away would be sold in the near future colored the way in which she understood and experienced her current labor participation; rather than being oppressive, her labor participation was seen as a reasonable expectation by Kam, not the least because it would be of limited duration.

In comparison with Kam's family, however, most families had been running their businesses for many years and had not discussed what would happen in the future. Not surprisingly, the few families in which parents and children did not agree about the future of their businesses experienced more tension than those in which neither parents nor children wanted their businesses to continue. For instance, in a few families, young people attempted to persuade their parents to sell up, despite the fact that their parents were reluctant to do so. For these young people, the main objective was to persuade their parents to sell their take-aways so that they would no longer feel tied to their FWCs.

For instance, Annie was active in trying to influence her parents to sell their business. Along with her siblings, Annie had been unhappy for some time about having to help out. Not only did Annie refuse to accept payment for helping out, so that her parents would feel guilty about wanting her assistance, but Annie also pointed out that their weekly turnover had been gradually eroded by increased competition from many other take-away businesses. During the course of my second interview with her, Annie revealed that, in response to her pressure, her parents were now seriously considering selling up: "They've [parents] been trying to sell it for the past half year. My dad was getting very worn down and my mother hated going to the shop. And we were putting pressure on them to sell." In another family, Pue-man explained that although no clear decision had been made about selling the shop, no one in the family (including parents) wanted to run the business anymore:

> *Pue-man:* I'm hoping to go into higher education. Actually my dad's thinking of selling the shop. That'd be good. No one wants to work there. And if I do go on for higher education, I'd be leaving in October. And my second sister [who is older than her] wants to start her own life; she's getting a bit fed up already.

> *M.S.:* So no one really wants to work there.

> *Pue-man:* No. And business is not very good. It would be hard to employ anyone, and my mum don't want to work, and my brother can do a little bit of work, but he should be at home. I'm planning to live away; I definitely want to leave home. My second sister says that as soon as we sell the shop, she's gonna move away.

Therefore, a number of factors tended to combine for families who were considering selling their take-aways. First, children's labor became increasingly unavailable as they left home, and pursued their own lives, thus endangering the viability of the business. Even for those "good" children who had remained committed to helping out, the strain of continuing to uphold their FWCs could be difficult for both children and parents. Second, either the children, or both parents and children, wanted the children to pursue outside careers, rather than take over the shop. Third, parents had health problems that made the arduous lifestyles required in take-aways difficult; also, some parents were getting older and wanted to retire. Last, take-aways were under increasing competitive pressure from the spread of other fast-food businesses nearby, including Chinese, other ethnic, and pizza and kebab businesses.

Although children's labor in these families tended to be very steady and reliable over the years, Chinese families' reliance upon children's labor was not static and could change over time. At different points in their family and business histories, these families tended to encounter similar pressures and transitions regarding children's labor participation:

1) the incorporation of children's labor into these family-based businesses;
2) the diversification and intensification of their labor as children learned a wider variety of tasks and took on more caring work;
3) the transition to children leaving home;
4) determining the future of the take-away, whether by selling the business or a child taking over.

The children could be active in shaping their family's adaptations and responses to changing social and economic circumstances. Just as children could be involved in negotiating and re-allocating their work roles as older children left home, some children tried to persuade their parents to sell their businesses.

Paradoxically, however, selling the shop did not automatically herald a clear-cut transition to a more relaxed lifestyle or an easing of tension in these families. Becoming "just a family," without a family work contract, could involve a major adjustment, and could entail some difficulties in these families.

Just a Family

Despite the fact that many Chinese young people felt very ambivalent about helping out and did not want to devote their careers to running take-aways, the actual or anticipated selling of their take-away businesses could still be complicated. This was because many of these individuals had trouble imagining what it would be like to be "just" a family. A commonly reported difficulty with selling the family business was that some parents were left with too much time and without hobbies or other social activities. This was because many parents had been so confined to their shops that they had not had much time or opportunity to socialize or develop other interests. In a follow-up interview with Annie, who had tried to persuade her parents to sell up (discussed earlier), I found out that their business was sold shortly after my second interviews with her and her sister. Annie had been so eager to sell their business, that she had not anticipated any negative consequences:

M.S.: How has the transition to closing the shop been?

Annie: It's opened a door to many other problems. He [father] just sits there. Very lethargic. He deserves to sit down after all these years, but he has no purpose in life. I'm out all the time now, and I feel guilty about that. It gets on my nerves to see them. They [her parents] just hog the place.

Annie also had some difficulty in adjusting to her new-found freedom:

M.S.: Are you happy about the shop being sold?

Annie: Yeah. I just can't get used to the weekends. Unbelieveable. I've never had a guilt-free weekend for about fifteen years. I don't know what to do. "Have a nice weekend." I've never gotten used to that phrase because I've never had a nice weekend in my life. I'm not in the rhythm. I don't know what people do on weekends. I'm so conditioned.

Pue-lai, too, was concerned about how her parents would occupy themselves if they sold their business in the coming years:

M.S.: What will your parents do if they sell?

Pue-lai: I don't know [laughs]. That's the problem; they stay in the house. My dad had been offered, not a job, it's a hobby. To teach how to do this dragon dancing. He wants to be a teacher. He wouldn't earn much, but enough to survive for a week.

In another family, Laura looked forward to having more time with her family, without working together. For Laura, selling the business was envisioned as an opportunity to build up close family relationships, based upon feelings of intimacy that differed from the kind of solidarity and strong sense of family ties which many respondents associated with upholding a FWC:

M.S.: How are you feeling about the idea of the shop being sold?

Laura: Um [pause] it will be strange, because I don't know what it's like, living without the shop; it's always been a part of our lives. It will be interesting. In a way, I'm looking forward to it cause in a way it will be the family unit. You can come home, you don't have the hassles of working all the time. This way you can spend some time together. It will be a time to spend in building up relationships; I don't feel that we have that. I don't think I've ever had that kind of relationship, that real closeness in the family. It would be nice to do that, to come in from work and to just talk to each other.

However, Laura also expressed concerns about how her father, who had been much more isolated in the shop than her mother, would adapt to life without the shop:

M.S.: So, when the shop closes it will be a big change in your lives?

Laura: Yeah. It was good because my mum's gone out and have another bit of her life [her mother had joined a Chinese women's group] so that when she retires there is something else, whereas with my father, he hasn't really had that. He doesn't know [what to do] with himself. He's already said that: "What am I gonna do with myself?" He makes that out for an excuse for not wanting to retire, because he doesn't really have, he doesn't want to do anything else. She wants to retire more than he does. He should be retired now; he's 67. He wants to keep the business in that he knows that the children will be around. He senses that once the business closes, we're all gonna leave.

For many children, such as Laura, who had been working together with their families for many years, it was difficult to conceive of their lives or family relationships without them revolving around their FWCs. Not only children but also parents could be anxious about how they would be, as "just a family." As Laura noted, her father was concerned about his children leaving home once the business was sold. For her father, this could be extremely traumatic, since he had led a very insular life, with little contact with people other than his wife and children.

In another family, the question of the future of the business was very important because the future of the take-away *and* the future of the family were seen to be inextricably tied; as such, the prospect of not having the business could be quite destabilizing and worrying. According to Colin, who reported that working together had entailed a great deal of conflict between his parents and between him and his father, "It's very insecure; it could break up at any time. I think as soon as the shop's finished, the family's finished." Although family relations had been terribly frayed by the conflicts and stress brought on by working together, one of the reasons why Colin had remained committed to running his family's business was that, ironically, the shop had also kept his family together. Therefore, as some of these young people indicated above, the dissolution of their FWCs could be bittersweet—it was regarded with some apprehension because it could portend the potential break-up of the family, as they had known it for many years.

Running Take-aways in the Future

One issue that requires more investigation in future studies of the Chinese and other immigrant groups in Britain and the United States is the question of if and in what ways will future generations of young people continue to concentrate in ethnic businesses. Although some children in these families, particularly sons, were able to rely upon their take-away businesses as an employment option, take-away businesses as a safety net against unemployment could not be taken for granted. A number of young people reported that the catering trade was now reaching a "saturation point," in terms of the number of fast-food businesses in their area. Furthermore, many take-aways could not actually absorb more than one child who was looking for paid employment, given the small size of these businesses and the somewhat unpredictable turnover in them. This saturation point in catering has been noted by the Home Affairs Committee Report on the Chinese (G. B. Parliament, 1985b:ixiv):

"Some are unable to find employment even in catering: the recession has meant that the catering sector can no longer absorb all available Chinese labour, except in the less desirable kitchen jobs."

Another key question that arises is, even if some Chinese young people do follow in their parents' footsteps by running take-aways of their own, will they necessarily rely upon their family members in the ways their parents had? In other words, will FWCs be reproduced in the next generation of owners, or will they be confined to families headed by immigrant parents?

Reliance upon Family Labor in the Future?

The cases of sons (nonrespondents) in two families who worked full-time in their parents' take-aways suggest that they might repeat a pattern of reliance upon their spouses' and children's labor, as their own parents had done.[3] Both of these sons, who were married, were raised in Hong Kong and had limited English language abilities and educational qualifications. Their wives worked full-time with them in their take-aways (alongside these sons' parents), thus creating, as Sai noted, an "extended family network."

Interestingly, in both of these families, not only sons but also married daughters and their husbands participated in their parents' take-away businesses. In Sai's family, her elder sister (who worked as a machinist at home) and her husband (who was a bookkeeper) also helped out occasionally in her parents' shop, with her sister's husband doing the bookkeeping (as discussed in the last chapter, Sai believed that her brother would expect his daughter to help out). In the other family, Yee-ling's husband worked full-time in her family's shop, along with Yee-ling's married brother and his wife. Yee-ling worked as a Chinese community worker, but she continued to work on Friday nights along with her husband, brother, and her sister-in-law. Thus the addition of a daughter in-law or son-in-law to these family economies provided a significant labor contribution and enabled elderly parents to retire or to reduce their work roles in their businesses. Once grandchildren were born, retired parents often performed considerable childcare in these families.

As for children's labor participation, it is unlikely that a new generation of take-away owners will rely upon their children to the same extent (or in the same ways) that their parents had. Except for those individuals who have serious limitations in their English language abilities, new generations of Chinese parents are less likely to rely upon their children for caring work. Like the handful of "liberal" parents of minor children, future parents may not want their children to be central to the running of the family business. Furthermore, given many young peoples' vehemence about not being automatically associated with the take-away, it is unlikely that they would want their own children to experience what they themselves had gone through.

For instance, in one case in which a son took over the business, Fai stressed the importance of setting limits on helping out for his own (hypothetical) children:

> M.S.: Could you imagine involving your own family in a business, with children, like the way you helped out?
>
> Fai: Um, to a certain extent. But not to such a great deal of time. Less involved. Allocate them more time for their own leisure, but let them work just to get the feel. Just part time.

In the future, more variation in the nature and degree of family involvement for both children and spouses in these businesses is likely. In addition to the twenty-five families running take-away businesses, I interviewed a few take-away owners who were considerably younger than the parents in the main sample. For instance, Joanne, age 28, was born in Hong Kong and came to Britain when she was 9 years old. She grew up in Oxford, where her father had owned Chinese restaurants. Although she herself had not helped out in these restaurants, she married a man who took over his parents' take-away business. She now worked full-time at the counter and managed the business.

> M.S.: With two young daughters, when the girls are older, will they start helping out in the shop?

Joanne: I wouldn't like them to. As far as I'm concerned, I would like them to go to university, if I can support them. I want them to be able to choose their own life. Not like with me and Tony's [husband] parents. Let them choose whatever they want to do.

M.S.: Are you saying that it's not right for children to help out?

Joanne: They can help, but for their actual career, I would never want them to do what we're doing, as a career. Because it's not much of a career. It's a living, you could say. You could never ever [pause] there's no completion in it. If you're a lawyer or doctor, you could be a good one or a lousy one. With a take-away, it's no career. It's a living. I don't expect them to help. But if they want to, then why not? But I don't expect them to or want them to. Most of the Chinese who come to the country now, most of them would find a job which is a career. Anyway, there's too much competition; they're not guaranteed a good business anymore. All the [Chinese] friends I know are getting office jobs, anything. Something different to take-aways. At least you get nine-to-five hours. The Chinese are looking for a way out of the take-aways.

Unlike most of the (older) parents in this study, Joanne states that she does not expect her children to help out. In addition to the fact that Joanne does not rely upon her children for caring or shop labor, her main concern is that her children have the ability "to choose their own life."

A Strictly Business Venture

Some young people said that the only way in which they would consider running a take-away was as a strictly business venture, run with employees, rather than with family members. While take-aways could never constitute their careers, a few respondents of both sexes did say that they would not mind owning a take-away business, on the side, as a money-making venture, in addition to a professional career. With such businesses, young people envisioned overseeing them rather than actually working in them. According to Herbert Gans (1992:178), such views accord with patterns of immigrant business entrepreneurship in the United States. "In most instances, the immigrant establishments grew more modestly, with the second generation perhaps taking over as owners but letting others, often from a later wave of the European immigration as well as blacks, Hispanics and others, do the work that required long hours and physical labour." These young peoples' desire to keep the take-aways a business-only venture revealed that they did not want to reproduce the FWCs that had been central to their own lives.

In addition to some younger take-away business owners, such as Joanne, I found a few Chinese people (outside of the 25 family sample) who had moved from professional waged employment to take-away business ownership (unfortunately, no figures were available on such job transitions). Such moves were motivated predominantly by financial considerations.

For instance, Harry, age 43, had obtained his university qualifications in Scotland, and had worked as a social worker in Britain. He reported that he had become frustrated by his job options. He also felt that, as a Chinese person, his mobility was more constrained, in relation to white social workers. As a result, he had recently opened a take-away business with his wife. He hoped to make some money and exercise more autonomy in his life. Harry reported that he would not expect his children to help out if they did not want to and said that he would probably continue relying upon employees. At the time of interview, Harry and his wife employed two non-Chinese part-timers in their business. Harry's case suggests that rather than being unable to enter into the wider labor market, as had been the case for many first-generation Chinese take-away owners (most of whom had little or no education), he had hit a "glass ceiling" in terms of his upward mobility. Small business ownership was a preferred option for Harry and his wife, despite the high risks of business failure.

Similarly, in one of the three families in which children had minor work roles, both parents had given up their jobs as a radiographer and nurse to start a take-away business. According to Chris, a key motivation for moving into the catering trade was that his parents wanted to earn more money, in order to send Chris and his sister to private schools. Thus rather than expecting their children to work a great deal in their take-aways, Chris' parents wanted to do all they could to ensure that their children would *not* end up in catering. Furthermore, like many of the other parents in these families, Chris reported that his parents wanted more control over their work lives:

> It's more a thing they can call their own. My dad, he's always drummed into us that they came here with very little, and now they have quite a bit. Trying to achieve more and more. . . . At the moment, there have been quite a few success stories. Many people are looking to emulate that. It's getting a bit saturated. Hopefully, we've been established, so we won't be affected, but at the moment, there are so many people going into take-aways, who had other jobs before. People who were in computing, nursing, stake a claim. Or people who are unemployed.

However, at least on the basis of anecdotal evidence, the cases of people leaving professional jobs and entering catering still seem to be the exception rather than the norm. Most of the young people in this study stated that they wanted, as Joanne (discussed above) expressed, "a way out of the take-away."

The Future of the Chinese in Britain

We can only speculate about the future of Chinese people and the catering industry in Britain, given that many Chinese young people are still pursuing their studies. Although they understood why their parents had considered the take-away trade their best livelihood option, the young people in these families wanted to leave the Chinese catering sector and did not want to be exclusively associated with this racialized economic niche. Rather, many of the respondents felt that it was incumbent upon them to redefine what it meant to be Chinese in Britain—independent of the take-away.

The fact that most Chinese parents spoke little or no English, the labor-intensive nature of the take-away business, and the intense interaction of home and work lives were crucial in shaping the centrality of children to these family livelihoods. It seems that the production of food on a small scale, as a labor-intensive activity, is particularly conducive to reliance upon children's labor. Take-away businesses could incorporate the labor of children in the kitchen, as well as at the counter, as an everyday part of these families' lives.

Children's labor was not only productive in terms of their family economies, but it was also a labor of love performed by children for their parents. That is, their labor could not be understood solely in terms of its economic rationality for ethnic businesses and immigrant family adaptation. An examination of the intersection of family relationships and obligations, the work and economic pressures involved in ethnic businesses, and issues of cultural identity is necessary for a full understanding of the nature and terms of children's work in ethnic businesses.

Based upon the case of families running Chinese take-away food businesses in Britain, I have argued against dire assessments of immigrants' reliance upon ethnic businesses as purely exploitative and denigrating. In their influential study of Korean immigrants in Los Angeles, Ivan Light and Edna Bonacich (1988:435) point out that: "Immigrant entrepreneurs are victims of world capitalism. They have been forced from their beloved homelands. They often suffer lives of great hardship and deprivation. Nevertheless, by participating in capitalism enthusiastically, and by pursuing its competitive values, they help to perpetuate the system that created their own oppression." Although immigrant entrepreneurs' lives are unquestionably hard, this characterization of them as "victims of world capitalism" does not fit the experiences of these Chinese families, especially from the perspective of British-born children in these families. At the very least, immigrant business owners and their families need to be accorded more agency and control. However, I would also temper wholly positive representations of ethnic businesses, as an avenue for economic and social mobility—as has been argued by some analysts such as Portes and Zhou (1992:511): "In lieu of a slow and painful process of assimilation as a precondition for economic ascent, we are confronted with a different story in which newcomers create the conditions for their own mobility, bypassing in the process the psychologically enfeebling consequences of discrimination."

Such analysts have argued that ethnic enclaves, such as Chinatown in New York City or the Cuban ethnic economy in Miami, provide opportunities for immigrants who cannot easily gain access to the broader labor market. The opportunities afforded by the Chinese ethnic economy in Britain are more questionable.4 In a study of Chinese peoples' education and employment in Britain and the United States, Cheng (1994:247–48), found that the benefits were greater for individuals with fewer qualifications than for those who were better educated; the latter could get better returns for their qualifications in the wider labor market, even taking potential discrimination into account: "Although the great majority of Chinese in Britain work in the catering industry, the enclave economy does not provide equitable chances of reaching the service class, nor does it reduce risks of unemployment, compared with the wider labour market. Therefore the ethnic enclave economy does not have a positive effect on occupational success."

Chinese young people reported that their parents, and their families more generally, were able to exercise more autonomy in their lives, and believed that they were provided with better opportunities for upward mobility through small business ownership. But the context in which "newcomers create the conditions for their own mobility" is, in fact, extremely bounded. Although catering was the best livelihood option seen by most of these Chinese families, their labor market options were greatly limited. Concentration in the Chinese catering industry did not mean that these families were able to bypass the "psychologically enfeebling consequences of discrimination." Rather, Chinese young people and their families had to contend regularly with racial discrimination and stereotyping—both inside and outside of the take-away. Such a positive characterization of ethnic enclaves tends to underestimate the racial harassment and the social marginalization experienced by many immigrant groups (and perhaps the internecine competition within ethnic business communities).

Nevertheless, most of the children in this study reported that they and their families had, on the whole, benefited from ethnic entrepreneurship. While some analysts have rightly emphasized the gendered nature of rewards in (native) Chinese family firms (Greenhalgh, 1994), the question of who does and does not benefit is less clear-cut in generational terms for Chinese families running take-away businesses in Britain. In the context of the disruptive experiences associated with immigration and the social and economic marginalization of Chinese parents in the take-away trade, their children may stand, ultimately, to gain much *more* than their parents. Despite the fact that many children encountered difficulties, and in a few cases, even hardship, as a result of their participation in their FWCs, most young people tended to stress their parents' difficulties in adapting to a new life in Britain, their limited choices, and hard work. It was clearly too late for their parents, who had no other livelihood options, but most of these young people noted that they had or would have much wider opportunities than their parents. Although ethnic businesses have allowed various immigrant groups, such as the Chinese in Britain, to achieve some degree of economic security and upward mobility, more research is needed on the complex social costs to this success (see the conclusion of Light and Bonacich 1988:429–36), including the long-term implications of the continuation or demise of ethnic businesses, both for future generations and the broader ethnic community.

The stringent expectations around the FWC, and their fundamental reliance upon the labor and assistance of children distinguish the relations of production in Chinese take-away businesses, and in ethnic businesses more generally, from the running of "native" family businesses. Although all small family businesses are likely to share many characteristics, particularly in relation to business pressures and ideologies around the family, what was specific about these FWCs were the conditions that gave rise to their creation—these families' experiences of immigration, the Chinese concentration in the ethnic catering sector, ethnic minority status in Britain, and many parents' reliance upon their children for caring labor. Although ideologies of family or family relationships are not necessarily any stronger or more "special" in

these Chinese families than in nonimmigrant white British families (contrary to some mythologizing about Chinese families),
Chinese family members running take-away businesses were subject to particular pressures to uphold their FWCs, and to attribute
positive meanings to their labor, given their experiences of social
marginalization, economic vulnerability, and various forms of
racism. Because Chinese families had to contend with the disrup-
tions of immigration and the pressures of working together as a
family, as well as stereotypical racialized identities, many of these
Chinese young people believed that their relationships and the
meanings attached to family were especially strong.

Most young people recognized that working together as a family was relatively widespread among Chinese families running
take-aways in Britain, but the formation of these FWCs was not
necessarily intrinsically Chinese or exclusive to Chinese immigrant families. While the meanings associated with helping out
clearly derived, in part, from traditional Confucian ideologies
stressing collective needs and familial piety, these FWCs emerged
and took on meaning as a Chinese practice in Britain, due to these
families' widespread concentration in the catering sector and
their need to adapt, socially and economically, to life in Britain.
Therefore, rather than remain static, immigrant family ideologies
and values (such as embodied in the FWC) may adapt to changing social and economic conditions (Kibria 1994).

It is possible that variants of the family work contract may operate in other immigrant groups running small, family-based enterprises in Western advanced capitalist societies. More needs to
be known about why some ethnic groups may rely upon children's labor while others do not. The investigation of differences
in the nature and extent of children's labor and responsibilities in
other ethnic businesses would require a comparative analysis of a
number of important factors, such as legal restrictions, the educational and social backgrounds of immigrant parents, cultural
norms and practices, and in particular, the nature and require-
ments of the business itself.

There are a number of implications of Chinese young people

gradually moving out of catering and of declining family involvement in take-aways for the nature and operation of the Chinese catering industry in Britain. Future (nonimmigrant) owners of take-aways may have to rely on nonfamily and even possibly non-Chinese workers, given that restrictive British immigration has cut off the supply of cheap immigrant labor from the Far East (Pang, 1993).Without a doubt, these families' concentration in the catering trade and in family-run take-aways enhanced Chinese peoples' sense of cultural identity—given their common experiences of migration, racism, and highly stressful experiences of working in a family business. Bonacich and Modell's (1980) classic analysis of Japanese American business ownership found an economic basis to Japanese ethnic solidarity. As future generations of Japanese Americans left the ethnic economy and found jobs in the wider labor market, their ethnic solidarity was also said to diminish. There seems to be little doubt that for other groups, such as Korean merchants in the United States, their sense of ethnic solidarity has also been enhanced by their economic segregation and the intergroup conflicts resulting from their business dealings (Min,1996b). This would suggest that the exiting of future generations from the Chinese catering sector may result in the decline in Chinese ethnic solidarity in Britain. However, it is unlikely that the labor market diversification of Chinese people in the future will result in any straightforward decline in Chinese ethnic identity. Their status as a distinct racialized minority group in Britain will ensure that they will not be able to "opt out" of being Chinese very easily (Waters, 1990). Rather than simply decline, Chinese ethnic solidarity and cultural identity are likely to undergo gradual change, accompanying Chinese peoples' economic and social diversification in Britain, including the growth of various Chinese subgroups comprised of those who stay in catering and those who enter into the wider professions.

In addition to their changing concentration in the ethnic catering sector, a key factor that will influence the ethnic ties and identities of the Chinese in Britain is the recent "handover" of Hong Kong to China, which occurred in July 1997. After the Tiananmen Square massacre in 1989, more Hong Kong people exerted pressure on the British government to honor its responsibilities towards the 3.25 million Hong Kong British passport holders (Chan and Chan, 1997:123). The British government has phased in a plan to give 50,000 heads of households and their families British right of abode under the 1990 Nationality Act. According to Chan and Chan (1997:124), a total of 128,392 people (48,336 principal beneficiaries and their 80,056 dependents) had registered under the right of abode scheme at the end of 1995. This new immigration has been targetted at well-educated and professional people who possess not only human, but also business capital, such as business managers, administrators, and senior civil servants (Segal 1993, in Pang 1993). In all probability, this gradual settlement will considerably change the nature of the Chinese presence in Britain (Henley Center, 1990). This influx of new Hong Kong Chinese has implications for both the Chinese community and for Chinese peoples' relations with the wider British society. It will be interesting to see how the impending diversification of the Chinese in Britain, particularly in terms of their employment, may shape Chinese peoples' family economies, (including the roles of children within them), their understandings of family, and Chinese cultural identity in the years to come.

Appendix A:
Locations of
Take-away Businesses

Most of the families (fifteen of twenty-five) in this study owned businesses in the southeast of England, particularly in the Greater London area: Leyton, Upper Holloway, Edgware, Millwall, Dalston, Islington (2), Pimlico, Penge, Croydon, Plaistow, West Hampstead, Dulwich, Walthamstow, and Streatham.

In addition to the businesses in the above parts of London, eight families owned businesses in nearby counties surrounding London, including Middlesex, Essex, Surrey, Kent, and Berkshire.

Further afield, I interviewed one family whose business was located in Manchester, a large city in the north of England, and another family in Gosport, located on the southern coast of England.

Appendix B:
Background Information
on Young People

This study was mainly based upon interviews with the following 42 young people. Those young people who requested pseudonyms are indicated below with an asterisk (*) beside their name. Interviews with the mothers in five of these families are indicated by bullets.

Sole Interviews

Name	Age	Birthplace	Occupation
Fai (m)	25	Hong Kong	Take-away
Jack m)	25	Yemen	Take-away
Yee Ling (f)	30	Hong Kong	Chinese community worker
Sai (f)	25	Hong Kong	Housing officer
Chris (m)	17	Britain	Sixth form student
David (m)	23	Britain	Computer analyst
Kam (f)	26	Hong Kong	Looking for work (M.F.A.)
Sui (f)	33	Hong Kong	Chinese community worker

Sibling Interviews

Name	Age	Birthplace	Occupation
Anna (f)*	24	Britain	M.A. student
Mary (f)*	26	Britain	University administrator
Richard (m)	24	Hong Kong	Take-away
Karen (f)	18	Britain	Studying for A-levels
Susan (f)	20	Britain	University
Mabel (f)	18	Britain	Take-away
June (f)*	22	Britain	University
Lisa (f)*	20	Britain	University
Tina (f)*	19	Britain	University
Kelly (f)*	18	Britain	Studying for A-levels
Theresa (f)•	20	Britain	Design school
Stephen (m)•	18	Britain	University
Jacqui (f)*	22	Britain	Refugee worker
Sarah (f)*	23	Britain	Secondary school teacher
Colin (m)•	20	Britain	Computer programmer
Simon (m)•	17	Britain	Unemployed; left college
Foon (m)	25	Hong Kong	Engineer
Wong (m)	27	Hong Kong	Computer programmer
Colin (m)	26	Hong Kong	Take-away
Peter (m)	25	Hong Kong	Ph.D. student
Sue (f)	22	Britain	Looking for work (M.A.)
Ming (f)	19	Britain	University
Wai-sun (m)•	22	Britain	Looking for work (B.A.)
Ming (f)•	19	Britain	University
Laura (f)*•	21	Britain	Secretary—temping
Kevin (m)*•	18	Britain	Studying for A-levels
Pue-man (f)	19	Britain	University
Pue-lai (f)	22	Britain	Photo lab
Helen (f)	23	Britain	Looking for work (B.A.)
Rita (f)	24	Britain	Currency trader
Annie (f)•	22	Britain	University
Shirley (f)•	26	Britain	Secretary
Ann (f)	24	Britain	Take-away
Paul (m)	22	Britain	Ph.D. student

Notes

Chapter 1: The Role of Family Ties in Ethnic Businesses

1. In Britain, the legal limits of employing children under 16 are as follows: No child under age 13 can be employed, except young farmers at least 10 years old, as well as young actors. Children cannot work before 7 a.m. or after 7 p.m. Nor can children work more than two hours on any school day or on a Sunday (Pond and Searle, 1991). Since these regulations cover any child who works in a trade carried out for profit, whether or not the child is paid, these regulations apply to family businesses. At the time of writing, the British government was considering tightening child labor legislation so that the number of working hours would be further restricted during school terms and school holidays.

2. As Maclennan et al. (1985:31) pointed out, "Prohibiting children who are under the legal age from helping out on the family farm or in the shop while under the watchful eye of parents is seen as an unreasonable interference by the state in family life." In fact, the International Labor Organization distinguishes between forms of child labor and work within the family (Morrow, 1992).

3. Furthermore, some of the media coverage of the Chinese in Britain has suggested that it is their stubborn pride and refusal to seek help which have kept such difficulties hidden. As such, Chinese families and children have been predominantly depicted as victims of their own enduring cultural traditions, such as "saving face" and "self-reliance" (Chinese Information and Advice Center, 1985).

4. Post-war international migration involved huge displacements of labor, in which individual migrants from less developed countries sold their labor power in Western societies (Castles and Kosack, 1973; Cohen, 1987). In continental Europe, the *Gastarbeiter* ("guest worker") system was used to recruit workers during the period of post-war economic expan-

sion, as in the case of Turkish workers in Germany. Within Britain, Asians (people from the Indian subcontinent), as well as African Caribbeans, were recruited to act as "replacement labor" in occupational sectors deserted by white people, such as foundries, cotton and wool textiles, and public transport (Peach, 1968; Nowikowski, 1984).

5. The growth and reported vitality of various ethnic businesses, most of which are small businesses, has been marked in comparison with the relative and gradual marginalization of the "native" small business sector as a whole in most Western societies. Before the early 1970s, the small business sector had been in steady decline for decades in many Western economies (Bechofer and Elliott, 1981; Steinmetz and Wright, 1989).

6. The growth of ethnic businesses, as a form of self-employment, has been seen by some analysts as a positive response to unemployment, either as a response to being made redundant or as a means of protecting oneself from periods of unemployment (Pahl, 1984). Conservative government initiatives in the 1980s promulgated self-employment as a palliative to recession and unemployment. The ideological emphasis on entrepreneurship promoted under the Thatcher governments included the ideals of "self-help" and independence. For instance, the Enterprise Allowance Scheme introduced under Thatcher (like the United States Self-Employment Act 1985) was aimed at assisting the unemployed to become "entrepreneurs"—a term which suggests an unrealistically innovative and glamorous process involved in the creation of a new economic enterprise based on a new product or service (Curran and Burrows 1987:165).

7. For instance, many Eastern European Jewish immigrants to the United States in the late-nineteenth and early-twentieth centuries set up apartment-based sweatshops—an inexpensive way of setting up a business in the garment industry (Gold and Phillips, 1996). More recently, Dominican immigrants in New York City have established small businesses such as bodegas (small stores catering primarily to Hispanic Caribbeans) and gypsy cabs (Grasmuck and Pessar, 1996).

8. There is now widespread recognition of the inadequacy of linear assimilation models, which were largely premised upon the experiences of white European immigrants (see Warner and Srole, 1945; Gordon, 1964). Generally, it is understood that forms of racial exclusion and prejudice still exist in white majority societies such as Britain and the United States. Analysts in the United States, such as Rumbaut and Portes (1990), have argued that immigrant groups encounter disparate "modes of incorporation," whereby some groups are said to encounter societal prejudice (e.g., Cambodians), while others supposedly do not (e.g., Eastern European immigrants). Therefore, "race" and persistent patterns of racial exclusion continue to be fundamental in making sense of the differential status attainment and mobility of various groups.

9. However, analysts of West Indians in the United States have questioned the image of West Indian immigrants as successful entrepreneurs, particularly in direct comparison with African Americans (see Kasinitz, 1992; Bashi, 1996). In fact, most of the post-1965 Caribbean immigrants to the United States are concentrated in low-level service-sector jobs that do not lead to capital accumulation or control over resources (Kasinitz, 1992:107).

10. Similarly, Korean rotating credit associations, known as *kyes,* have been instrumental in providing Korean immigrants with start-up capital to open businesses (Light and Bonacich, 1988). Pakistani *kommitti* (Boissevain et al., 1990) and Vietnamese *hui* (Gold, 1992) also operate in a similar fashion.

11. In the United States, the term Asian usually refers to individuals of Far Eastern origin, such as Japanese, Chinese, Korean, or Vietnamese people.

12. Studies of native small business owners have observed that married women, and the family in general, can provide a hidden asset during the early stages of business formation (see Bechofer et al., 1974a; Scase and Goffee, 1980a).

13. British research on female business owners is growing. Women owners tend to specialize in retailing and the service sector (Goffee and Scase, 1987). Unlike businesses owned by men, which rely upon their spouses for assistance, women owners rarely get assistance from their spouses in their enterprises (Curran and Burrows, 1987).

14. However, recent sociological work on children in Britain suggests that we need to reexamine children's work more seriously (Leonard, 1990; Hood-Williams, 1990; Morrow, 1992). Child labor and children's economic contributions to their parents' households in Western societies are still more prevalent than is thought (Goddard and White, 1982; Morrow, 1992; Hutson and Cheung, 1992). With the persistence of unemployment and rising poverty among working-class families in Britain, recent studies reveal that young peoples' economic contributions to their parents' households may be quite significant, and that their productivity is, to some extent, determined by these families' economic needs (Allat and Yeandle, 1992; Hutson and Jenkins, 1989; Jones, 1992). These findings suggest that we need to rethink deep-seated assumptions about the dependence and productivity of children in Western family economies more generally.

15. The decline in children's labor was quite variable regionally and very gradual over time. This decline occurred in tandem with domestic ideologies that valorized the dependency of wives and children on a male breadwinner (Davidoff and Hall, 1987). Of course, class differences were significant in terms of what types of families actually enacted middle-class ideals about a protected childhood.

16. In fact, some studies of "primitive" and peasant agricultural economies have attempted to calculate the productive input of children's labor to family economies (e.g., White, 1974; Cain, 1977). The ratio of dependents to earners is said to vary, over the course of "family development" (Sahlins, 1974; Yanagisako, 1979; Chayanov, 1986).

17. The traditional Chinese family has been characterized as patriarchal and patrilineal (Freedman, 1958; Wolf, 1972), and studies of the overseas Chinese have tended to examine the strength of traditional Chinese family patterns by illustrating how Chinese traditions are adapted through gradual acculturation (e.g., Lee, 1960; Hsu, 1971; Sung, 1967, 1987).

18. Very little empirical investigation of how family obligations and responsibilities are fulfilled more generally has been done (but see Finch, 1989; Rossi and Rossi, 1990; Finch and Mason, 1993; Wallace et al., 1994).

19. In Britain, students can leave school at the age of 16; or, if they study for A-levels—examinations used for university entrance—they continue in school for another two years. These last two years are called the "sixth form."

Chapter 2: Chinese Migration and the Establishment of Take-aways in Britain

1. While various studies of the Chinese have provided background on their settlement and adjustment in various parts of Britain (e.g. Broady, 1955; Ng, 1968), Watson's (1975; 1977a) studies of a particular clan lineage from the New Territories of Hong Kong were among the first to examine the centrality of the catering industry and of chain migration for the gradual growth and settlement of Chinese communities in Britain. Many of the subsequent studies of the Chinese have focused upon their concentration in the catering trade (see Chan, 1986; Baxter, 1988; Pang, 1993; Parker, 1995). Although Chinese take-away businesses are well suited for a study of children's labor participation, none of these studies has centrally addressed the issue of Chinese children providing labor in their family take-away businesses.

2. It is very possible, however, that this estimate is too low, reflecting the likely under-counting in the Census.

3. As a result of the Opium War of 1840, China ceded the island of Hong Kong to Britain under the Nan King Treaty of 1842. Subsequently, under the Convention of Peking in 1898 Hong Kong was leased to Britain until 1997 (Chan and Chan, 1997).

4. Until the 1940s, Cantonese farmers had grown mostly rice on their land. As skilled and specialized refugees from the Guangdong province in Southern China came to rural Hong Kong to grow vegetables and rear poultry, a "vegetable revolution" occurred (Shang, 1984:20).

5. In a handful of families, however, parents had met and married in Britain; significantly, these parents tended to be younger than most of the parents in the sample.

6. For instance, many of the recent Korean immigrants to the United States are middle-class, university educated individuals who have concentrated in the small business sector. Despite their high levels of education, Korean immigrants have not been able to apply their credentials in the United States, and they tend to possess limited English language abilities (Min, 1988; Park, 1997).

7. Keith Hart's (1982) work on informal economies has shown that they depend heavily upon evading formal sector constraints.

8. Taped interview with Chinese accountant Charles Ho, in Queensway, London, August 11, 1992.

9. Depending upon where businesses were located, the source of their regulars could vary a great deal. For instance, some shops were located near council estates, where the residents from these estates constituted the bulk of their trade. Other shops were on high streets [main streets], or near markets, and relied more upon passing trade.

Chapter 3: "The Shop Runs Our Lives"

1. Although most young people were extremely courteous toward me, and considered my queries thoughtfully, there were times in the course of these interviews when I was reminded of the limits of my understanding, because my own family experiences had been radically different from theirs.

2. In contrast with these Chinese families, in her broad study of children's work in England, Morrow (1992:151) found that "Asian [Indian, Bangladeshi, or Pakistani] boys in particular [were] more likely to be working in family concerns than any other category of working children" in her study.

3. A study done by the Commission for Racial Equality (Chan, 1986:2) found differences in the business management among families running both Chinese take-aways and restaurants in London and Edinburgh. Catering business owners in Edinburgh were said to be more likely to employ extra workers so that they could spend more time with their families than catering business owners in London. Chan attributed this disparity to the claim that Edinburgh had a more middle-class Chinese population than London did. Although there may indeed be some regional differences in the backgrounds of various Chinese populations in Britain, Chan did not distinguish between take-aways and restaurants in his study—a crucial distinction in terms of the family-only basis of take-aways. Furthermore, Chan did not elaborate upon whether financial considerations or value and

lifestyle differences were primary in explaining why Chinese people reportedly hired more employees in Edinburgh than London.

4. However, in one family, their employee, Kim, was spoken of as practically a family member. Kim had been with their family for a number of years, as a part-time student, and was trusted and much relied upon.

Chapter 4: Helping Out

1. This is not to suggest that other kinds of relationships, such as with fictive kin (see, e.g., Stack, 1974), or close friendships, in different cultural contexts, cannot take on these dynamics. However, on the whole, these kinds of fictive ties are not as universally recognized as being binding in most Western societies.

2. We do not know if this would have been the case for children working in Western small businesses.

3. Although I use the terms "cultural identity" and "ethnicity" synonymously throughout this book, I primarily use cultural identity because it seems to suggest a less fixed identity and more plural forms of identification.

4. The reinforcement of ethnic identity, however, is not necessarily confined to racial antagonisms or tensions with the white majority. In the United States, African American boycotts of Korean businesses, and the conflicts between these two groups, has been said to enhance younger Koreans' sense of ethnic identity (Min, 1996b).

5. Portes and Zhou (1993) have recently argued that the "incorporation" of the new second generation is likely to be "segmented" (Portes and Zhou, 1993)—shaped by various social and economic conditions, as well as by resources held by particular groups (see also Rumbaut, 1994).

Chapter 5: Upholding and Negotiating the Family Work Contract

1. As Finch (1989:8) has argued, notions of duty and obligation are prescriptive concepts, "locked into a particular view of the moral order of the social world, not an empirical description of what happens in practice" (1989:8).

2. For instance, in their study of young people in farm families, Wallace et al. (1994:528) found that, "Both farm diversification and the diversification of family roles are subject to continual negotiation between family members." Through negotiation, children in these families exercised some influence in terms of their work roles on the farm, rather than simply being directed by their parents.

3. For example, Parker's (1995) study of Chinese young people in Britain and Gardner and Shukur's (1994) study of young Bengalis in Britain dismiss the notion of being between two cultures as overly simplistic.

4. Although Hong Kong is officially bilingual (English and Cantonese), the majority of the Hong Kong population speaks Cantonese as their first language (Taylor, 1987). Cantonese and Hakka were the most commonly spoken dialects among these families, but overseas Chinese people speak many different dialects, not only in Britain, but also in Southeast Asia and in North America (Bozorgmehr and Der-Martirosian, 1994). In addition to Cantonese and Hakka, other main dialects spoken in Britain are Mandarin, spoken by those from mainland China, and Hokkien, the main dialect of the Malay Chinese (Taylor, 1987).

5. Some of these young people (both BBCs and Hong Kong-born) reported that although they spoke both English and a Chinese dialect, they felt inadequate in the usage of both languages.

6. Children were often left in the care of grandparents in the New Territories. In his study of the Man clan in Britain and Hong Kong, Watson (1977a:201) found that two-thirds of the Man children born in Europe were sent back to be raised by their paternal grandmothers in rural Hong Kong—what Watson calls "grandparent socialization." It is now much more common for families to raise their children with them in Britain than it was a few decades ago.

7. Developmental research on Western families has suggested that most families undergo a period in the family life cycle, often starting with adolescence, when children press for more independence in anticipation of leaving home and when parents gradually loosen their authority and control over their children (Aldous, 1978; Rossi and Rossi, 1990). However, in her study of Scottish young adults living at home, Jones (1992:26) argues that the transition from dependence to independence is a gradual process that can take a long time; in fact, there are "processes whereby young people grow up while still in the home," for instance, by making economic contributions to the household (see also Wallace, 1987).

8. Individualism has been said to be an important outgrowth of waged work, for as more employment opportunities became available, individual family members, especially children, increasingly prioritized their own needs and preferences at the expense of family needs (Shorter, 1975). For instance, French peasant families underwent major changes in the ways children married and left home, in the context of employment opportunities and normative changes (Segalen, 1987). Thomas and Znaniecki's (1927) study of Polish immigrants to the United States in the

early twentieth century pointed to how individual family members' pursuits gained ground with the rise of individualistic norms and increased economic opportunities. However, even with the increasing availability of waged work, there was evidence that traditional attitudes and values influenced individuals' decisions (especially daughters) in consideration of family needs and strategies (Tilly and Scott, 1978).

9. The fact that some young people in higher education were being financially assisted by their parents may have meant that these young people felt obliged to continue helping out, but a number of those in full-time employment (who either lived with their parents or within a reasonable distance from them) also helped out. Therefore, children's continuing commitments to help out could not only be explained by their expectations of material compensation.

Chapter 6: Siblings' Labor Commitments and Family Reputations

1. Given the small number of sibling sets I had access to, I was unable to discern any clear pattern distinguishing relationships between sisters versus those between brothers. Although Helen and Rita may have shared a close relationship as sisters, I also found other sister sets in which they reported differences in labor commitments and difficulties arising from such perceived disparities.

2. Despite the attribution of these polarized cultural identities, as either British or Chinese, respondents noted that Chinese people in Britain did not constitute an entirely homogeneous group. For instance, some young people made distinctions between BBCs (British-born Chinese) and Chinese young people who were from Hong Kong, who were studying in British universities. Furthermore, a few young people also referred to Vietnamese people of Chinese ethnic origin, who were seen to have had very different experiences from those of BBCs. The attribution of Chinese or British cultural identities, therefore, had to be understood in terms of idealized family reputations.

3. In Britain, school leaving age is 16, for those who do not prepare for entrance into university.

4. However, Nazli Kibria (1998) has recently argued that Asian Americans, such as people of Japanese, Chinese, or Korean heritage, occupy an ambiguous position in American race relations, vis-à-vis the white majority and African Americans. Kibria thus raises the question of whether Asian Americans constitute an ethnic group that will gradually assimilate like white Europeans before them.

Chapter 7: Looking to the Future

1. Until very recently, most large-scale surveys of ethnic minority groups in Britain (including those of youths) have tended to exclude the Chinese (e.g., the Policy Studies Institute study *Black and White Britain,* 1984), and have predominantly focused upon people of African Caribbean and Asian origin.

2. Ten families in this study owned the leaseholds on their businesses, while ten others owned the freeholds on their businesses (young people in five families did not provide this information). Those who owned freeholds could sell (lease) their businesses to a leaseholder for some years, but the property would revert back to them eventually.

3. These sons were the brothers of two different respondents in this study. They were not siblings who had been interviewed; rather, their situations were reported by their siblings.

4. Min Zhou has noted that the British Chinese ethnic economy seemed more closed than it was in various Chinese enclaves in the United States (personal communication at the American Sociological Association Meeting, Washington, D.C., August 21, 1995).

Bibliography

Adkins, Lisa. 1995. *Gendered Work*. Buckingham, U.K.: Open University Press.

Alba, Richard. 1988. The twilight of ethnicity among Americans of European ancestry: The case of Italians. In *Ethnicity and Race in the U.S.A.,* ed. Richard Alba. New York: Routledge.

Aldous, Joan. 1978. *Family Careers: Development and Change in Families.* New York: John Wiley.

Aldrich Howard. 1980. Asian shopkeepers as a middle-man minority. In *The Inner City: Employment and Industry,* ed. Alan Evans and David Eversley. London: Heinemann.

Aldrich, Howard and Albert Reiss. 1976. Continuities in the study of ecological succession. *American Journal of Sociology* 81(4): 846–866.

Alexander, Claire. 1996. *The Art of Being Black*. Oxford: Clarendon.

Allan, Graham. 1985. *Family Life: Domestic Roles and Social Organisation.* Oxford: Blackwell.

Allat, Pat. 1996. Conceptualizing parenting from the standpoint of children. In *Children and Families,* ed. Julia Brannen and Margaret O'Brien. London: Falmer.

Allat, Pat and Susan Yeandle. 1992. *Youth Unemployment and the Family: Voices of Disordered Times.* London: Routledge.

Alvarez, Lizette. 1995. Interpreting new worlds for parents. *The New York Times,* October 1. Metro Report: L29 and L36.

Anderson, Michael. 1980. *Approaches to the History of the Western Family, 1500–1914.* London: Macmillan.

Ang, Ien. 1994. On not speaking Chinese. *New Formations* 24 (November):1–18.

Anthias, Floya. 1983. Sexual divisions and ethnic adaptation: The case of Greek Cypriot Women. In *One Way Ticket: Female Migration and Labour,* ed. Annie Phizacklea. London: Routledge & Kegan Paul.

Anthias, Floya and Nira Yuval-Davis. 1983. Contextualising feminism—gender, ethnic and class division. *Feminist Review* (15): 62–75.

Anwar, Muhammad. 1979. *The Myth of Return: Pakistanis in Britain*. London: Heinemann.

———1981. Between two cultures: A study of relationships between generations in the Asian community in Britain. London: Commission for Racial Equality.

Aries, Phillipe. 1972. *Centuries of Childhood*. London: Peregrine.

Auernheimer, Georg. 1990. How "black" are the German Turks? In *Childhood, Youth, and Social Change*, ed. Lynne Chisholm, Peter Buchner, Heinz-Hermann Kruger, and Phillip Brown. Basingstoke, U.K.: Falmer Press.

Back, Les. 1993. Race, identity and nation within an adolescent community in South London. *New Community* 19(2): 217–33.

Ballard, Catherine. 1979. Conflict, continuity and change. In *Minority Families in Britain*, ed. Verity Saifullah Khan. London: Macmillan.

Ballard, Roger, ed. 1994. *Desh Pardesh: The South Asian Presence in Britain*. London: Hurst & Company.

Ballard, Roger and Catherine Ballard. 1977. The Sikhs: The development of South Asian settlements in Britain. In *Between Two Cultures: Migrants and Minorities in Britain* ed. James Watson. Oxford: Blackwell.

Barth, Frederik. 1969. *Ethnic Groups and Boundaries*. London: Allen & Unwin.

Bashi, Vilna. 1996. "We don't have that back home": Race, racism, and the social networks of West Indian immigrants. Paper presented at the Annual Meeting of the American Sociological Association, 16–20 August, New York City.

Baxter, Susan. 1988. A political economy of the ethnic Chinese catering industry. Ph.D. dissertation, University of Aston.

Baxter, Susan and Geoff Raw. 1988. Fast food, fettered work: Chinese women in the ethnic catering industry. In *Enterprising Women*, ed. Sallie Westwood and Parminder Bhachu. London: Routledge.

Bechofer, Frank, Brian Elliott, Monica Rushforth, and Richard Bland. 1974a. The petit-bourgeois in the class structure: The case of small shopkeepers. In *The Social Analysis of Class Structure*, ed. Frank Parkin. London: Tavistock.

——— 1974b. Small shopkeepers: Matters of money and meaning, *Sociological Review* 22: 465–80.

Bechofer, Frank and Brian Elliott, Brian. 1981. Petty property: The survival of a moral economy. In *Comparative Study of an Uneasy Stratum*, ed. Frank Bechofer and Brian Elliott. London: Macmillan.

Becker, Gary. 1981. *A Treatise on the Family*. Cambridge: Harvard University Press.

Becker, Harold. 1960. Notes on the concept of commitment. *American Journal of Sociology* 66: 32–40.

Benedict, Benedict. 1968. Family firms and economic development. *Southwestern Journal of Anthropology* 24(1): 1–19.

————— 1979. Family firms and firm families: A comparison of Indian, Chinese, and Creole firms in Seychelles. In *Entrepreneurs in Cultural Context*, ed. Sidney Greenfield, Arnold Strickon, and Robert Aubey. Albuquerque: University of New Mexico Press.

Bertaux, Daniel and Isabel Bertaux-Wiame. 1981. Artisanal bakery in France: How it lives and why it survives. In *The Petite Bourgeoisie: Comparative Study of an Uneasy Stratum*, ed. Frank Bechofer and Brian Elliott. London: Macmillan.

Bhabha, Homi. 1990a. Interrogating identity: the post-colonial prerogative. In *The Anatomy of Racism*, ed. David Goldberg. Minneapolis: University of Minnesota Press.

————— 1990b. The third space. In *Identity: Culture, Community, Difference*, ed. Jonathon Rutherford. London: Lawrence and Wishart.

————— 1994. *The Location of Culture*. London: Routledge.

Bhachu, Parminder. 1985. *Twice Migrants: East African Sikh Settlers in Britain*. London: Tavistock Publications.

Blalock, H. M. 1967. *Toward a Theory of Minority Group Relations*. New York: J. Wiley Press.

Bloch, Maurice. 1973. The long term and the short term: the economic and political significance of the morality of kinship. In *The Character of Kinship*, ed. Jack Goody. Cambridge: Cambridge University Press.

Boissevain, Jeremy. 1984. Small entrepreneurs in contemporary Europe. In *Ethnic Communities in Business*, ed. Robin Ward and Richard Jenkins. Cambridge: Cambridge University Press.

Boissevain, Jeremy, Jochen Blaschke, Hanneke Grotenbreg, Isaac Joseph, Ivan Light, Marlene Sway, Roger Waldinger, and Pnina Werbner. 1990. Ethnic entrepreneurs and ethnic strategies. In *Ethnic Entrepreneurs*, ed. Roger Waldinger, Howard Aldrich, and Robin Ward. Newbury Park, Calif.: Sage.

Boissevian, Jeremy and Hanneke Grotenbreg. 1987. Ethnic enterprise in the Netherlands: The Surinamese of Amsterdam. In *Entrepreneurship in Europe*, ed. Robert Goffee and Richard Scase. London: Croom Helm.

Bonacich, Edna. 1973. A theory of middleman minorities. *American Sociological Review* 38: 583–94.

Bonacich, Edna and John Modell. 1980. *The Economic Basis of Ethnic Solidarity: A Study of Japanese Americans*. Berkeley: University of California Press.

Boyd, Robert. 1990. Black and Asian self-employment in large metropolitan areas. *Social Problems* 37: 258–74.

Bozorgmehr, Mehdi and Claudia Der-Martirosian. 1994. Minorities within a minority. *Origins and Destinations: 41 Essays on Chinese America*. Chinese Historical Society of Southern California and UCLA Asian American Studies Center.

Brah, Avtar. 1992. Women of South Asian origin in Britain. In *Racism and Antiracism*, ed. Peter Braham, Ali Rattansi and Richard Skellington. London: Sage.

Brannen, Julia. 1988. The study of sensitive subjects. *Sociological Review* 36: 552–63.

——— 1995. Young people and their contributions to household work, *Sociology* 29(2): 317–38.

——— 1996. Discourses of adolescence. In *Children in Families*. ed. Julia Brannen and Margaret O'Brien. London: Falmer.

Brannen, Julia and Margaret O'Brien, eds. 1996. *Children in Families* London: Falmer.

Brennan, J. M. and P. D. McGeevor. 1990. Ethnic minorities and the graduate labor market. London: Commission for Racial Equality.

Broady, Maurice. 1955. The social adjustment of Chinese immigrants in Liverpool. *Sociological Review* 3: 65–75.

Brown, Colin. 1984. *Black and White Britain: The Third PSI Survey*. London: Heinemann.

——— 1992. "Same difference": The persistence of racial disadvantage in the British employment market. In *Racism and Anti-racism*, ed. Peter Braham, Ali Rattansi, and Richard Skellington. London: Sage.

Cain, Mead. 1977. The economic activities of children in a village in Bangladesh. *Population and Development Review* 3(3) 201–28.

Cannon, Lynn, Elizabeth Higginbotham, and Marianne Leung. 1991. Race and class bias in qualitative research on women. In *The Social Construction of Gender*, ed. Judith Lorber and Susan Farrell. Newbury Park, Cailf.: Sage.

Carby, Hazel. 1982. White woman listen! In *The Empire Strikes Back*. Centre for Contemporary Cultural Studies, Birmingham, U.K.: University of Birmingham.

Cariño, Benjamin. 1996. Filipino Americans: Many and varied. In *Origins and Destinies*, Silvia Pedraza and Ruben Rumbaut. Belmont, Calif.: Wadsworth.

Cashmore, Ellis and Barry Troyna, eds. 1982. *Black Youth in Crisis*. London: Allen & Unwin.

Castles, Stephen, Heather Booth, and Tina Wallace. 1984. *Here For Good: Western Europe's New Ethnic Minorities*. London: Pluto.

Castles, Stephen and Godula Kosack. 1973. *Immigrant Workers and Class Structure in Western Europe*. London: Oxford University Press.

Chan, Alfred. 1986. Employment prospects of Chinese youth in Britain: A research report. London: Commission for Racial Equality.

Chan, Yiu Man and Chan, Christine. 1997. The Chinese in Britain. *New Community* 23(1):123–31.

Chan, J. M. and Y. W. Cheung, 1985. Ethnic resources and business enterprise: A study of Chinese businesses in Toronto. *Human Organisation* 44(2): 142–53.

Chayanov, A. V. 1986. *A. V. Chayanov on the Theory of Peasant Economy.* Trans. Daniel Thorner, Basile Kerblay, and R. E. Smith. Madison: University of Wisconsin Press.

Cheal, David. 1983. Intergenerational family transfers. *Journal of Marriage and the Family* 45: 805–13.

——— 1991. *Family and the State of Theory.* Hemel Hempstead, U.K.: Harvester Wheatsheaf.

Cheng, Yuan. 1994. *Education and Class: Chinese in Britain and the U.S.* Aldershot, U.K.: Avebury Press.

Child, I. L. 1943. *Italian or American?* New Haven: Yale University Press.

Chinese Information and Advice Center. 1985. Statement in response to the Home Affairs Committee Report. London: Chinese Information and Advice Center.

Chisholm, Lynne, Peter Buchner, Heinz-Hermann Kruger, Phillip Brown, eds. 1990. *Childhood, Youth, and Social Change.* Basingstoke, U.K.: Falmer Press.

Chung, Y. K. 1990. At the palace: Researching gender and ethnicity in a Chinese restaurant. In *Feminist Praxis,* ed. Liz Stanley. London: Routledge.

Cicourel, Aaron. 1982. Living in two cultures: The everyday world of migrant workers. In *Living in Two Cultures.* Paris: UNESCO.

Clifford, James and Gary Marcus, eds. 1986. *Writing Culture: The Poetics and Politics of Ethnography.* Berkeley: University of California Press.

Cohen, Abner. 1974. The lesson of ethnicity. In *Urban Ethnicity,* ed. Abner Cohen. London: Tavistock.

Cohen, Robin. 1987. *The New Helots: Migrants in the International Division of Labour.* London: Gower.

Collins, P. H. 1990. *Black Feminist Thought.* London: Harper Collins.

Constantinides, Pamela. 1977. The Greek Cypriots: Factors in the maintenance of ethnic identity. In *Between Two Cultures: Migrants and Minorities in Britain* ed. James Watson. Oxford: Blackwell.

Corrigan, Paul. 1989. Gender and the gift: The case of the family clothing economy. *Sociology* 23(4): 513–34.

Crissman, Lawrence. 1967. The segmentary structure of the urban overseas Chinese communities. *Man* 2(2): 185–204.

Cummings, Scott, ed. 1980. *Self-help in Urban America: Patterns of Minority Business Enterprise.* Port Washington, N.Y.: Kennikat Press.

Curran, James and Roger Burrows. 1987. The social analysis of small business: Some emerging themes. In *Entrepreneurship in Europe,* ed. Robert Goffee and Richard Scase. London: Croom Helm.

Davidoff, Leonora and Catherine Hall. 1987. *Family Fortunes.* London: Hutchinson.

Davin, Anna. 1982. Child labour, the working-class family, and domestic ideology in 19th century Britain. *Development and Change* 13: 633–52.

Delphy, Christine and Diana Leonard. 1992. *Familiar Exploitation.* Cambridge, U.K.: Polity Press.

Department of Employment. 1988. Ethnic origins and the labour market. *Employment Gazette* (March).

Dex, Shirley. 1983. Second generation school leavers. In *One Way Ticket: Female Migration and Labour,* ed. Annie Phizacklea. London: Routledge & Kegan Paul.

Drew, David and Bekia Fosam. 1994. Gender and ethnic differences in education and the youth labour market: A statistical review. Paper presented at the British Sociological Association Conference, Sexuality in Social Context, Sheffield Hallam University, 28–31 March.

Drury, Beatrice. 1991. Sikh girls and the maintenance of an ethnic culture. *New Community* 17(3): 387–401.

Eades, Jeremy, ed. 1987. *Migrants, Workers, and the Social Order.* Association of Social Anthropologists Monographs 2b.

Easey, Walter. 1979. Child labour in Hong Kong. London: Anti-Slavery Society.

Edwards, Rosalind. 1990. Connecting method and epistemology: A white woman interviewing black women. *Women's Studies International Forum* 13: 477–90.

Elder, Glen. 1974. *Children of the Great Depression.* Chicago, Ill.: University of Chicago Press.

————— 1985. Perspective on the life course. In *Life Course Dynamics: Trajectories and Transitions,* ed. Glen Elder. Ithaca, N.Y.: Cornell University Press.

Ennew, Judith. 1982. Family structure, unemployment and child labour in Jamaica, *Development and Change* 13: 551–63.

Erikson, Erik. 1968. *Identity, Youth, and Crisis.* New York: W.W. Norton.

Espiritu, Yen Le. 1992. *Asian-American Panethnicity: Bridging Institutions and Identities.* Philadelphia, Pa.: Temple University Press.

Faraday, Annabel and Kenneth Plummer. 1979. Doing life histories. *Sociological Review* 27: 773–98.

Feagin, Joe and Nikitah Imani. Racial barriers to African American entrepreneurship: An exploratory study. *Social Problems* 41(4): 562–84.

Fernandez-Kelly, Patricia and Richard Schauffler. 1994. Divided fates:

Immigrant children in a restructured U.S. economy. *International Migration Review* 28(4): 662–89.

Ferree, M. M. 1985. Between two worlds: German feminist approaches to working-class women and work. *Signs* 10(3): 517–36.

Fewster, Carol. 1990. The great wall of silence. *Social Work Today* (15 February): 14–15.

Finch, Janet. 1983. *Married to the Job.* London: Unwin Hyman.

———— 1984. "It's great to have someone to talk to": The ethics and politics of interviewing women. In *Social Researching: Politics, Problems, Practice,* ed. Colin Bell and Helen Roberts. London: Routledge & Kegan Paul.

———— 1989. *Family Obligations and Social Change.* Cambridge: Polity Press.

Finch, Janet and Dulcie Groves, eds. 1983. *A Labour of Love: Women, Work and Caring.* London: Routledge & Kegan Paul.

Finch, Janet and Jennifer Mason. 1993. *Negotiating Family Responsibilities.* London: Routledge.

Firth, Raymond, Jane Hubert, and Anthony Forge. 1970. *Families and their Relatives.* London: Routledge & Kegan Paul.

Fitchett, Norman. 1976. Chinese children in Derby. Derby, U.K.: Bishop Lonsdale College.

Foner, Nancy. 1978. *Jamaica Farewell.* London: Routledge & Kegan Paul.

Fong, L. K. W. 1981. Chinese children in Liverpool. Diploma in Special Education thesis, University of Liverpool.

Fortes, Meyer. 1969. *Kinship and the Social Order.* Chicago, Ill.: Aldine.

Fox, Alan. 1974. *Beyond Contract.* London: Faber & Faber.

Frankenberg, Ruth. 1993. *White Women, Race Matters.* Minneapolis: University of Minnesota Press.

Freenborne, J. D. M. 1980. The Chinese communities in Britain: With special reference to housing and education. Ph.D. thesis, University of London.

Freedman, Maurice. 1958. *Lineage Organisation in Southeastern China.* London: Athlone.

Gans, Herbert. 1962. *The Urban Villagers, Group and Class in the Life of Italian-Americans.* New York: The Free Press.

———— 1979. Symbolic ethnicity: The future of ethnic groups and cultures in America. *Ethnic and Racial Studies* 2(1): 1–20.

———— 1992. Second-generation decline: Scenarios for the economic and ethnic futures of the post-1965 American immigrants. *Ethnic and Racial Studies* 15(2): 173–92.

Gardner, Katy. 1995. *Global Migrants, Local Lives.* Oxford: Clarendon Press.

Gardner, Katy and Abdus Shukur. 1994. I'm Bengali, I'm Asian, and I'm living here. In *Desh Pardesh: The South Asian Presence in Britain,* ed. Roger Ballard. London: Hurst & Company.

Garvey, Anne. 1993. Over the counter. *The Guardian* (July 7).

Gates, Hill. 1987. *Chinese Working-Class Lives*. Ithaca, N.Y.: Cornell University Press.

Ghodsian, Mayer and Juliet Essen. 1980. The children of immigrants: Social and home circumstances. *New Community* 8(3): 422–29.

Gilroy, Paul. 1987. *There Aint No Black in the Union Jack*. London: Hutchinson.

———— 1993. *The Black Atlantic*. London: Verso.

Glazer, Nathan and Daniel Moynihan. 1963. *Beyond the Melting Pot*. Cambridge, Mass.: MIT Press.

———— eds. 1975. *Ethnicity: Theory and Experience*. Cambridge, Mass.: Harvard University Press.

Glenn, Evelyn. 1983. Split household, small producer and dual wage earner: An analysis of Chinese-American family strategies. *Journal of Marriage and the Family* (February): 35–46.

Glenn, Evelyn and Stephanie Yap. 1994. Chinese American families. In *Minority Families in the United States,* ed. Ronald Taylor. Englewood Cliffs, N.J.: Prentice-Hall.

Goddard, Victoria and Benjamin White. 1982. Child workers and capitalist development. *Development and Change* 13: 465–77.

Goffee, Robert and Richard Scase, eds. 1987. *Entrepreneurship in Europe*. London: Croom Helm.

Goffman, Erving. 1963. *Stigma*. Englewood Cliffs, N.J.: Prentice-Hall.

———— 1969. *Presentation of Self in Everyday Life*. Harmondsworth, U.K.: Penguin.

Gold, Steve. 1992. *Refugee Communities*. Newbury Park, Calif.: Sage.

Gold, Steve and Bruce Phillips. 1996. Mobility and continuity among Eastern European Jews. In *Origins and Destinies*, ed. Silvia Pedraza and Ruben Rumbaut. Belmont, Calif.: Wadsworth.

Gordon, Milton. 1964. *Assimilation in American Life*. New York: Oxford University Press.

Gove, Walter, James Grimm, Susan Motz, and James Thompson. 1973. The family life cycle: Internal dynamics and social consequences, *Sociology and Social Research* 57(2): 182–95.

Grasmuck, Sherri and Patricia Pessar. 1996. Dominicans in the United States: First and second generation settlement. In *Origins and Destinies*, ed. Silvia Pedraza and Ruben Rumbaut. Belmont, Calif.: Wadsworth.

Great Britain Parliament. 1985a. *Swann Committee Report: Education for all*. Cmd 9453.

———— 1985b. *Chinese Community in Britain Report*.

Greenhalgh, Susan. 1994. De-Orientalizing the Chinese family firm. *American Ethnologist* 21(4):746–75.

Hall, Stuart. 1989. Cultural identity and cinematic representation. *Framework* 36.

———— 1991. Old and new identities, old and new ethnicities. In *Culture, Globalization and the World System,* ed. Anthony King. Binghamton: State University of New York.

Hammersley, Martin and Paul Atkinson. 1983. *Ethnography: Principles in Practice.* London: Routledge.

Harding, Sandra. 1987. *Feminism and Methodology.* Bloomington: Indiana University Press.

Hareven, Tara. 1982. *Family Time and Industrial Time.* New York: Cambridge University Press.

Harris, Olivia. 1981. Households and their boundaries. *History Workshop Journal* 13: 143–52.

Hart, Keith. 1982. *The Political Economy of West African Agriculture.* Cambridge: Cambridge University Press.

Hartmann, Heidi. 1981. The unhappy marriage of marxism and feminism. In *Women and Revolution,* ed. Lydia Sargent. Boston: South End Press.

Henley Centre. 1990. The economic impact of the arrival in the UK from Hong Kong of 50,000 heads of households and their dependants. Prepared for *Public Eye* by Professor Bernard Corry and others. U.K., Henley-on-Themes.

Hewitt, Roger. 1986. *White Talk, Black Talk.* Cambridge: Cambridge University Press.

———— 1992. Language, youth and the destabilisation of ethnicity. In *Ethnicity in Youth Culture,* ed. Cecilia Palmgren, Karin Lovgren, and Goran Bolin. Stockholm: Stockholm University.

Ho, David. 1989. Continuity and variation in Chinese patterns of socialization, *Journal of Marriage and the Family* 51(February): 149–63.

Hoel, Barbro. 1982. Contemporary clothing "sweatshops": Asian female labour and collective organisation. In *Women, Work, and the Labour Market,* ed. Jackie West. London: Routledge & Kegan Paul.

Hood-Williams, John. 1990. Patriarchy for children: On the stability of power relations in children's lives. In *Childhood, Youth, and Social Change,* ed. Lynne Chisholm, Peter Buchner, Heinz-Hermann Kruger, and Phillip Brown. Basingstoke, U.K.: Falmer Press.

Hsu, Francis. 1971. *The Challenge of the American Dream: The Chinese in the U.S.* Belmont, Calif.: Wordsworth.

Hutson, John. 1987. Fathers and sons: Family farms, family businesses and the farming industry. *Sociology* 21(2), 215–29.

Hutson, Susan and Wai-yee Cheung. 1992. Saturday jobs: Sixth-formers in the labour market and the family. In *Families and Households,* ed.Cathy Marsh and Sara Arber. London: Macmillan.

Hutson, Susan and Richard Jenkins. 1989. *Taking the Strain: Families, Unemployment and the Transition to Adulthood.* Milton Keynes, U.K.: Open University Press.

Iganski, Paul and Geoffrey Payne. 1996. Declining racial disadvantage in the British labour market. *Ethnic and Racial Studies* 19(1): 113–34.

Jackson, Brian and Anne Garvey. 1974. The Chinese children of Britain. *New Society* 30: 9–12.

————— 1975. *Chinese Children.* U.K.: National Education Research and Development Trust.

James, Allison and Alan Prout, eds. 1990. *Constructing and Reconstructing Childhood.* London: Falmer Press.

————— 1996. Strategies and structures: Towards a new perspective on children's experiences of family life. In *Children in Families,* ed. Julia Brannen and Margaret O'Brien. London: Falmer Press.

Jayaweera, Hiranthi. 1993. Racial disadvantage and ethnic identity: The experiences of Afro-Caribbean women in a British city. *New Community* 19(3): 383–406.

Jenks, Christopher. 1996. The postmodern child. In *Children and Families: Research and Policy.* London: Falmer Press.

Jo, M. H. 1992. Korean merchants in the black community: Prejudice among the victims of prejudice. *Ethnic and Racial Studies* 15(3): 395–411.

Jones, David. 1987. The Chinese in Britain: Rebirth of a Community. *New Community* 14: 245–47.

Jones, Gill. 1992. Short-term reciprocity in parent-child economic exchanges. In *Families and Households,* ed. Cathy Marsh and Sara Arber. London: Macmillan.

Jones, Trevor. 1993. *Britain's Ethnic Minorities.* London: Policy Studies Institute.

Joseph, Gloria. 1981. The incompatible menage a trois: marxism, feminism, and racism. In *Women and Revolution,* ed. Lydia Sargent. Boston: South End Press.

Josephides, Sasha. 1988. Honour, family, and work: Greek Cypriot women before and after migration. In *Enterprising Women,* ed. Sallie Westwood and Parminder Bhachu. London: Routledge.

Kasinitz, Philip. 1992. *Caribbean New York.* Ithaca, N.Y.: Cornell University Press.

Khan, V. S. 1977. The Pakistanis: Mirpuri villagers at home in Bradford. In *Between Two Cultures: Migrants and Minorities in Britain,* ed. James Watson. Oxford: Blackwell.

————— ed. 1979. *Minority Families in Britain: Support and Stress.* London: Macmillan.

Kibria, Nazli. 1994. Household structure and family ideologies: The dynamics of immigrant economic adaptation among Vietnamese refugees. *Social Problems* 41: 81–96.

———— 1997. The construction of "Asian American": reflections on intermarriage and ethnic identity among second-generation Chinese and Korean Americans. *Ethnic and Racial Studies* 20 (3): 523–44.

———— 1998. The contested meanings of "Asian American": Racial dilemmas in the contemporary U.S. *Ethnic and Racial Studies* 21(5): 939–58.

Kim, Ilsoo. 1981. *New Urban Immigrants: The Korean Community in New York.* Princeton, N.J.: Princeton University Press.

Kim, Kwang Chung and Won Moo Hurh. 1988. The burden of double roles: Korean wives in the USA. *Ethnic and Racial Studies* 11(2):151–67.

Klein, David. 1982. The problem of multiple perception in family research. Draft chapter prepared for *Interpersonal Perception in Families,* ed. L. Larson and J. White forthcoming.

Knott, Kim and Sajda Khokher. 1993. Religious and ethnic identity among young Muslim women in Bradford. *New Community* 19(4): 593–610.

Kuo, Wen. 1995. Coping with racial discrimination: The case of Asian Americans, *Ethnic and Racial Studies* 18(1): 109–27.

Ladbury, Sarah. 1984. Choice, chance, or no alternative? Turkish Cypriots in business in London. In *Ethnic Communities in Business,* ed. Robin Ward and Richard Jenkins. Cambridge: Cambridge University Press.

Lai, Ah-Eng. 1982. The little workers: A study of child labour in the small-scale industries of Penang. *Development and Change* 13: 565–85.

Lasch, Christopher. 1977. *Haven in a Heartless World.* New York: Basic Books.

Lee, Rose Hum. 1960. *The Chinese in the United States of America.* Hong Kong: Hong Kong University Press.

Lem, Winnie. 1988. Household production and reproduction in rural Languedoc. *The Journal of Peasant Studies* 15(4): 500–529.

Leonard, Diana. 1990. Persons in their own right: Children and sociology in the UK. In *Childhood, Youth, and Social Change,* ed. Lynne Chisholm, Peter Buchner, Heinz-Hermann Kruger, and Phillip Brown. Basingstoke, U.K.: Falmer Press.

Lewis, Jane. 1986. Anxieties about the family and the relationship between parents, children and the state in twentieth-century England. In *Children of Social Worlds,* ed. Martin Richards and Paul Light. Cambridge: Polity Press.

Lewis, Jane and Barbara Meredith. 1988. *Daughters Who Care.* London: Routledge.

Li, Peter. 1988. *The Chinese in Canada.* Toronto: Oxford University Press.

Light, Ivan. 1972. *Ethnic Enterprise in America: Business and Welfare Among Chinese, Japanese, and Blacks.* Berkeley: University of California Press.

———— 1980. Asian enterprise in America. In *Self-help in Urban America*, ed. Scott Cummings. Port Washington, N.Y.: Kennikat.

———— 1984. Immigrant and ethnic enterprise in North America. *Ethnic and Racial Studies* 7(2): 195–216.

Light, Ivan and Edna Bonacich. 1988. *Immigrant Entrepreneurs: Koreans in L.A., 1965–1982*. Berkeley: University of California Press.

Light, Ivan, Georges Sabagh, Mehdi Bozorgmehr, Claudia Der-Martirosian. 1993. Internal ethnicity in the ethnic economy. *Ethnic and Racial Studies* 16(4): 581–97.

Lin, M. W. 1989. *Chinese Liverpudlians*. Wirral, U.K.: Liver Press.

Loewen, J. W. 1971. *The Mississippi Chinese: Between Black and White.* Cambridge, Mass.: Harvard University Press.

Loizos, Peter. 1981. *The Heart Grown Bitter: A Chronicle of Cypriot War Refugees.* Cambridge: Cambridge University Press.

Lovell-Troy, Lawrence. 1980. Clan stucture and economic activity: The case of Greeks in small business enterprise. In *Self-help in Urban America,* ed. Scott Cummings. Port Washington, N.Y.: Kennikat.

Lyman, Stanford. 1974. *Chinese Americans.* New York: Random House.

MacLennen, Emma, John Fitz, and Jill Sullivan. 1985. *Working Children.* London: Low Pay Unit Pamphlet No. 34.

Marsh, Cathy and Sara Arber, eds. 1992. *Families and Households.* London: Macmillan.

Massey, Douglas, Rafael Alarcon, Jorge Durrand, and Humberto Gonzalez. 1987. *Return to Aztlan.* Berkeley: University of California Press.

Mauss, Marcel. 1954. *The Gift.* London: Cohen and West Ltd.

McKee, Lorna and Margaret O'Brien. 1983. Interviewing men: Taking gender seriously. In *The Public and the Private,* ed. Eve Gamarnikow, David Morgan, Daphne Taylorson, and June Purvis. London: Heinemann.

Meillasoux, Claude. 1984. *Maidens, Meals, and Money.* Cambridge: Cambridge University Press.

Merton, Robert. 1972. Insiders and outsiders. *American Journal of Sociology* 78: 9–47.

Min, P. G. 1988. *Ethnic Business Enterprise: Korean Small Business in Atlanta.* New York: Center for Migration Studies.

———— 1991. Cultural and economic boundaries of Korean ethnicity: A comparative analysis. *Ethnic and Racial Studies* 14: 225–41.

———— 1996a. The entrepreneurial adaptation of Korean immigrants. In *Origins and Destinies,* ed. Silvia Pedraza and Ruben Rumbaut. Belmont, Calif.: Wadsworth.

———— 1996b. *Caught in the Middle.* Berkeley: University of California Press.

———— 1998. *Changes and Conflicts.* Boston: Allyn and Bacon.

Mitchell, J. C. 1983. Case and situation analysis. *Sociological Review* 31: 187–211.

Mo, Timothy. 1982. *Sour Sweet.* London: Vintage.

Modood, Tariq. 1994. Political blackness and British Asians. *Sociology* 28(4): 859–76.

Modood, Tariq, Sharon Beishon, and Satnam Virdee. 1994. *Changing Ethnic Identities.* London: Policy Studies Insitute.

Modood, Tariq, Richard Berthoud, and Jane Lakey. 1997. *Ethnic Minorities in Britain.* London: Policy Studies Institute.

Moen, Phyllis and Elaine Wethington. 1992. The concept of family adaptive strategies. *Annual Review of Sociology* 18: 233–51.

Morrow, Virginia. 1992. A sociological study of the economic roles of children, with particular reference to Birmingham and Cambridgeshire. Ph.D. thesis, University of Cambridge.

Nagel, Joanne. 1994. Contstructing ethnicity: Creating and recreating ethnic identity and culture. *Social Problems* 41(1): 152–76.

Niehoff, Justin. 1987. The villager as industrialist: Ideologies of household manufacturing in rural Taiwan. *Modern China* 13: 278–309.

Nelson, Candace and Marta Tienda. 1988. The structuring of Hispanic ethnicity. In *Ethnicity and Race in the U.S.A.*, ed. Richard Alba. New York: Routledge.

Newby, Howard. 1977. Paternalism and capitalism. In *Industrial Society: Class Cleavage and Control,* ed. Richard Scase. London: Allen and Unwin.

Ng, K. C. 1968. *The Chinese in London.* London: Institute for Race Relations.

Nowikowski, Susan. 1984. Snakes and ladders: Asian business in Britain. In *Ethnic Communities in Business,* ed. Robin Ward and Richard Jenkins. Cambridge: Cambridge University Press.

Oakley, Ann. 1981. Interviewing women: A contradiction in terms. In *Doing Feminist Research,* ed. Helen Roberts. London: Routledge & Kegan Paul.

Omi, Michael and Howard Winant. 1986. *Racial Formation in the United States.* New York: Routledge.

Owen, David. 1992. Ethnic minorities in Great Britain: Settlement patterns. National Ethnic Minority Data Archive 1991 Census Statistical Paper No. 1 Coventry, U.K.: Centre for Research in Ethnic Relations, University of Warwick.

———— 1993. Ethnic minorities in Great Britain: Age and gender structure. National Ethnic Minority Data Archive 1991 Census Statistical Paper No. 2 Coventry, U.K.: Centre for Research in Ethnic Relations, University of Warwick.

Oxfeld, Ellen. 1993. *Blood, Sweat, and Mahjong.* Ithaca, N.Y.: Cornell University Press.

Pahl, Ray. 1984. *Divisions of Labour.* Oxford: Basil Blackwell.

Pang, Mary. 1993. Catering to employment needs: The occupations of young Chinese adults in Britain. Ph.D. thesis, University of Warwick.

Park, Kyeyoung. 1997. *The Korean American Dream.* Ithaca, N.Y.: Cornell University Press.

Park, Robert. 1950. *Race and Culture.* New York: Free Press.

Parker, David. 1994. Encounters across the counter: Young Chinese people in Britain. *New Community* 20(4): 621–34.

———— 1995. *Through Different Eyes: The Cultural Identities of Young Chinese People in Britain.* Aldershot, U.K.: Avebury Press.

Parkin, Frank, ed. 1974. *The Social Analysis of Class Structure.* London: Tavistock.

Patterson, Orlando. 1975. Context and choice in ethnic allegiance: A theoretical framework and Caribbean case study. In *Ethnicity: Theory and Experience,* ed. Nathan Glazer and Daniel Moynihan. Cambridge: Harvard University Press.

Peach, Ceri. 1968. *West Indian Migration to Britain.* Oxford: Oxford University Press.

Pedraza, Silvia and Ruben Rumbaut, eds. 1996. *Origins and Destinies.* Belmont, Calif.: Wadsworth Publishing.

Perez, Lisandro. 1994. Cuban families in the United States. In *Minority Families in the United States,* ed. Ronald Taylor. Englewood Cliffs, N.J.: Prentice-Hall.

Phizacklea, Annie. 1982. Migrant women and wage labour: The case of West Indian women in Britain. In *Women, Work and the Labour Market,* ed. Jackie West. London: Routledge & Kegan Paul.

———— ed. 1983. *One Way Ticket: Female Migration and Labour* London: Routledge & Kegan Paul.

———— 1988. Entrepreneurship, ethnicity, and gender. In *Enterprising Women,* ed. Sallie Westwood and Parminder Bhachu. London: Routledge.

———— 1990. *Unpacking the Fashion Industry.* London: Routledge.

Phoenix, Ann. 1988. Narrow definitions of culture. In *Enterprising Women,* ed. Sallie Westwood and Parminder Bhachu. London: Routledge.

Pieterse, Jan. 1995. Globalization as hybridization. In *Global Modernities,* ed. Mike Featherstone, Scott Lash, Roland Robertson. London: Sage.

Pile, Steve. 1991. Securing the future: "survival strategies" amongst Somerset dairy farmers. *Sociology* 25(2): 255–74.

Pistrang, Nancy. 1990. Leaping the culture gap. *Social Work Today* (15 February): 16–17.

Pleck, Joseph. 1977. The work-family roles system. *Social Problems* 24(4): 417–27.

Pond, Chris and Ann Searle. 1991. *The Hidden Army: Children at Work in the 1990s.* London: Birmingham City Education Department and the Low Pay Unit.

Portes, Alejandro. 1987. The social origins of the Cuban enclave economy in Miami. *Sociological Perspectives* 30(4): 340–72.

Portes, Alejandro and Robert Bach. 1985. *Latin Journey: Cuban and Mexican Immigrants in the United States.* Berkeley: University of California Press.

Portes, Alejandro and Douglas MacLeod. 1996. What shall I call myself? Hispanic identity formation in the second generation. *Ethnic and Racial Studies* 19(3): 523–47.

Portes, Alejandro and Robert Manning. 1986. The immigrant enclave: Theory and empirical examples. In *Competitive Ethnic Relations,* ed. Susan Olzak and Joane Nagel. Orlando, Fla.: Academic Press.

Portes, Alejandro and Richard Schauffler. 1996. Language acquisition and loss among children of immigrants. In *Origins and Destinies,* ed. Silvia Pedraza and Ruben Rumbaut. Belmont, Calif.: Wadsworth.

Portes, Alejandro and Min Zhou. 1992. Gaining the upper hand: Economic mobility among immigrant and domestic minorities. *Ethnic and Racial Studies* 15(4): 491–522.

———— 1993. The new second generation: segmented assimilation and its variants among post-1965 immigrant youth. *Annals of the American Academy of Political and Social Sciences* 530 (November): 74–96.

Pryce, Kenneth. 1979. *Endless Pressure.* Harmondsworth, U.K.: Penguin.

Qureshi, Hazel. and Ken Simons. 1987. Resources within families: Caring for elderly people. In *Give and Take in Families,* ed. Julia Brannen and Gail Wilson. London: Allen and Unwin.

Qvortrup, Jens. 1985. Placing children in the division of labour. In *Family and Economy in Modern Society,* ed. Paul Close and Rosemary Collins. Basingstoke, U.K.: Macmillan.

Rainbird, Helen. 1991. The self-employed: Small entrepreneurs or disguised wage labourers? In *Farewell to Flexibility,* ed. Anna Pollert. Oxford: Blackwell.

Ram, Monder and Ruth Holliday. 1993. Relative merits: Family culture and kinship in small firms. *Sociology* 27(4): 629–48.

Rapp, Rayna, Ellen Ross, and Renate Bridenthal. 1979. Examining family history. *Feminist Studies* 5(1): 174–200.

Reissmann, Catherine. 1991. When gender isn't enough: Women interviewing women. In *The Social Construction of Gender,* ed. Judith Lorber and Susan Farrell. Newbury Park, Calif.: Sage.

Ribbens Jane and Rosalind Edwards. 1995. Introducing qualitative research on women in families and households. *Women's Studies International Forum* 18(3): 247–58.

Rinder, Irwin. 1959. Strangers in the land: Social relations in the status gap. *Social Problems* 8: 253–60.

Roberts, Helen. *Doing Feminist Research*. London: Routledge & Kegan Paul.

Roche, Jeremy. 1996. The politics of children's rights. In *Children in Families*, ed. Julia Brannen and Margaret O'Brien. London: Falmer Press.

Rodgers, Guy and Guy Standing, eds. 1981. *Child Work, Poverty and Underdevelopment*. Geneva: International Labor Organization.

Rosaldo, Michelle. 1974. Woman, culture, and society: A theoretical overview. In *Woman, Culture, and Society*, ed. Michelle Rosaldo and Louise Lamphere. Stanford, Calif.: Stanford University Press.

Rosenblatt, Paul , Leni de Mik, Roxanne Anderson, and Patricia Johnson. 1985. *The Family in Business*. San Francisco, Calif: Jossey-Bass.

Rossi, Alice and Peter Rossi. 1990. *Of Human Bonding: Parent-Child Relations Across the Life Course*. New York: Aldine De Gruyter.

Rumbaut, Ruben. 1994. The crucible within: Ethnic identity, self-esteem, and segmented assimilation among children of immigrants. *International Migration Review* 28(4): 748–94.

Rumbaut, Ruben and Alejandro Portes. 1990. *Immigrant America*. Berkeley: University of California Press.

Runnymede Trust. 1986. The Chinese community in Britain: The Home Affairs Committee Report in context. The Runnymede Trust.

Sahlins, Marshall. 1965. On the sociology of primitive exchange. In *The Relevance of Models in Social Anthropology*, ed. Michael Branton. London: Tavistock.

————— 1974. *Stone Age Economics*. London: Tavistock.

Said, Edward. 1978. *Orientalism*. London: Routledge & Kegan Paul.

Salaff, Janet. 1981. *Working Daughters of Hong Kong*. Cambridge: Cambridge University Press.

Sanders, Jimy and Victor Nee. 1987. Limits of ethnic solidarity in the enclave economy. *American Sociological Review* 52: 745–74.

————— 1996. Immigrant self-employment: the family as social capital and the value of human capital. *American Sociological Review* 61: 231–49.

Sargent, Lydia. ed. 1981. *Women and Revolution*. Boston: South End Press.

Scase, Richard and Robert Goffee. 1980a. *The Real World of the Small Business Owner*. London: Croom Helm.

————— 1980b. Homelife in a small business. *New Society* (October): 220–22.

Segalen, Martine. 1984. Avoir sa part: sibling relations in partible inheritance in Brittany. In *Interest and Emotion: Essays on the Study of Families and Kinship*, ed. Hans Medick and D.W. Sabean. Cambridge: Cambridge University Press.

————— 1987. Life-course patterns and peasant culture in France: A critical assessment. *Journal of Family History* 12(1–3): 213–24.

Shang, Anthony. 1984. *The Chinese in Britain*. London: Batsford.

Shaw, Alison. 1994. The Pakistani community in Oxford. In *Desh Pardesh*:

The South Asian Presence in Britain, ed. Roger Ballard. London: Hurst & Company.

Shorter, Edward. 1975. *The Making of the Modern Family.* London: Fontana/Collins.

Simmel, Georg. 1950. *The Sociology of Georg Simmel,* trans. and ed. K. Wolff. Illinois: Free Press.

Simpson, M. M. 1987. *Children of the Dragon,* Bradford, U.K.: Bradford and Ilkley Community College.

Siu, Paul. 1952. The sojourner. *American Journal of Sociology* 58: 34–44.

Solomos, John. 1989. *Race and Racism in Britain.* London: Macmillan.

Sombart, Werner. 1967. *Luxury and Capitalism.* Ann Arbor, Mich.: University of Michigan Press.

Song, Miri. 1995. Between "the front" and "the back": Chinese women's work in family businesses. *Women's Studies International Forum* 18(3): 285–98.

———— 1997a. Children's labour in ethnic family businesses: The case of Chinese take-aways in Britain. *Ethnic and Racial Studies* 20(4): 690–716

———— 1997b. "You're becoming more and more English every day": Investigating Chinese siblings' cultural identities. *New Community* 23(3): 343–62.

———— 1998. Hearing competing voices: Sibling research. In *Feminist Dilemmas in Qualitative Research,* ed. Jane Ribbens and Rosalind Edwards. London: Sage.

Song, Miri and David Parker. 1995. Commonality, difference, and the dynamics of disclosure in in-depth interviewing. *Sociology* 29(2): 241–56.

Sowell, Thomas. 1981. *Ethnic America.* New York: Basic Books.

Stack, Carol. 1974. *All Our Kin: Strategies for Survival in a Black Community.* New York: Harper & Row.

Steinberg, Stephen. 1981. *The Ethnic Myth.* Boston: Beacon Press.

Steinmetz, George and Erik Wright. 1989. The fall and rise of the petty bourgeoisie. *American Journal of Sociology* 94(5): 973–1018.

Stopes-Roe, Mary and Raymond Cochrane. 1990. *Citizens of this Country.* Clevedon, U.K.: Multilingual Matters.

Sulloway, Frank. 1996. *Born to Rebel.* Boston: Little, Brown & Company.

Sung, Betty Lee. 1967. *Mountain of Gold: The Story of the Chinese in America.* New York: Macmillan.

————1987. *The Adjustment Experience of Chinese Immigrant Children in New York City.* New York: Center for Migration Studies.

Sway, Marlene. 1988. *Familiar Strangers.* Urbana: University of Illinois Press.

Taylor, Monica. 1987. *Chinese Pupils in Britain.* London: NFER.

Taylor, Ronald. 1994. Minority families in America: an introduction. In *Minority Families in the United States,* ed. Ronald Taylor. Englewood Cliffs, N.J.: Prentice-Hall.

Thomas, W. and F. Znaniecki. 1927. *The Polish Peasant in Europe and America*. New York: Dover Publications.

Thompson, Marcus. 1974. The second generation—Punjabi or English?, *New Community* 3(3): 242–48.

Thompson, Paul. 1988. *The Voice of the Past*. Oxford: Oxford University Press.

————— 1995. Transmission between generations. In *Childhood and Parenthood*, ed. Julia Brannen and Margaret O'Brien. London: Institute of Education.

Tilly, Louise and Joan Scott. 1978. *Women, Work and Family*. New York: Routledge.

Troyna, Barry and Richard Hatcher. 1992. *Racism in Children's Lives*. London: Routledge.

Tuan, Mia. 1995. "Forever foreigners" or "hononary whites?": The salience of ethnicity for multigeneration Asian ethnics. Paper presented at the American Sociological Association Annual Meeting, Community of Communities: Shaping Our Future, Washington, D.C., August 19–23.

Ungerson, Claire. 1987. *Policy is Personal: Sex, Gender and Informal Care*. London: Tavistock.

Van Den Berghe, Pierre. 1970. *Race and Ethnicity*. New York: Basic Books.

Vigil, James. 1988. *Barrio Gangs: Street Life and Identity in Southern California*. Austin, Tex.: University of Texas Press.

Virdee, Satnam. 1995. *Racial Violence and Harassment*. London: Policy Studies Institute.

Walby, Sylvia. 1990. *Theorizing Patriarchy*. Cambridge: Polity Press.

Waldinger, Roger. 1986. *Through the Eye of the Needle*. New York: New York University Press.

Waldinger, Roger, Howard Aldrich, and Robin Ward. 1990. *Ethnic Entrepreneurs: Immigrant Business in Industrial Societies*. Newbury Park, Calif.: Sage.

Wallace, Claire. 1987. *For Richer, For Poorer: Growing Up In and Out of Work*. London: Tavistock.

Wallace, Claire, David Dunkerley, Brian Cheal, and Martyn Warren. 1994. Young people and the division of labour in farming families. *The Sociological Review* 42: 501–30.

Wallerstein, Immanuel. 1974. *The Modern World System*. New York: Academic Press.

Wallman, Sandra. 1978. Boundaries of "race": Processes of ethnicity in England. *Man* 13: 200–217.

Walton, Helen. 1986. White researchers and racism. Working paper no. 10. Manchester, Eng.: Manchester University Press.

Ward, Robin. 1985. Minority settlement and the local economy. In *New

Approaches to Economic Life, ed. Bryan Roberts, Ruth Finnegan and Duncan Gallie. Manchester, Eng.: Manchester University Press.

Ward, Robin and Richard Jenkins, eds. 1984. *Ethnic Communities in Business: Strategies For Economic Survival.* Cambridge: Cambridge University Press.

Ward, Robin and Frank Reeves. 1984. West Indians in business in Britain. In *Ethnic Communities in Business: Strategies for Survival,* ed. Robin Ward and Richard Jenkins. Cambridge: Cambridge University Press.

Warde, Alan. 1990. Household work strategies and forms of labor. *Work, Employment, and Society* 4(4): 495–515.

Warner, W. L. and Leo Srole. 1945. *The Social Systems of American Ethnic Groups.* New Haven: Yale University Press.

Waters, Mary. 1990. *Ethnic Options: Choosing Identities in America.* Berkeley: University of California Press.

———— 1994. Ethnic and racial identities of second-generation black immigrants in New York City. *International Migration Review* 28(4): 795–820.

———— 1996. Optional ethnicities: For Whites only? In *Origins and Destinies,* ed. Silvia Pedraza and Ruben Rumbaut. Belmont, Calif.: Wadsworth.

Watson, James. 1975. *Emigration and the Chinese Lineage: The Mans in Hong Kong and London.* Berkeley: University of California Press.

———— 1977a. The Chinese: Hong Kong villagers in the British catering trade. In *Between Two Cultures: Migrants and Minorities in Britain,* ed. James Watson. Oxford, Eng.: Blackwell.

———— 1977b. ed. *Between Two Cultures: Migrants and Minorities in Britain.* Oxford, Eng.: Blackwell.

Weinreich, Peter. 1979. Ethnicity and adolescent conflict. In *Minority Families in Britain,* ed. Verity Saifullah-Khan. London: Macmillan.

Werbner, Pnina. 1987. Enclave economies and family firms: Pakistani traders in a British city. In *Migrants, Workers, and the Social Order,* ed. Jeremy Eades. Association of Social Anthropologists Monographs 2b.

———— 1988. Taking and giving: Working women and female bonds in a Pakistani immigrant neighborhood. In *Enterprising Women,* ed. Sallie Westwood and Parminder Bhachu. London: Routledge.

West, Jackie, ed. 1982. *Work, Women, and the Labour Market.* London: Routledge & Kegan Paul.

Westwood, Sallie and Parminder Bhachu, eds. 1988. *Enterprising Women.* London: Routledge.

Wheelock, Jane. 1991. Small businesses, "flexibility" and family work strategies. Sunderland Polytechnic Business School Research Paper, Sunderland, U.K.

White, Benjamin. 1974. The economic importance of children in a Japanese village. In *Population and Social Organization*, ed. Moni Nag. The Hague: Mouton Publishers.

White, Lynn and David Brinkerhoff. 1981. Children's work in the family: Its significance and meaning. *Journal of Marriage and the Family* 43: 789–98.

Williams, Fiona. 1989. *Social Policy: A Critical Introduction*. Cambridge, U.K.: Polity Press.

Willmott, Phyllis and Michael Young. 1960. *Family and Class in a London Suburb*. London: Routledge & Kegan Paul.

Wilson, Kenneth and W. Allen Martin. 1982. Ethnic enclaves: A comparison of the Cuban and black economies in Miami. *American Journal of Sociology* 88(1): 135–60.

Wilson, Kenneth and Alejandro Portes. 1980. Immigrant enclaves: An analysis of the labor market experiences of Cubans in Miami. *American Journal of Sociology* 86(2): 295–319.

Wilson, Patricia and Ray Pahl. 1988. The changing sociological construct of the family. *Sociological Review* 36: 233–72.

Wilson, Peter and John Stanworth. 1986. Growth and change in black minority enterprise in London. *International Small Business Journal* 4(3): 13–27.

Wolf, Margery. 1972. *Women and the Family in Rural Taiwan*. Stanford, California: Stanford University Press.

Wong, Bernard. 1988. *Patronage, Brokerage, Entrepreneurship and the Chinese Community in New York*. New York: AMS Press.

Wong, Lornita. 1992. *Education of Chinese Children in Britain and the USA*. Clevedon, U.K.: Multilingual Matters.

Wong, S. L. 1985. The Chinese family firm: a model. *British Journal of Sociology* 36(1): 58–72.

Wright, E. O. 1985. *Classes*. London: Verso.

Yanagisako, S. J. 1979. Family and household: The analysis of domestic groups. *Annual Review of Anthropology* 8: 161–205.

Yancey, William, Eugene Ericksen, and Richard Juliani. 1976. Emergent ethnicity: A review and reformulation. *American Sociological Review* 41(3): 391–403.

Yang, C. K. 1974. The Chinese family: The young and the old. In *The Family: Its Structures and Functions*, ed. R. L. Coser. London: Macmillan.

Zenner, Walter. 1988. Jewishness in America: Ascription and choice. In *Ethnicity and Race in the U.S.A.*, ed. Richard Alba. New York: Routledge.

Zhou, Min. 1992. *Chinatown:The Socioeconomic Potential of an Urban Enclave*. Philadelphia, Pa: Temple University Press.

Zhou, Min and Carl Bankston. 1994. Social capital and the adaptation of the second generation: The case of Vietnamese youth in New Orleans. *International Migration Review* 28(4): 821–45.

Index